Appointment of Judges
THE JOHNSON PRESIDENCY

An Administrative History of the Johnson Presidency Series

Appointment of Judges
THE JOHNSON PRESIDENCY

By Neil D. McFeeley

 University of Texas Press, Austin

First edition, 1987

Requests for permission to reproduce material from
this work should be sent to:
    Permissions
    University of Texas Press
    Box 7819
    Austin, Texas 78713-7819

Library of Congress Cataloging-in-Publication Data
McFeeley, Neil.
    Appointment of judges, the Johnson presidency.
    (An Administrative history of the Johnson presidency
series)
    Includes index.
    1. Judges—United States—Appointment, qualifications,
tenure, etc.   2. Johnson, Lyndon B. (Lyndon Baines),
1908–1973.   I. Title.   II. Series: Administrative history
of the Johnson presidency.
KF8776.M34   1987   347.73'2034   86-24936
ISBN 0-292-70377-5   347.30714

To my mother and the memory of my father, William J. McFeeley

Contents

Tables

Foreword

This is the sixth of a group of publications collectively designed to comprise An Administrative History of the Johnson Presidency. The first study, by Emmette S. Redford and Marlan Blissett, *Organizing the Executive Branch: The Johnson Presidency,* was published in 1981. The second, by Richard L. Schott and Dagmar S. Hamilton, *People, Positions and Power: The Political Appointments of Lyndon Johnson,* was published in 1983. The third, by W. Henry Lambright, *Presidential Management of Science and Technology: The Johnson Presidency,* was published in 1985. The fourth and fifth studies, published in 1986, were James E. Anderson and Jared E. Hazleton, *Managing Macroeconomic Policy: The Johnson Presidency,* and Emmette S. Redford and Richard E. McCulley, *White House Operations: The Johnson Presidency.* This fuller study by Neil D. McFeeley will complement that by Schott and Hamilton to present a view of presidential exercise of the key function of appointment.

The concept of administration employed in this series of studies has been comprehensive. It encompasses operation of the infrastructure of administration, including the structure and staffing of the executive branch, and budgeting for its operation. The first two published studies were in this area. The concept also includes both implementation of public policy and the mixture of policy development and implementation at the top levels of the executive branch and includes management of the interrelated processes.

As the series has evolved, authors have concentrated their attention on the management of the substantive aspects of administration at the highest level of the executive branch. How President Johnson managed the executive branch to achieve the objectives of law and presidential purpose is the broad question which jointly they strive to answer.

Our goal is an authentic and substantial historical record based primarily on the documentary materials in the Lyndon B. Johnson

Library and on interviews with many people who assisted President Johnson. We hope this historical record, as presented from a social science perspective, will amplify knowledge of administrative processes and of the tasks and problems of the presidency both generally and during the Johnson presidency.

The study is being financed primarily by a grant from the National Endowment for the Humanities, with additional aid from the Lyndon Baines Johnson Foundation, the Hoblitzelle Foundation, and the Lyndon B. Johnson School of Public Affairs of the University of Texas at Austin.

The findings and conclusions in publications in this series do not necessarily represent the view of any donor.

EMMETTE S. REDFORD
Project Director

JAMES E. ANDERSON
Deputy Director

Acknowledgments

There are a number of people whom I would like to thank for their help in this project. First is Professor Emmette S. Redford of the University of Texas, whose support in including this book as part of his series on the administration of the Johnson presidency led to its publication by the University of Texas Press. Emmette epitomizes the terms "gentleman" and "scholar" and I appreciate his professional and personal encouragement. I also appreciate the editorial help provided by Professor James Anderson of the University of Houston and Dr. Richard McCulley, as well as the editors at the University of Texas Press. Professor Sheldon Goldman of the University of Massachusetts generously opened his extensive files on judicial appointees to me. The late Ray McNichols, United States district judge for the District of Idaho, discussed his nomination with me.

I wish to acknowledge the two summer research grants provided by the Lyndon Baines Johnson Foundation and some administrative support given by Robert Blank, chairman of the Political Science Department of the University of Idaho. The Lyndon B. Johnson Library and the librarians there were of immeasurable help in this work, as were Evelyn Brandt and Helen Petersen of the Library of the United States Court of Appeals for the North Circuit in Pasadena, California. David Bowie typed the manuscript.

A more personal note of thanks goes to Sarah, Austin, and Blaine, who gave and continued to give love and encouragement in this and all my efforts.

NEIL D. MCFEELEY

Appointment of Judges
THE JOHNSON PRESIDENCY

1. Introduction

Article II of the Constitution provides that the president shall nominate and, with the advice and consent of the Senate, shall appoint judges to the federal courts. That responsibility is a significant one, for federal judges, especially in the last several decades, have come to exercise a great deal of power. The president who appoints them may shape American society through his appointees' decisions. This book details how the nomination responsibility was carried out in the administration of Lyndon B. Johnson. It explores the management process by which information was filtered and transmitted to the president and through which the president's criteria for selection would prevail. The book also discusses the various actors who played a role in judicial selection, especially those with a continuing responsibility in this area.

On matters of importance and high public visibility the president will typically be personally involved in all phases of the decision process. In all cases he must rely on a management process through which his assistants in and out of the White House contribute information, analysis, and advice. Professors Emmette S. Redford and Marlan Blissett have described these two aspects of the presidency as the president and the "subpresidency." The term *subpresidency* is used

> to denote all those who have served the president—continuously or ad hoc, in an institutional capacity or otherwise—in the exercise of his responsibilities. This included [in the Johnson presidency] on occasion individuals in departments or independent agencies who had separate official responsibilities but whose loyalties to the president led them to look at problems from a presidential perspective.[1]

These two aspects of the presidency emerge from a study of judicial appointments. The president can take on virtually the entire responsibility of searching out and deciding upon nominees for a few particularly significant judicial positions, as on the Supreme Court, but he cannot spend any appreciable amount of time or other resources on individual selection of the mass of nominees. Instead, he must rely on the assistance of a subpresidency operating in the judicial-selection area. The success of both the personal and institutional aspects of decisionmaking depends upon the ability of the president to create and sustain a process through which information flows to him and by which his decisions are effectively communicated to those performing the selection function.

President Johnson played a personal role in several judicial selections, particularly those for the Supreme Court, but a few others as well. He was highly interested in and aware of the importance of his nominations to the federal courts. But most of those nominees were actually selected by the subpresidency under general guidelines set by the president. The subpresidency for judicial selection in the Johnson administration included a number of constants: the Department of Justice, certain White House assistants, the American Bar Association's (ABA) Committee on Federal Judiciary, and a "merit search" operation headed by John W. Macy, Jr., who also served as chairman of the Civil Service Commission. To a greater extent than in other Johnson subpresidencies, then, departmental officials were a regular and structured part of the judicial selection subpresidency.[2] The attorney general and deputy attorney general played a major role. And even more unusual was the virtual incorporation into the official process of the ABA Committee, making it a continuing and influential part of the judicial selection subpresidency. The Johnson subpresidency was a combination of traditional elements and some new actors. This book explores both the personal involvement of Lyndon Johnson and the role of the subpresidency in judicial selection.

As noted earlier, the primary subject of this book is the process of managing judicial selection. Management of process has implications both for administration and for democratic theory. No president can personally carry out or even carefully oversee the expanding responsibilities of the office. At most he can reserve the essential decisions for himself and guide those who implement the rest. But to do this he must develop a process that provides for the transmission to him of information relevant to his decisionmaking on major issues and necessary for maintaining general control. The communication must facilitate his exercise of those functions without overburdening him with extraneous information and decisions. The process must coordinate and thus control the various actors.

Well-structured filtering and transmission processes can enable the most heavily burdened officials, public or private, to reserve their control, retain their options, and accomplish their objectives. In the case of the president—an elected public official—structured process and collaborative effort, accompanied by presidential guidance, can give validity to the democratic objective of control of fundamental decisions by representatives of the people. Communication and control were the goals of the process and to a large extent those goals were met, as Johnson generally was able to accomplish his objectives in the area of judicial selection.

The following chapters show the continuous interest in judicial selection displayed by President Johnson. They describe the process developed and the varied actors involved. They set out the criteria Johnson specified for judicial candidates. They detail how the integrated process worked. By doing these things an in-depth understanding is provided of both the continuing and novel elements in presidential management of a process that is both distinctive and significant for public welfare.

The Importance of Judicial Selection

Judges on federal constitutional courts, according to Article III of the Constitution, "shall hold their office during good behavior." Once a president appoints a judge, that judge cannot be removed from the bench except by impeachment. Yet impeachment has seldom been used. "Furthermore, not only is the selection of a federal judge irrevocable by ordinary means, it is unconditional as well."[3]

Several presidents have regretted the "unconditional" nature of their appointments and have been openly critical of "their" judges. For example, Theodore Roosevelt called Justice Oliver Wendell Holmes a "bitter disappointment" and, after Holmes had joined in an "anti-antitrust" decision, stated that "I could carve out of a banana a judge with more backbone than that."[4] Dwight Eisenhower is reported to have called his appointment of Earl Warren as chief justice "the biggest damn fool mistake I ever made" and was also disappointed with the liberalism of another of his appointees to the Court, William Brennan. When Eisenhower was later asked if he had made mistakes as president, he responded, "Yes, two, and they are both sitting on the Supreme Court."[5] And Harry Truman, also plainly speaking, replied when asked the same question:

> Tom Clark was my biggest mistake. No question about it. . . . He hasn't made one right decision that I can think of. And so when

you ask me what was my biggest mistake, that's it. Putting Tom
Clark on the Supreme Court of the United States.

Truman also commented on another appointment: "I appointed [ex-
Senator] Bennett Clark to be an associate justice of the circuit court
of appeals. He was no damn good, though."[6]

Those judgments reflect both political and policy concerns. Presidents recognize the major impact judicial appointments have on political relationships and sometimes on political polls. They also recognize that judicial appointments have long-term effects on law and
social policy.

During the Johnson administration, 125 lifetime appointments to
the United States district courts, 41 appointments to the courts of
appeals, and two appointments to the Supreme Court of the United
States were effected.[7] In 1966 alone, Johnson made 63 lifetime judicial appointments, which up to that time was the largest number
ever made in a single year.[8] In addition, Johnson made some 13 appointments to the Court of Claims, Customs Court, and Court of
Customs and Patent Appeals. These are lifetime positions but will
not be discussed in detail in this study.

The judges Johnson appointed had to deal with major policy issues
of the 1960s and thereafter. Civil rights, criminal justice, and reap-
portionment were just some of the cases on the dockets of federal
judges in the years of the Johnson presidency and the decisions made
by the Johnson appointees on these and other issues had great importance for the individual litigants and for American society as well.
Federal judicial responsibility has increased dramatically in recent
decades as more and more disputes are brought before the federal
judiciary in this "litigious society" of ours.[9] The long-term significance of Johnson's judicial appointments is evident. Seventeen years
after leaving office, one of the Supreme Court justices, thirty-five of
the judges of the courts of appeals, and eighty-seven of the district
judges appointed by Johnson remain on the bench in active or senior
status. Almost two decades after Johnson left office, his decisions on
appointments to the courts are still having a significant impact on
the life of the nation. Those appointments remain a reflection of and
a reflection on the presidency of Lyndon B. Johnson and the man
himself.

Judicial Appointments in Johnson's Career

As noted earlier and as will be discussed in the following chapters,
Johnson was quite interested in and often personally involved with

the appointments process. One reason for this involvement may be because Johnson's elective political career began with a controversy over the appointment of federal judges. Indeed, one might argue that his political career also ended in a controversy over such appointments.

In 1937 Johnson was the young administrator of the National Youth Administration in Texas. President Franklin D. Roosevelt, following his overwhelming 1936 reelection, proposed that Congress expand the number of justices on the Supreme Court in order to allow the president to appoint new members who would be less hostile to New Deal legislation. This Court-packing plan, announced on 5 February 1937, met great opposition from the very start. Most constitutional scholars, newspapers, and members of Congress opposed it. Political leaders in Texas, including most members of the Texas State Senate, Senator Tom Connally, and Vice President John Nance Garner, were opposed. Even Speaker Sam Rayburn was at best lukewarm in support. It was in this period that Texas Congressman James P. Buchanan died of a heart attack on 22 February and a special election was called. Lyndon Johnson ran against several other candidates, and the one issue that separated Johnson from the others was his total support of Roosevelt, the New Deal, and the doomed Court-packing plan:

> But there is one candidate—Lyndon Johnson—who declared from the first that he supported the president wholeheartedly, including the controversial Supreme Court issue. I didn't have to hold back. I support Franklin Roosevelt the full way, all the way, every day. That's what I intend to do when elected as your representative in Congress, and that includes enlarging the Supreme Court of the United States. When that comes up, I'm not going to be out in the woodshed practicing ways to duck.[10]

Johnson's advocacy of the Court-packing plan carried him to victory and to a close relationship with the president and his intimate advisers. One of those advisers, Secretary of the Interior Harold Ickes, put the new congressman in touch with a brilliant young lawyer from Memphis named Abe Fortas, who was working in the department.[11] It has been argued that the Court-packing proposal was a victory for FDR since shortly after the plan was proposed there was a shift in the Court that allowed most New Deal legislation to be held constitutional. But the Court-packing plan was the greatest political mistake Roosevelt made; a lot of former supporters apparently did go "out in the woodshed" and the plan was never passed. Lyndon

Johnson's first exposure to the judicial appointment process was thus both controversial and had ambivalent results.

Thirty years later, in the last few months of his presidency, Johnson nominated Abe Fortas, that same New Dealer he had met as a young congressman, to the chief justiceship of the Supreme Court. He also nominated his friend Homer Thornberry to an associate justiceship. But these nominations occurred after Johnson's 31 March 1968 speech in which he announced he would not seek reelection; amid accusations of cronyism and charges that the president was a lame duck who was trying to usurp the rightful prerogatives of the next (Republican) president, the Senate refused to end a filibuster in opposition to Fortas and the nominations were withdrawn. Johnson's wish to see Fortas and Thornberry, men who shared his values and his concerns, serving as chief justice and associate justice when he left office was thwarted.

Yet even this bitter defeat did not end Johnson's involvement with the federal courts. He attempted to fill several lower court vacancies before he left office; after Richard Nixon became president several of those nominations were withdrawn in apparent violation of an agreement between the two administrations. In addition, the earlier Fortas hearings became the springboard for later revelations that led to Justice Fortas' resignation from the Supreme Court.

Study of Judicial Appointments

Despite these unfortunate episodes involving the appointment of federal judges, Johnson as president had an enormous opportunity to affect the quality of the judiciary and its influence on the nation through his many judicial appointments. Existing studies detail various aspects of Johnson's judicial appointments, but neither separately nor in the aggregate do they provide a complete or thorough analysis of the judicial selection process during the Johnson administration. Several studies deal with nominations to the Supreme Court and shed some light on the Johnson nominees.[12] There are several studies on the appointing process for the lower federal courts and on the socioeconomic backgrounds of lower-court nominees.[13] In addition, a number of more general works that deal with federal judges and the judicial appointment process are available.[14]

Those works provide a good background and perspective for this study. But for those concerned with judicial selection during the Johnson years they are not sufficient, for they do not concentrate on the Johnson appointments and do not fully explain the process of judicial selection and the philosophy behind those appointments.

This book differs from previous studies in that it provides an intensive investigation of the complete judicial selection process in the Johnson administration—though it does to a limited degree utilize information on other administrations for comparative purposes. Rather than relying on secondary sources exclusively, it is based largely on primary information gathered from a search of the rich archival files of aides, officials, and agencies at the Lyndon B. Johnson Library in Austin, Texas. These files include memorandums to the president from his White House advisers and the deputy attorney general concerning the nominations, and the president's replies. They contain letters from individuals on judgeships. Department of Justice lists of vacancies and of potential nominees for the positions as well as formal recommendations by the department are included, as are White House staff memos dealing with the politics of selection. There are oral histories of many of the participants in the selection process and of several appointees as well. This study utilizes those primary resources and therefore gains a different perspective from most other studies of this topic. (An exception to this would be Harold W. Chase's description of the Kennedy process in *Federal Judges* because Chase was given access to Department of Justice files and personnel; but even Chase did not have access to White House office files.)

This type of investigation obviously has a number of advantages. The researcher is able to view the process as it was rather than only an after-the-fact account. A detailed investigation of particular incidents is possible rather than only a view of the aggregate process. The "how" and "why" of the process can be addressed, rather than just the results. Finally, the outsider can get an inside look at judicial appointments.

There are, however, some limits to this method of study. The written records, although quite extensive, obviously do not record everything:

. . . increasingly, much of modern government is conducted off the record in conversations, private telephone calls, and other personal communications. Especially in a sensitive area such as the recruitment and evaluation of prospective appointees, much potentially rich material never found its way into documentary sources; it remains only as memory traces in the minds of the participants themselves.[15]

Jack J. Valenti, a close aide to Johnson, stressed that the president preferred not to have memorandums on such "sensitive subjects" as appointment matters; "He told me, 'One day somebody's going to be crawling through files and finding out some of these memorandums you are writing, and I'd get rid of them.' So I dealt with the president almost exclusively on an oral basis."[16]

Thought processes are not written down. Formal letters from senators recommending one or several candidates are in the files, but as Joseph F. Dolan, assistant deputy attorney general, points out:

> Justice officials . . . know that such letters are often written only to satisfy certain constituents or to pay political debts. Only by personal conversation with the senator can the Justice official know which candidate, if any, the senator really favors.[17]

Although Justice Department files contain some memorandums describing such conversations, not all of those personal conversations and "real" recommendations appear in the records. Oral histories, although useful, are to some extent edited versions of thought processes.

To a very limited degree, the written records have also been edited. President Johnson, in his deed of gift of his papers to the presidential library, specified that material that would subject individuals to injury, embarrassment, or harassment be restricted. Also, Federal Bureau of Investigation (FBI) reports on potential appointees are closed. So too are most of the office files maintained by John W. Macy, Jr., the president's "talent scout," although these files are gradually being made available for research. Schott and Hamilton note that

> another important reservoir of information, also beyond our reach, is the numerous Dictabelt recordings of presidential telephone conversations that Johnson directed be closed to researchers until fifty years after his death. Undoubtedly, much rich and revealing information concerning the president's personal reactions to prospective appointees, as well as his role in the appointments process, lies hidden in these recordings.[18]

And of course the files of senators, who play a major role in initiating many candidacies, are not available to give a nonadministration perspective.

Even with these limitations, the original archival records of the Johnson administration provide a valuable and unique perspective on the process of judicial selection. This book uses those sources to describe the Johnson selection process and to examine the criteria of choice developed by President Johnson. Case studies are utilized to illustrate the interplay of process and criteria at the various levels of participation in selection of judges and in the first and last years of the Johnson presidency. The bulk of the book, of course, is devoted to the description and discussion of the Johnson process, a process that to a great extent allowed President Johnson successfully to direct the selection of federal judges.

2. The Historical Development of the Appointments Process

In order to understand the process of judicial appointment in the Johnson administration it is necessary to understand the general process as it has developed historically. This will provide more context for the study of the Johnson process and will provide a perspective from which to judge the conventional and the unique elements of that process.

The process of judicial appointment is based on only two constitutional provisions. Custom, political practice, and presidential judgment complete the process.

Constitutional Provisions for Judicial Appointment

Article II of the Constitution specifies that the president "shall nominate, and by and with the Advice and Consent of the Senate, shall appoint . . . Judges of the supreme Court, and all other Officers of the United States." That statement was the result of extensive debate and compromise in the Constitutional Convention and was a part of larger issues faced by the framers. Included in the Virginia Plan, which set the agenda for the convention, was a proposal for the creation of a national judiciary to be chosen by the legislature. Advocates of this plan, including Benjamin Franklin, George Mason, Elbridge Gerry, and Edmund Randolph, feared executive tyranny and believed that a group would be better informed about the qualifications of nominees than would a single individual. On 5 June, this proposal came up for discussion and met opposition from those who feared the inability of the legislature to choose qualified candidates. James Wilson argued that

experience shewed the impropriety of such appointments by numerous bodies. Intrigue, partiality, and concealment were the necessary consequences. A principal reason for unity in the Executive was the officers might be appointed by a single responsible person. . . .

James Madison noted that

beside the danger of intrigue and partiality, many of the members were not judges of the requisite qualifications. The Legislative talents, which were very different from those of a Judge, commonly recommended men to the favor of Legislative Assemblies.

Madison, however, did not then favor executive appointment and suggested that appointment might be made by the Senate.[1] Alexander Hamilton, a proponent of a strong executive, suggested that judges be "appointed or nominated by the Executive to the Senate, which shall have the right of rejecting or approving," but this suggestion did not attract any support.

In the next two months several different plans for appointments were proposed, including the New Jersey Plan's provision for appointment by the executive and the support by Nathaniel Gorham of Massachusetts for Hamilton's proposal for executive appointment with advice and consent of the Senate, "a method which he said had been used in Massachusetts for 140 years."[2] By this time Madison too favored the Hamilton proposal, but the draft reported by the Committee on Detail on 6 August provided for appointment of Supreme Court justices by the Senate. However, Gouverneur Morris and James Wilson led opposition to this proposal. Finally, near the end of the convention, the Special Committee on Postponed Matters proposed on 4 September that the president should have the appointing power subject to advice and consent of the Senate. This compromise was acceptable to large states and small states, North and South, and proponents of both executive strength and legislative power and was accepted after "lively debate" and written into the Constitution with an amendment authorizing the president to make recess appointments.[3]

It has been argued that the Constitution does not require presidential appointment nor senatorial confirmation for appointments below the Supreme Court level. The constitutional provision states that "the Congress may by Law vest the Appointment of such inferior Officers, as they think proper, in the President alone, in the Courts of Law, or in the Heads of Departments." The argument is that lower federal judges are "inferior officers"—inferior in the sense of "lower than" the Supreme Court and inferior in the sense that they are officers of "such inferior Courts as the Congress may from time to time ordain and establish."[4] Notwithstanding this argument, in 1891 Congress provided that "there shall be appointed by the President of the United States, by and with the advice and consent of the Senate, in each circuit an additional circuit judge." And in 1948 it was "provided explicitly for the first time that all circuit and district judges be appointed with the advice and consent of the Senate. This is in the law to this day."[5] So for two centuries federal judges have been nominated by the president, confirmed by a simple majority vote of the Senate, and formally appointed by the president.

Article II of the Constitution also grants the president power "to fill up all Vacancies that may happen during the Recess of the Senate, by granting Commissions which shall expire at the End of their next Session." The president uses the authorization to make regular appointments, subject to Senate consent. Sometimes the Senate refuses to assent, as it did when George Washington granted a recess appointment as chief justice to John Rutledge, who had injudiciously criticized the Senate's ratification of the Jay Treaty. Other presidents have met Senate opposition to their recess appointments; for example, Eisenhower's recess appointments of Earl Warren, William Brennan, and Potter Stewart all encountered some opposition. The Senate has also passed laws withholding salaries from many recess appointees in order to discourage the president from making too many such appointments.[6] But presidents can gain advantages by recess appointments: "By having a candidate assume the position while the Senate is not in session, the president gains the advantage of having his appointee in place and at work when the Senate returns to business. To defeat the candidate would be to disrupt the judicial business that the judge has gotten involved with during the recess appointment."[7] A recess appointment may be made to persuade the Senate to accept an individual whom it might not otherwise have accepted. This was the case with President Kennedy's appointment of Irving Ben Cooper to the District Court for the Southern District of New York in 1961. Earlier, Kennedy's nomination of Cooper had met stiff opposition from the ABA and had lapsed without Senate action. Cooper was given a recess appointment, and when the Congress reconvened in 1962 the support of Cooper's on-the-job performance by the sitting judges on the District Court persuaded the Senate to confirm him.[8]

A controversy about recess appointments concerns the meaning of "Vacancies that may happen during the Recess." Some, including most senators, have concluded that only those vacancies that occur during a recess can be filled by an interim appointment.[9] Presidents, however, have argued that any vacancies existing during a recess may be filled without prior Senate approval, and they have acted on that belief. Although the Constitutional Convention debates are silent on this topic, the broad interpretation has been upheld by at least one federal court.[10]

A final act in the appointment process is both a formality and a real power: the president must sign the formal appointment papers. An incoming president has the power to withdraw the pending nominations of the preceding president. This action has occurred often, especially when there has been a shift in party control of the presidency. Most recently, Ronald Reagan withdrew a nomination pending from the Carter administration.[11]

The Actual Process of Appointment

The process of judicial appointment is much more complicated and involves many more players than the formal constitutional requirement indicates. Over time, several new participants have become involved and their interactions have increased the complexity of the selection process. These new players perform two general types of roles: initiating and screening.[12] These roles are not entirely distinct and various participants play both roles.

Initiators

These participants are the ones who gather and suggest names and support individual candidates. The primary constitutional actor in the process is the president. Individual presidents differ in their concern with and participation in the judicial selection process. William H. Taft as president (and later as chief justice) was very personally involved in the selection of federal judges: "Taft chose his jurists with great care."[13] William P. Rogers noted that President Eisenhower often talked with judicial candidates before submitting his nomination.[14] And Joel Grossman reports that President Kennedy occasionally overruled the attorney general's recommendations for judicial nominations because of political pressures.[15]

Although presidents play a personal role in the process, particularly in selecting Supreme Court justices, they have delegated the recruitment responsibility to others. Before the 1840s the secretary of state performed this clearance function for judges and all federal officials. But during the Pierce administration, at the urging of Attorney General Caleb Cushing, the president delegated the authority to make recommendations for judicial nominations to the Department of Justice.[16] The president retains the power to initiate personally consideration of a candidate, to provide criteria for selection, and to decide whether to accept the department's recommendations. He may delay filling a vacancy, thereby putting pressure on recalcitrant senators who may well be importuned by overworked sitting judges and local lawyers to go along with the president's candidate. "Refusal to nominate can be particularly effective when coupled with a suggestion 'leaked' to the press that a distinguished lawyer or state judge is the president's choice."[17]

Perhaps the most important influence presidents exercise over judicial appointments arises from the establishment of certain criteria, either implicit or explicit, for filling federal judicial vacancies. Even if the president is never directly involved in individual selections, the process is guided by the criteria he had set up. For example, Jimmy Carter specified that the nominating commissions he instituted should "make special efforts to seek out and identify well qualified women and members of minority groups."[18] Ronald Reagan—in his attempt to correct the perceived ideological imbalance resulting from the Carter selection process—has embraced the criteria in the 1980 Republican Party platform, which called for the appointment of judges who had the "highest regard for protecting the rights of law-abiding citizens," who opposed greater federal involvement in state matters, and who "respect traditional family values and the sanctity of innocent human life."[19]

But, with the exception of Supreme Court appointments, the Department of Justice has the primary executive role in selecting the great majority of federal judges. Modern presidents do not have the time to select from among the many candidates and so the attorney general's formal letter of recommendation usually results in the nomination of a candidate chosen largely by the Department of Justice. "In most cases the choice of a federal judge is the attorney general's to make—provided only that he makes it within the framework of the relevant norms of behavior which operate on the selection process" and within the guidelines of the president's criteria.[20]

In most recent administrations, except in highly visible cases where the attorney general or the president himself may be involved, it is the deputy attorney general's office that plays the major role in recruitment and selection: "With the exception of those few nominations that are likely to become major public issues, recruiting judges is essentially a staff operation in the name of the Attorney General—and ultimately in the name of the President."[21] The staff of the deputy's office obtains information on prospective candidates and makes lists of possible nominees in conjunction with or after negotiations with other powerful interests, including party officials, bar leaders, and especially senators from the state where the vacancy exists. Senatorial cooperation is particularly essential in district court appointments, while the department has more leeway in positions on the courts of appeals and District of Columbia courts, which are not "reserved" for specific states.[22] Concerning vacancies on the courts of appeals, Goldman notes that "the first reality is that the president's men in the Justice Department, i.e., the Attorney General and the Deputy Attorney General and his assistants, are primarily responsible for the judicial selection. . . . These officials use their vast network of friends, acquaintances, and friends of friends as a source for possible appointees."[23]

Some presidents have also depended on their White House staff to screen judicial nominees from a political perspective and to maintain communication with the Department of Justice to ensure that presidential wishes are carried out. And the members of the White House staff's congressional liaison team may be quite important in verifying the Department of Justice's understandings about senatorial preferences for candidates and communicating them to the president. In addition, the liaison team may become vital in gaining and maintaining support for the administration's nominee in close confirmation votes.

The Reagan administration has made some substantial changes in the executive branch selection process. While in previous administrations the deputy attorney general's office had been primarily responsible for judicial selection, the Reagan administration has shifted the selection focus in the Department of Justice to the Office of Legal Policy and has also created a post of Special Counsel for Judicial Selection. In addition, the Reagan administration created the "President's Committee on Federal Judicial Selection," a nine-member committee that "institutionalizes and formalizes an active White House role in judicial selection."[24] "The committee's weekly meetings bring together some of the president's most trusted advisers—Attorney General Edwin Meese, White House Chief of Staff Donald Regan, political adviser Ed Rollins, and presidential counsel Fred Fielding, who serves as chairman—as well as the president's assistants for personnel and legislative affairs, the head of the Justice Department's Office of Legal Policy and three other top Justice officials."[25] The committee recommends candidates and discusses Department of Justice recommendations. Further centralization of the selection power in the White House occurs through the investigation of potential nominees by the president's personnel office, which takes place independent of the Justice Department's investigation.[26]

The framers of the Constitution contemplated presidential initiative and a "negative" influence by the Senate.[27] Alexander Hamilton, in explaining and perhaps advocating an interpretation of the clause he had originally suggested in the convention, wrote in *The Federalist*, No. 12:

> It will be the office of the President to NOMINATE, and with the advice and consent of the SENATE to APPOINT. There will, of course, be no exertion of choice on the part of the Senate. They may defeat one choice of the Executive and oblige him to make another; but they cannot themselves CHOOSE—they can only ratify or reject the choice of the President. They might even entertain a preference to some other person at the very moment they were assenting to the one proposed, because there might be no positive ground of opposition to him; and they could not be sure, if they withheld their assent, that the subsequent nomination would fall upon their favorite, or upon any other person in their estimation more meritorious than the one rejected.

Despite Hamilton's argument, to a great extent the intention of the framers has been reversed; in judicial selection and especially in district court appointments it is the senators of the president's party from the state where the vacancy exists who initiate the recruitment process and play the leading role in selection and appointment.[28] In *The Advice and Consent of the Senate,* Joseph Harris concludes that senators have historically exercised domination over judicial selection; Joseph Dolan, assistant deputy attorney general in the Kennedy administration, characterized the Senate's power over judicial selection (especially district court) in more practical terms: "The Constitution is backwards. Article II, Section 2 should read: 'The Senators shall nominate, and by and with the consent of the President, shall appoint.'"[29]

President Jimmy Carter and his attorney general Griffin Bell attempted to change the traditional selection process and therefore the traditional role of the Senate by implementing a campaign pledge and instituting "merit selection" by establishing nominating commissions for both district courts and courts of appeals.[30] This concept met opposition from James Eastland, chairman of the Senate Judiciary Committee, and others, and no legislation was passed requiring the commissions. Instead, Carter's executive order of February 1977 established nominating commissions for only the courts of appeals.[31] However, Carter urged senators to set up nomination commissions for district judge selection, and they were established in some thirty states. Analyses of these commissions indicate that although particularly the district commissions were less than completely successful in removing power from senators, the commissions in general did appear to produce higher-quality candidates. They also opened up the nominating process by tapping more minorities and women, and overall, did transfer power to the executive.[32] However, Ronald Reagan's administration reverted to the traditional method of judicial selection, with influence centered in the hands of Republican senators. On 6 March 1981, Attorney General William French Smith released a memorandum that announced the change and stated that the Department of Justice, "in making recommendations to the President for judicial appointments, will invite Republican members [of the Senate] to identify prospective candidates for federal district judgeships."[33]

The *Washington Post* commented on the Reagan process:

> By eliminating the judicial selection panels former attorney general Griffin Bell struggled to create, the administration made itself vulnerable to suspicions that senators, once again, are going to control the appointment of federal judges in their home states. Only time, and a series of judicial nominations, will reveal whether Mr. Smith has yielded too much to the senators of his party.[34]

Surprisingly, many senators have continued to use the panels in making recommendations for district courts.[35]

In any event, the Reagan administration has usually deferred to Republican senators or their panels in naming district court nominees, and when there is no Republican senator, has often turned to state party leaders.[36] No circuit court panels remain, however, and the traditional process—senators pushing for candidates, but needing to get the acceptance of the White House and the Justice Department, who have more flexibility in this multistate choice—has returned.[37]

Under either method of selection, but especially under the traditional method, the Senate's role is an important one. The key to this role lies in the practice of "senatorial courtesy": the propensity of the Senate to support an individual senator, especially of the president's party, who opposes a nominee from his state. Senatorial courtesy has a long history. The custom began in 1789, when George Washington's nomination for naval officer of the Port of Savannah, Georgia, was rejected in light of the opposition of Georgia's senators.

More recently, both Franklin Roosevelt and Harry Truman had judicial nominations rejected by the Senate because of objections from home-state senators. The power of senatorial courtesy is not absolute, but it is a strong factor in Senate deliberations.[38]

The result of this custom is that the candidate of the home-state senators, after Justice Department and other checks, is usually the district court, and often the court of appeals, nominee of the president. When both senators belong to the president's party, agreements are usually worked out in which they either jointly recommend candidates or alternate when vacancies occur. When one senator is from the opposite party, he or she usually has less power, although in certain states such senators have exercised an important role, either through agreements with the other senator or the administration or by threats to fight the nomination. When neither senator is from the president's party, the congressional delegation or the state party organization plays a significant, although not usually primary, role. Even though senatorial courtesy exerts a powerful effect on the judicial selection process, presidents who are prepared to wage an all-out effort to secure nomination despite a senator's opposition may sometimes be successful.[39]

Besides senators, a variety of other individuals make recommendations for judgeships. Usually these recommendations are directed to the senators concerned in an attempt to persuade them to endorse an individual, but sometimes they are directed to the Department of Justice or to the White House. Party officials, interest group representatives, attorneys, and private citizens often offer names. In addition, while "the sitting judiciary has no official role in the selection of federal judges, . . . it is not surprising that in virtually *all* cases the views of some judges are solicited or offered."[40] If the sitting judge has the ear of a senator, the Justice Department, or the president, and is a judge of considerable reputation, his or her view can affect a candidacy. For example (as will be discussed in the next chapter), Massachusetts District Court Judge Charles Wyzanski, a well-known jurist, opposed the "political" nomination in 1965 of Francis X. Morrissey to the Massachusetts court and wrote a very strong letter to the Senate Judiciary Committee criticizing Morrissey's legal credentials. The ABA Committee also consults sitting judges concerning prospective nominees. In 1952 President Eisenhower gave a recess appointment to Ernest Tolin. During the confirmation process, two of Tolin's fellow judges wrote a highly critical letter to the Judiciary Committee stating that he was not qualified. (Tolin was nevertheless confirmed and took his seat on the district court.)[41] Chief Justice William Howard Taft exercised perhaps the greatest overall influence by a sitting judge; he apparently influenced the selection of Justices George Sutherland, Pierce Butler, and Edward Sanford and was quite active in lower court selection as well.[42]

Another source of pressure in the selection process, usually unrecognized by the public but often of great significance, is the candidates themselves; often attorneys wage extensive, although unpublicized, campaigns for judicial office, and sitting judges campaign for "promotion" to higher courts. The ideal may be that the office should seek the individual; but in reality the individual who wishes to become a federal judge must make his or her interest clear through direct contact with senators or the Justice Department, or more usually by soliciting letters of endorsement from other attorneys, sitting judges, political figures, and state bar associations. It may appear unseemly for a distinguished attorney to run for judicial office, but many have done so because federal judgeships are highly valued. As Grossman notes, "[W]ith the exception of a few well-known lawyers or political figures who may literally be 'chosen' by the recruiting agents, the candidate who does not make at least a minimum effort in his own behalf is likely to remain a private citizen."[43]

Screeners

Once an individual is nominated or is seriously considered for the federal judiciary, participants act to screen the person from a variety of perspectives in an attempt to avoid an unsuitable appointment. The major screening is performed by the Senate in the confirmation process.[44]

The formal process of Senate confirmation begins after the nomination is submitted to the president. At this point, senatorial courtesy may come into play. Formerly, the senator would have only to state that he or she found the nominee "personally obnoxious" in order for courtesy to prevail; Chase suggests that more persuasive arguments are now expected.[45] For the past twenty-five years, senatorial courtesy has been effectuated through the device of the "blue slip."[46] The Senate Judiciary Committee sends a blue form to senators from the state where the vacancy exists asking for their views on the nominee. The form reads:

Dear Senator:

Will you kindly give me, for the use of the Committee, your opinion and information concerning the nomination of (name, district, name of former judge.)

Under a rule of the Committee, unless a reply is received from you within a week from this date, it will be assumed that you have no objection to this nomination.

Respectfully,
(Signature)
Chairman

Although the slip states that support is evidenced by the nonreturn of the form, in reality senators who object to a nomination do not return the blue slip and the committee usually delays or does not schedule hearings.

Recent years saw a brief break from this tradition of individual veto exercised without public knowledge or committee discussion. When Edward Kennedy assumed the chairmanship of the Judiciary Committee in 1979, he announced that the committee would continue to distribute the blue slips but would no longer automatically reject the nominee if the blue slip were not returned; instead, the committee would vote whether or not to consider a nomination in the absence of a blue slip.[47] Kennedy also instituted another change in committee procedures: he established an investigatory staff to "examine the backgrounds of the nominees independent of the Justice Department so that the committee could make its own evaluations."[48] All nominees were required to fill out a questionnaire covering their personal finances, political background, and legal qualifications.[49] However, Kennedy's innovations were short-lived; in 1981 Strom Thurmond became chairman of the Judiciary Committee. Despite the comment of Attorney General William French Smith that he "did not foresee or encourage" a return to the blue-slip procedure, Thurmond reinstituted the custom of the blue slip.[50]

The nomination is referred to the Judiciary Committee and the chairman sends out the blue slips and schedules public hearings. In lower court nominations the hearings are usually conducted by a subcommittee of three appointed by the chairman; in cases when senatorial endorsements have been received the hearing is usually a formality. The nominee is introduced, makes a brief, perfunctory appearance, and hears laudatory remarks by the sponsoring senators or others. Philip Kurland comments that the "Senate as a whole ordinarily acknowledges [senatorial courtesy] by paying less attention to the confirmation process of a federal judge than to the price of bean soup in the Senate restaurants."[51] But in controversial nominations the hearings may be prolonged and the testimony heated. In a few instances hearings on controversial nominees have lasted for several months and occasioned much testimony from various groups.

Delaying hearings is one way the committee, which sees itself as a watchdog for the public interest, can affect the process. In addition, committee hearings afford opportunity for damaging testimony, and the committee may recommend against confirmation. None of these are definitive in the sense that they alone can defeat a nomination, but the possibility of their occurrence may discourage the president from submitting a name or may persuade a candidate to withdraw or may rally majority support in the Senate when a nominee's weaknesses are exposed. However, a determined president and a majority of the Senate can override the Judiciary Committee. Chase reports that President Kennedy's nomination of Thurgood Marshall to a court of appeals position was delayed by the committee for many months but nevertheless was successful because of Kennedy's support and Senate pressure on the committee.[52]

Of course, in the difficult confirmations especially, the White House–senatorial liaison team actively tries to gain support for the president's nominee. After the subcommittee finishes its work, the full committee votes, issues its recommendation, and the nomination goes to the floor of the Senate, where in most cases the nominee is quickly confirmed. If the nomination is opposed, further debate may occur or a filibuster may be brought against the nomination. If a majority vote is received, as in most instances when the Judiciary Committee has approved, the Senate has performed its "consent" function and the president may formally commission the judge.

A major extraconstitutional actor in the appointment process since 1947 has been the Standing Committee on Federal Judiciary of the American Bar Association. This role of the legal profession in judicial selection was anticipated in the Constitutional Convention: in an attempt to relieve the antagonism generated by the debate over whether the legislature or the executive should have the power, Benjamin Franklin

> in a brief and entertaining manner related a Scotch mode, in which the nomination proceeded from the Lawyers, who always selected the ablest of the profession in order to get rid of him, and shared his practice among themselves. It was here he said the interest of the electors to make the best choice, which should always be the case if possible.[53]

It is doubtful that Franklin expected that 160 years later his light comment would become, to a great extent, a reality.

In any event, the organized bar has attempted to participate in judicial selection since it was founded in 1878, partly in opposition to the liberal decisions of the Supreme Court.[54] In 1908, the ABA's Committee on Professional Ethics commented in the canons of ethics of the association that "it is the duty of the Bar to endeavor to prevent political considerations from outweighing judicial fitness in the Selection of Judges."[55] The ABA and its leadership maintained a continuing but episodic interest in judicial selection for forty years, particularly in response to what various bar leaders called the "socialist menace," the "threatened subversion of the judiciary," and the "downgrading of property rights." The ABA (including ex-President Taft and six other former presidents of the association) expressed vitriolic opposition to the nomination in 1916 of Louis Brandeis, whom it characterized as "not a fit person to be a member of the Supreme Court."[56] As early as 1924 an ABA committee urged the "principle of bar selection" for federal as well as state judges, and to an extent William D. Mitchell, Herbert Hoover's attorney general, informally acceded to the bar. In 1931 he reported that "early in this Administration I publicly asked from the Bar of the country assistance and trustworthy information about men under consideration for judicial office, and the response has been gratifying."[57] Encouraged by this, the association created in 1932 a Special Committee on Federal Appointments to advise the Senate Judiciary Committee; its advice was never requested and it was discontinued two years later.[58] However, twelve years later, in 1946, the association established a Special Committee on the Judiciary that soon after its formation "was invited by the chairman of the Senate Judiciary Committee to either testify or file a recommendation on each nomination given a hearing. Thus, the collective views of the committee would become a regular factor in the confirmation process."[59] In 1949, the ABA changed the special committee to a permanent Standing Committee on Federal Judiciary.

That committee judges the qualification of candidates for lifetime federal judgeships and its rankings, which range from "not qualified" to "qualified," "well qualified," and "exceptionally well qualified," have come to be a powerful element of the process. The Senate Judiciary Committee receives the committee reports and they are made a part of the formal hearings. President Eisenhower lent great weight to the bar committee's participation when he commented in 1956 that "I believe also that we must never appoint a man who doesn't have the recognition of the American Bar Association."[60] His administration had previously reached an agreement with the committee to judge candidates; thus, the ABA "became the first non-governmental or extra-governmental participant to acquire an officially recognized role in federal judicial selection."[61] All administrations since that time, including Democratic administrations that have not shared viewpoints with the ABA leadership, have entered into agreements to work and cooperate with the Standing Committee.

The Carter administration did have a more distant relationship with the ABA committee because of its use of circuit nominating panels and analogous district court commissions established by most senators.[62] The Reagan administration has also been less willing to utilize the ABA committee in the prenomination stage. It has generally not sought preliminary ratings on anyone but the actual candidate chosen by the White House and is the first Republican administration in thirty years that has not pledged to reject anyone rated "not qualified" by the ABA.[63] But the Reagan administration has worked closely with the ABA committee after a choice has been made, and the ratings of the committee remain important.[64]

The influence of the ABA committee has varied, but it is usually a substantial screening device. The Department of Justice usually requests informal reports on candidates under consideration before final decisions are made. The committee investigates a candidate's prior trial experience and judicial temperament, and it surveys fellow attorneys in the area.[65] It requires the candidate to fill out a personal-data questionnaire. The chairman then reports the committee's informal rating to the Justice Department. "If the Justice Department decided that the candidate will probably be the nominee, the Deputy Attorney General asks the Committee to supply a 'formal report' on the candidate."[66] That report is made confidentially to the Justice Department and, if the nomination proceeds, to the Judiciary Committee. Although the bar committee does not exercise veto power, most administrations have been hesitant to nominate candidates rated "unqualified"; such a rating is ammunition for opponents in Senate hearings and for editorial writers in newspaper columns.[67]

The participation of the committee has been praised and condemned. It is asserted that the independent scrutiny of committee review helps keep unfit persons off the federal bench, that political hacks can be prevented from trading presidential or senatorial IOUs for judicial office, and that the proper interests of the organized bar in this area of the legal process are protected by the committee.[68] But the committee has received criticism as well. Grossman questions whether a private group should have so much influence in a governmental process.[69] Philip Kurland, himself a distinguished law professor, states that "with all due respect to my own profession, the submission of names for approval to any segment of that profession, national, state, local, or individual, is both inappropriate and undesirable where the Senate is charged with duties of advice and consent. Since the bar is anything but a representative political body, it affords no legitimating function in this regard."[70] Many have accused the committee and the ABA in general, particularly in the past, of representing elite interests and philosophies: "Until recent years it was virtually a tradition of the American Bar Association that its leaders comprise those who achieved high economic success in the legal profession and who entertained deeply conservative viewpoints on economic and social questions. These leaders managed the affairs of the Association and set the tone and temper of its activities." Only recently have any females or minorities served on the Standing Committee.[71] This perspective may have produced biased evaluations and favored white, male corporate attorneys. The committee's standards on age and trial experience have also been criticized, as have the secrecy and idiosyncracy of the evaluative process.[72] Notwithstanding these criticisms, the Standing Committee on Federal Judiciary of the ABA continues to play a leading role in federal judicial selection.

While the ABA remains the most influential interest group, a variety of other groups may also participate in the screening stage as they attempt to veto candidates they consider unacceptable or promote nominees they favor. "The tendency for interest groups to attempt to influence federal judicial selection has, of course, long been characteristic of American Politics."[73] The efficacy of those efforts varies from group to group and from era to era as some groups gain more sympathetic hearings from various administrations or Senates. During the Carter years, the Department of Justice sent names of prospective nominees not only to the ABA but also to the predominantly black National Bar Association and the Federation of Women Lawyers for their evaluation.[74]

The Department of Justice may clear candidates with certain groups, and groups may testify in behalf of or in opposition to certain nominees. This tactic can be successful, as seen in the 1930 defeat of John Parker, whose nomination to the Supreme Court was opposed by labor groups and the NAACP, and in the 1970 defeat of Harold Carswell, who was also opposed by civil rights groups. More usually, though, if the nomination has reached the Senate confirmation stage, interest-group opposition fails, as seen in the victories of Louis Brandeis in 1916 against conservative opposition, Thurgood Marshall in 1961 and 1967 against anti–civil rights groups, William

Rehnquist in 1972 against ACLU opposition, John Paul Stevens in 1975 despite opposition from the National Organization for Women, and Sandra Day O'Connor in 1981 over opposition from the Moral Majority and antiabortion forces.[75] Less visible and more individualized attempts to influence the process are usually more effective than group activity at the Senate hearing stage.[76]

The media may also play a screening role. They may uncover or disseminate information to the senators as well as the public that may affect selection or confirmation; they may also attempt to suggest or evaluate candidates in editorials or political columns.[77]

Finally, a few others are involved in the screening process. The FBI runs an investigation, at the request of the Department of Justice, on all serious candidates for judgeships. These investigations are extensive probes into the background, associations, and character of the candidate. FBI investigations are usually pro forma, but an adverse report is enough to stop a candidacy. The FBI file is confidential; it is received by the deputy attorney general's office and an official orally presents the substance of the file to the chairman of the Senate Judiciary Committee. "If the chairman wishes to look at the file, he will do so but only in the presence of the officer. . . . As a practical matter, therefore, the members of the Judiciary Committee only know what the Department of Justice or the chairman of the Judiciary Committee wishes to tell them."[78] The Internal Revenue Service is also consulted by the Department of Justice to make sure that the candidate's income tax returns have been filed on time and correctly.

These, then, are the formal and informal rules and actors in the federal judicial selection process. Although every administration has had a slightly different process, in general it involves the same players and the same rules interacting in more or less unique ways for each vacancy.

Criteria for Federal Judicial Appointments

Articles I and II of the Constitution specify that legislators and executives must possess certain minimal qualifications of citizenship and age. But Article III is silent as to judicial qualifications; constitutionally, federal judges need not be citizens, residents, over eighteen, or even lawyers. Today, custom and the involvement of the ABA demand a law degree for any candidate, and the Congress has required that district judges be residents of the district before appointment.[79] In practice, there is more localism than this requirement imposes. Richardson and Vines report that 66.6 percent of the district judges and 77.1 percent of the appeals judges were born in the state or the circuit, respectively, and that 60.5 percent of district judges and 86.4 percent of appeals judges were locally educated.[80]

The framers rejected the Continental model, which provided for a judiciary constituting a separate civil service system with specialized education and a particular career pattern, and left it to the president and the Senate to work out appropriate qualifications. "One result of the lack of constitutional guidance was that the process of judicial selection came to reflect the political standards and balances of each generation."[81] Yet those additional criteria differ to some degree from one administration to the next and thus reflect the political balance of the moment. They also reflect political and other standards of presidents. The importance of the political standards can be seen in the fact that the percentage of lower court appointees from the same party as the appointing president historically has been well over 90 percent. From the time of Grover Cleveland (who appointed *all* Democrats) until today, the lowest percentage of appointments from the same political party was made by William H. Taft, who cared more for the correct legal philosophy than the party label. Yet even he appointed over 82 percent Republicans.[82]

Presidents expect their nominees to share many of their political and policy views, and senators seldom endorse their political opponents. All presidents claim they wish to appoint "outstanding," "well-qualified," the "best" individuals, but different presidents judge qualifications differently. President Eisenhower wished for experienced judges and gave great weight to ABA ratings.[83] President Kennedy wanted nominees of "incorruptible character" who could "temper justice with mercy."[84] President Nixon was more candid than most in stating his criterion for selection: "First and foremost, they had to be men who shared my legal philosophy." He continued that he was determined to appoint "competent, experienced men who are sensitive to the [proper] role of the judiciary." The proper role, according to Nixon campaign speeches, was one of "strict construction" of the Constitution and support of the "peace forces" against the "criminal forces."[85]

Carter attempted to create an "independent" federal judiciary by calling for "merit selection" and affirmative action. Studies indicate that his process did open up the judiciary for groups traditionally excluded, but that most of his nominees shared his basically liberal Democratic philosophy.[86] And although President Reagan's counselor Edwin Meese stated that the president did not "have any litmus test in mind" for selecting judges, Reagan's nominees have generally agreed with his conservative philosophy and met the criteria of the 1980 Republican Party platform, which Reagan embraced.[87]

J. Woodford Howard, in his excellent study of courts of appeals, reports that his interviews with circuit judges themselves revealed four major factors in their appointments: "political participation, professional competence, personal ambition, plus an oft-mentioned pinch of luck. . . . Judgeships normally are rewards for political service. . . . To the politically active as well as to the party faithful go the prizes."[88] In order to be known to the executive or the senators, individuals must usually be active in party politics and must also be or have the reputation of being competent attorneys. Vocational choice is also important; some lawyers aspire to judicial office and plan their careers to work toward that goal. And a final factor, although not a criterion of presidential choice, is chance:

> The passage from the sea of eligibles to the narrow channels
> of candidacy, these judges generally agreed, requires luck. This
> usually meant a chance convergence of basic credentials with
> the politics of final selection—"knowing the right people at the
> right time."

Although Howard's list was drawn from judges of the courts of appeals, the factors also apply to other federal judges. Luck is an element, but the criteria set by presidents are the major factors in the appointment process.

The Constitution prescribes only the authority for selection and appointment of federal judges. Customs and political balances have combined to fill in the participants, their roles, and the criteria for selection. There is a general process, but because customs and the political balance change over time, the process changes from administration to administration. The next chapters examine the appointment process as it developed in the administration of Lyndon Johnson.

3. The Judicial Selection Process in a Presidential Transition

Every president's judicial selection process features a combination of unique aspects and components retained from previous administrations. Lyndon Johnson's process was no exception, but the development of his process was complicated by the fact that he was completing the term of an assassinated president. Several observers have noted that Johnson felt that the period from November 1963 until Johnson won election in his own right a year later was that of a caretaker or interim administration.[1] There was a period of transition in which elements of the John Kennedy process merged with the developing Johnson process and in which Kennedy criteria merged with Johnson criteria. Continuity during this period was a dominating theme. That continuity can be seen in the first year's nominations and in the appointment aides whom Johnson retained.

When Johnson took office in November of 1963 six judicial nominations made by President Kennedy had not yet been confirmed by the Senate. Homer Thornberry's nomination had been confirmed by the Senate but he had not yet been formally appointed. "With understandable and admirable loyalty to the late President, Johnson proceeded with the formalities required to ensure that these appointees would become federal judges."[2] Of course, Thornberry was a close friend of Johnson—indeed, the then vice president had made the initial recommendation for his nomination. Unfortunately, two of the other holdover nominees were highly controversial and caused the new president considerable trouble. George C. Edwards, Jr., nominated for the Court of Appeals for the Sixth Circuit, was confirmed only after a rather bruising round of hearings focusing on his early labor union leanings.[3]

Much greater problems arose with the nomination of David Rabinovitz for the District Court for Wisconsin. This nomination proceeding, begun in January 1963, had been held up during the last months of Kennedy's administration by the opposition of the Wisconsin State Bar Association and the American Bar Association, by whom Rabinovitz was rated "unqualified." It was alleged that the ABA's opposition to Rabinovitz, who had been legal counsel to the United Auto Workers (UAW) and whose appointment had been pushed by UAW President Walter Reuther, stemmed from his role as a labor lawyer. This point was apparent in a telegram sent on 21 November 1963 (before Kennedy's death) to James Eastland, chairman of the Senate Judiciary Committee. Some twenty-seven legal counselors to various unions, including J. Albert Woll of the AFL-CIO and Joseph L. Rauh, Jr., of the UAW urged the prompt confirmation of Rabinovitz and stated that "as labor lawyers we resent the attacks upon our colleague by anti-labor elements in Wisconsin and support his confirmation in the interest of fairness and justice."[4] This telegram was sent in response to the action of the Judiciary Subcommittee chairman, Senator Sam Ervin (D-N.C.), who on 20 November had said he would delay action on the Rabinovitz nomination.[5] Kennedy, in his last press conference, had been asked:

Q: Several months ago you nominated David Rabinovitz to be a Federal judge in western Wisconsin. Since that time the American Bar Association has opposed this nomination and a majority of lawyers polled by the State Bar Association said that he was unqualified. Do you still support this nomination, or in view of this opposition are you going to withdraw?

A: No. I'm for David Rabinovitz all the way. I know him very well, in fact, for a number of years and the American Bar Association has been very helpful in making the judgments but I'm sure they would agree that they're not infallible. The—Mr. [Louis] Brandeis was very much opposed—a good many judges have been opposed . . . some of them rather distinguished. And I'm for David Rabinovitz.[6]

The issue faced Johnson when he became president.

On 3 December 1963, in an editorial citing the adverse findings of the ABA concerning Rabinovitz, the *New York Times* urged the new president to withdraw the nomination.[7] But on that same day, in letters to White House aides Lawrence O'Brien, Kenneth O'Donnell, Theodore Sorenson, and Pierre Salinger, Rabinovitz, citing Kennedy's press conference comments, wrote, "I hope and pray that he [Johnson] will want to carry out what our dear, mutual friend, President Kennedy, so firmly declared on November 14, 1963."[8] Salinger responded, after seeking guidance from O'Donnell: "We're all standing behind you."[9] But the Judiciary Committee recessed without confirming Rabinovitz. President Johnson, upon the recommendation of Attorney General Robert F. Kennedy, then made Rabinovitz, along with three other of the Kennedy nominees, a recess appointment on 7 January 1964.[10] This interim appointment of Rabinovitz was effected just twelve minutes before Congress convened.[11] It was one of the very few such recess appointments Johnson made in his administration.[12]

The appointment was greeted with appreciation from many union sources, Jewish groups, and Democratic party officials in Wisconsin. Senator William Proxmire wrote to the president:

> Your recess appointment of David Rabinovitz as Federal Judge was an act of good sense and courage. . . . I especially appreciate your action because it was taken under extraordinarily difficult circumstances. The opposition to this appointment was powerful and determined. This was a brave decision on your part. I shall always be grateful for it.[13]

Judge Rabinovitz wrote to O'Brien to "acknowledge my deep feelings for the wonderful cooperation from the 'Whole Gang' at the White House."[14]

But it was not over. Johnson, again with the recommendation of Robert Kennedy, resubmitted the nomination in February, but again the Senate refused to confirm and adjourned in October with the appointment still unconfirmed.[15] Rabinovitz pleaded for another recess appointment by the president.[16] It appears that Johnson considered this action and inquired about the political effects in Wisconsin.[17] But despite his desire for continuity that first year, Johnson decided not to push any more on Rabinovitz and lose more political capital. In May 1965 he nominated James Doyle, who was rated "well-qualified" by the ABA, to the judgeship that had first become vacant over two years previously. Doyle was confirmed by the Senate.

Another nomination that, although not made in the first year, might also be considered part of Johnson's desire for continuity, or at least respect for the deceased president, was that of Francis X. Morrissey to the District Court for Massachusetts. The nomination of Morrissey, who had been Senator John Kennedy's secretary and was a longtime friend of the Kennedy family, was submitted in September 1965 at the repeated urging of Robert Kennedy and later of Senator Edward M. Kennedy and because of Johnson's perception of President Kennedy's intentions. In a letter to Johnson just before he left the administration, Robert Kennedy expressed the hope that he "would give sympathetic consideration to Frank Morrissey for appointment to the United States District Court for the District of Massachusetts."[18] In a memorandum to the president on 2 September, Attorney General Nicholas deB. Katzenbach noted that "Senator Edward Kennedy has consistently recommended Francis Morrissey [for the District Court]. . . . If you do not wish to submit the nomination of Judge Morrissey Senator Kennedy would appreciate the opportunity to discuss it with you in view of his very strong feelings."[19] And in a meeting with congressional leaders Johnson supported Morrissey:

> Mr. Johnson reportedly believes . . . that the late President made a private commitment to his father [Joseph P. Kennedy] to nominate Morrissey [for the judgeship] after the 1964 election. The President is said to feel that he should move forward with the nomination out of respect for his predecessor and a special favor to [former] Ambassador Kennedy.[20]

Thus, Johnson pushed the nomination of "a Kennedy-sponsored candidate whom the Kennedys manifestly never dared to nominate when one of them was President and another Attorney General."[21] The nomination was in trouble from the start—there were questions about Morrissey's legal training and professional competence; the ABA had rated him "unqualified." Morrissey's law degree was from a Georgia diploma mill, he had failed the bar examination twice, and he had had little legal experience before becoming a municipal judge. Later in the hearings it came out that at the same time Morrissey was claiming to be a resident of Georgia in order to gain admittance to the Georgia bar, he was also a candidate for a seat in the Massachusetts legislature.

Massachusetts District Court Chief Judge Wyzanski urged the Senate Judiciary Committee in a letter to reject the Morrissey nomination, stating that the "only discernible ground" for appointment was Morrissey's service to the Kennedy family rather than any legal ability.[22] The Judiciary Committee, in an unusual closed session on 13 October 1965 voted 6–3, with many abstentions, to approve the nomination. Soon after, however, media investigations revealed additional questionable aspects of Morrissey's legal training as well as other possible improprieties that raised more doubts about his testimony before the committee. (The *Boston Globe,* which ran a series of stories about the investigation, won a Pulitzer Prize for its efforts.) Several senators and newspapers announced their opposition, and on 19 October Johnson gave only lukewarm support by stating that he did not intend to withdraw the nomination "at this time."[23] Faced with this deteriorating situation, Senator Edward Kennedy asked on 21 October 1965 that the nomination be recommitted to the Judiciary Committee for further consideration. During the adjournment, when questions arose over possible recess appointments, Deputy Attorney General Ramsey Clark strongly recommended to the president that

> Judge Morrissey should not receive a recess appointment. The basis for Senator Kennedy's motion to recommit was to afford a full opportunity for Committee and Senate consideration. This purpose has not been fulfilled. In addition, hopefully either Judge Morrissey will withdraw his name from further consideration or Senator Kennedy will withdraw his recommendation. It would be most unfortunate under the present circumstances for Judge Morrissey to assume the Federal bench.[24]

Clark's hopes were realized: that same day, Morrissey wrote a letter to Johnson withdrawing his name from consideration.[25] Six months later, W. Arthur Garrity, also recommend by Senator Kennedy but receiving a thorough check from Johnson's team, was nominated to the vacancy and readily confirmed.[26]

More important than support for the small number of Kennedy recommendations was Johnson's substantial dependence on the Kennedy team. While Attorney General Robert Kennedy, who had dominated the process during his brother's presidency, was preoccupied during Johnson's incumbency with other matters, the Department of Justice continued the search for and recommendation of judges.[27] "The team at the Department of Justice remained the same, and they continued to carry on their activities connected with judicial selection as they had done while President Kennedy was alive."[28] That team included Katzenbach, deputy attorney general, and the assistant deputy, Joseph F. Dolan. Dolan was particularly involved in identifying candidates, while Katzenbach often made the major decisions on whether the department should recommend individuals.

Because of the close relationship between President Kennedy and Attorney General Kennedy, in the Kennedy administration no "member of the White House staff participated actively in the process of judicial selection."[29] However, there were exchanges of information between Justice and various White House aides, particularly those involved in congressional liaison. These included Mike N. Manatos, who had responsibility for Senate relations, presidential advisers Lamy O'Brien and Kenneth O'Donnell, and Ralph A. Dungan, who was Kennedy's appointments adviser. Johnson kept these men, and their role in the judicial selection process remained relatively minor. Johnson did bring in several of his own personal advisers, such as Walter Jenkins, Jack Valenti, and Bill D. Moyers, whose role in the process increased as time wore on. Johnson also relied on trusted friends outside of government to advise him on various judicial appointments.[30] Most notable was longtime confidante Abe Fortas, who advised Johnson on the selection of federal judges until Johnson left office, even while himself serving as a justice of the Supreme Court.[31]

In sum, while some changes were occurring, the judicial selection process in Johnson's transition year remained similar to that under Kennedy, with the exceptions of the close relationship between President Kennedy and his brother, perhaps a slightly larger role and more-informed status for the White House staff, and Johnson's reach for outside advice. The Justice Department's team still made most of the significant judgments, with final approval from the president. For example, when William C. Doherty, ambassador to Jamaica, wrote to the president recommending a candidate for the Court of Appeals for the District of Columbia, it was Dolan, assistant deputy attorney general, who wrote the reply that O'Donnell, special assistant to the president, actually sent to Ambassador Doherty.[32]

But one thing that was different was the amount of time which passed during the selection process. For whatever reasons—his unfamiliarity with the process, his wish to be certain of the Senate's wishes, his desire to be personally sure of the qualifications of his nominees, rather than just accepting the Justice Department's assurances—Johnson often delayed making nominations for relatively long periods. Besides the Kennedy holdovers from 1963, in the entire year of 1964 only eighteen Johnson-initiated appointments were completed.

The delay can be seen in the selection of a judge of the Second Circuit Court of Appeals. On 13 December 1963, a vacancy arose because of the death of Judge Charles Clark, a Democrat from Connecticut. On 21 December Attorney General Kennedy (presumably with the concurrence of his deputy) recommended in a memorandum to the president that the appointee be a Democrat and an outstanding jurist from any of the three states making up the Second Circuit (Connecticut, Vermont, and New York):

> In my judgment the outstanding candidate would be Judge
> Edward Weinfeld, . . . the outstanding district court judge in New
> York, and, I believe, in the United States. . . . Because Judge
> Clark was from Connecticut it is likely that Senators Dodd and

Ribicoff will make a recommendation from that state. One possibility is Chief Judge [Robert P.] Anderson [of the District Court], who is a Republican, which would open up a vacancy on the district court in Connecticut. Anderson is a good judge, but there is no reason to appoint a Republican [and Weinfeld's qualifications are better].[33]

Following this up a week later, Deputy Attorney General Katzenbach sent a memo to O'Donnell informing him of the existing judicial vacancies on the courts of appeals and the status of the Second Circuit, including Robert Kennedy's recommendation.[34]

A month later, on 23 January 1964, Katzenbach sent another memo to O'Donnell concerning the vacancies and the developments that had occurred since the earlier memo. By this time, Senator Dodd from Connecticut was beginning to express interest in an appointment from his state, especially one that would help him politically. Katzenbach suggested that "Senator Dodd may well recommend Anderson, along with a Democrat for the District Court vacancy which would open up." He concluded: "We would still like to elevate Weinfeld. I have not discussed the matter with Senator Dodd. I cannot take any steps to fill this vacancy without some further guidance from you."[35] Several months later, Dolan sent a memo to Mike Manatos again reviewing the Second Circuit vacancy and noting that both Dodd and the department had received recommendations for Judge Anderson and for Eugene Rostow, Dean of the Yale Law School. Dolan wrote, "I have chatted with Senator Dodd several times about the vacancy and he appears to feel that Anderson's appointment would be more helpful to him politically." It was apparent by this time that the White House had decided to favor geographic representation and go along with the Democratic senator's wishes. The department responded that before any recommendation of Anderson was made, it was important that the appointment of a successor to Anderson on the District Court for Connecticut be thought through. Dodd said "that it will be difficult politically for him to recommend, between now and the election, an appointee for the District Court other than a lawyer of Italian descent," and pointed to Lieutenant Governor Samuel Tedesco and U.S. Attorney Robert Zampano.[36] Soon after, stories of the contest over the still nonexistent district court vacancy appeared in the press, and on 12 July the *New York Times* reported that the Anderson elevation was delayed by the failure of Connecticut Democrats to agree on a successor and especially by Dodd's failure to choose between Tedesco and Zampano.[37]

Those stories may have prompted action, because on 17 August 1964, Robert P. Anderson was appointed to the United States Court of Appeals for the Second Circuit and Robert Zampano was appointed to the District Court for the District of Connecticut.[38] It is interesting to note the time it took to fill the original vacancy (eight months), the White House concern about the senator's wishes, and the overruling, to an extent, of the attorney general's original recommendation because of geographic considerations.

Changes from the Kennedy-Johnson process to a more uniquely Johnson process began in the early fall of 1964. A major change came about when Robert Kennedy resigned as attorney general on 3 September 1964 in order to run for the Senate from New York.[39] Nicholas Katzenbach was named acting attorney general to replace Kennedy. Joseph Dolan also soon resigned and became Edward Kennedy's administrative assistant in the Senate. There were changes in the White House too, as Ralph Dungan left in late November to become ambassador to Chile. Walter Jenkins, Johnson's trusted aide who was somewhat involved in judicial selection, also resigned in October 1964.[40] And a week after the election, Johnson asked John Macy, chairman of the United States Civil Service Commission, to act also as his personnel adviser. So by shortly after the election, a somewhat different team had taken over the judicial selection process, which itself was changing to a Johnson process.

A sidelight to this discussion of the transition-year process is that the Republican candidate for the presidency in 1964, just as would the candidate in 1968, made the "liberal" courts and the "criminal-coddling" judges appointed by the administration a campaign target. Barry Goldwater, in a speech in September 1964, charged that the federal courts sacrificed law and order in order "to give criminals a sporting chance to go free." He pledged that if he were elected he would use the appointment power to "redress constitutional interpretations in favor of the public." A few days later, Johnson's deputy attorney general Katzenbach (without naming Goldwater) termed such criticism of the courts "uninformed and irresponsible."[41]

Johnson's defeat of Goldwater enabled him to reshape the judicial appointment process. The next chapter will discuss the developed Johnson process of judicial selection and the major actors in that process.

4. The Developed Johnson Process of Judicial Selection

With the huge election victory of 3 November 1964, the transition year came to an end, and Lyndon B. Johnson was president in his own right. He felt less hesitance in making changes in the process and in bringing in his own people; although it should be recognized that there was no abrupt break with the past, there was a perceptible shift to a judicial selection process in which Johnson and the White House staff played a more prominent role.

When a vacancy occurred, the process usually began at the Department of Justice, especially with the deputy attorney general and his assistant. The department had extensive files on many candidates, which it retained for five years after initial consideration.[1] In addition, it had sources in most states that it contacted for possible candidates when a vacancy arose and that it used to check on candidates suggested by senators. There was routine checking with the (John W.) "Macy operation" (to be discussed later) and extensive political negotiations with the senators and White House aides involved (particularly W. Marvin Watson, Jr., and later Larry E. Temple). There may also have been communication with the more informal advisers such as Abe Fortas, and informal FBI and ABA checks on possible nominees. Often the president was notified of and concerned with these preliminary steps and may have been personally involved in the selection. Many times the initial information would be provided to the president in his "night reading," which he took into his private chambers overnight.[2] In the morning he would often make comments on the documents, either directing the Justice Department to go ahead with or to stop a candidacy or specifying that his aides should get further directions personally from him to transmit to Justice. Often the comments would state, "Marvin [Watson] or Larry [Temple]—See me." With White House concurrence, the Department of Justice would have formal FBI and ABA investigations (and sometimes Democratic National Committee and IRS checks, also) run and then send over the formal memo of recommendation. In the later years especially, before proceeding any further White House aides might bring in the prospective nominee for a personal interview to determine the personal credentials and loyalty before making the final recommendation to the president. The president, if he concurred, would sign the nomination form and send it to the Senate and the Judiciary Committee, headed by Senator James Eastland (D-Miss.), for confirmation hearings and vote.

Of course, one of these steps usually included, especially if no interview was conducted, checking with the prospective nominee to see if he or she were interested in the nomination. Most were eager for the chance, and many have noted that an appointment to a federal judgeship is every attorney's goal. But on a few occasions, the candidate refused. Fortas, for example, tried to decline the nomination to the Supreme Court and sent a letter to that effect to the president.[3] And William T. Coleman, Jr., declined nomination to the Court of Appeals for the Third Circuit, suggesting that he could be more valuable serving the Negro community in a position of economic and legal leadership.[4] However, on at least a few occasions nominees were not asked or informed but simply announced. For example, Fortas was told only moments before Johnson announced him as a nominee to the Supreme Court.[5] And Johnson's close friend Homer Thornberry first received news about his elevation to the court of appeals from a newspaper reporter who asked for a statement.[6]

Finally, the nominee would be informed that his or her nomination had been submitted to the Senate. In the early years this notification was often done formally by telegram, as exemplified by a telegram sent by the president in April 1964 to an Idaho attorney: "I have sent your nomination to be United States District Judge for the District of Idaho to the Senate today."[7] Later, there seemed to be less formal notification by the White House to the nominee and on occasion the White House or the Justice Department would win political points by allowing the home-state senator to inform the nominee.

The Macy Operation

One of the unique parts of the selection team was the "Macy operation." John Macy had been appointed chairman of the Civil Service Commission by President John F. Kennedy and began his relationship with Johnson when he served on the President's Committee on Equal Opportunity, which Johnson chaired as vice president. Soon after his election, Johnson persuaded Macy to put on a second hat as a presidential aide, working one shift as civil service commissioner and another in the Executive Office Building advising the president on appointments.[8]

> Among presidential appointments advisers, Macy was unique in coming, not from the campaign or "political" side of the administration, but from a long career in the federal bureaucracy. Johnson told Macy quite frankly that he did not expect him to make political judgments about appointees. "I am aware that your political judgment probably isn't very good," the president said. "Others will make the political judgment. I want you to proceed in the same professional way that you proceed in the civil service."
>
> Macy speculates that, in addition to the advantage of having staff work done by someone who was knowledgeable in the field of personnel administration, his appointment gave a president interested in recruiting officers of high quality more leverage against requests for pure patronage appointments.[9]

Macy's function was of much greater significance in nonjudicial appointments. For those, he would prepare position profiles and match those with the names he had gathered from his many sources. For judicial appointments, he served more as a clearinghouse for names submitted by the Justice Department. As White House aide Larry Temple noted:

> The way the Presidential appointment process was set up . . . is that most of the Presidential appointments initiated with John Macy. . . . But those related to the legal end in any way or form— obviously all the Judicial appointments . . . —originated with the Department of Justice.[10]

And, in Macy's own words:

> To some degree the office was involved in some of the judicial appointments—but only in a limited degree. The Attorneys General, Nicholas Katzenbach and Ramsey Clark, were the responsible officials who dealt with the Judicial appointments. The actual papers came through this office of mine but largely to raise any particular policy issues that we felt the President might want to raise himself.[11]

So Macy's role in judicial selection was largely a formal one involving record-keeping and oversight. His office also received suggestions about appointments, which were passed on to the Department of Justice and the White House aide concerned. For example, in a memorandum to Marvin Watson commenting on a vacancy on the court for the Southern District of Illinois, Macy wrote: "For your information, we have received several letters like the attached from County Chairmen in Southern Illinois. I am also advising Ramsey Clark of this."[12] In turn, those officials and others would send communications involving judicial selection to Macy's office for filing: "Attached are several memos and letters in my possession relating to judicial appointments which I return to you as the person primarily responsible," wrote Clark.[13] Macy's office was also a convenient place for officials to direct requests they had received for assistance in gaining judicial posts, as seen in this memo from Harry C. McPherson, Jr., special counsel to the president, concerning a letter McPherson had received asking for help in getting a judicial appointment: "I have no axe to grind on the matter, and merely pass this on to you because I said I would get it to the chief body supplier for the Great Society."[14] And Macy every few weeks prepared a list of existing and anticipated vacancies in presidential appointment positions (including judicial vacancies), their regions, and the date of the vacancy.[15]

But Macy may have played a somewhat stronger role as well, particularly in the first few years of the operation. By being the clearinghouse for final approval, Macy put together all the various checks and may have exerted some influence over certain selections. A typical memorandum of the period from Macy to the president reads:

SUBJECT: Judge Frederick J. Nichol to be United States District
         Judge, District of South Dakota

I have reviewed the memorandum from the Deputy Attorney General and I support his recommendation that you nominate Judge Frederick J. Nichol to be United States District Judge for the District of South Dakota.

Judge Nichol has the strong support of Senator George McGovern of South Dakota.

The FBI investigation and the IRS check have been completed, and the necessary Congressional and National Committee clearances have been obtained.

Attached were a resume, the memorandum from Deputy Attorney General Clark, and the formal recommendation from Attorney General Katzenbach. At the bottom of Macy's memo, where there are blanks after "Approve," "Disapprove," and "See Me," Johnson had checked "Approve."[16] Nichol was nominated and appointed to the judgeship.

Another memo from Macy is of a more substantive nature and indicates that Macy was aware of the politics of judicial selection:

> SUBJECT: E. Mac Troutman and Charles B. Weiner to be United States District Judges for the Eastern District of Pennsylvania
>
> In the attached memoranda, the Attorney General and the Assistant [Deputy] Attorney General recommend the nomination of *Charles R. Weiner*, 44, and *E. Mac Troutman*, 52, for appointment. . . . The FBI investigation and the IRS check have been completed.
>
>   Weiner, a Democrat, has the endorsement of Senator [Joseph S.] Clark and is also supported by Mayor [Joseph M.] Barr and Thomas Minehart, the Democratic State Chairman. Troutman, a Republican, was recommended by Senator Hugh Scott and is acceptable to Senator Clark. Mayor Barr and Chairman Minehart, however, oppose Troutman's nomination. Nevertheless, I agree with the Attorney General that your best hope of breaking the impasse in Pennsylvania judicial nominations is to proceed with these two candidates. . . .
>
>   I recommend your approval.[17]

Both nominations were sent to the Senate in the middle of 1967.

But soon after this, the Macy operation appears to have been excluded from any major role in the judicial selection process. In an internal White House memorandum of 1 September 1967 to Watson from H. Barefoot Sanders, Jr., recently appointed legislative counsel to the president, Sanders wrote:

> I note that all nominations from the Justice Department—Federal Judges, U.S. Attorneys, U.S. Marshalls, etc.—are routed from here to John Macy for clearance.
>
>   This seems to me unnecessary duplication. I have no strong feelings about it, but unless there is some purpose being served by routing these nominations through Chairman Macy, I recommend that this procedure be cancelled.

"O.K." was written on the bottom of the memo.[18] The Macy role from then on appears to be merely record-keeping on judicial appointments, as indicated by a memorandum informing Macy that the president had signed a particular nomination.[19]

The Department of Justice

While the Justice Department did not have the almost sole official power over judicial selection that it did during the Kennedy years, it continued to play a significant role in the process. The department was, within the executive branch, the initiator of most actions, the major source of names, and the primary decisionmaker on most nominations.[20] The department often responded to senatorial initiative in recommending names, but it did not simply forward senatorial wishes. Instead, it independently checked on the qualifications of the candidates, and if they were not appropriate, would usually reject the individuals and search for other candidates. This is illustrated by a memo from then-Deputy Attorney General Katzenbach to a White House aide early in the Johnson presidency. Katzenbach, discussing a district court vacancy in Arkansas, reported that:

> Senator [John L.] McClellan [D-Ark.] . . . has recommended _____, who is unacceptable to us on the basis of ability and reputation. He would also be rated as not qualified by the ABA. We have told McClellan that we will not recommend _____.[21]

Even though McClellan was an influential senator, his candidate was not appointed.

When the White House initially received a suggestion for a judgeship, it referred the name to the department. The department would then proceed to do preliminary political and legal checks. For example, Jack Valenti of the White House staff sent Attorney General Katzenbach a memorandum in early 1966 reporting that an individual "has been brought to our attention" for a district judgeship. "Can you check the two Senators and see how they feel about him?"[22]

The major players dealing with judicial selection in the department were the attorney general, the deputy attorney general, and the assistant deputy attorney general. While their responsibilities in selection were flexible, it appears that the deputy had the primary responsibility overall and the assistant deputy worked closely with him and was involved in liaison with the ABA Committee on the Federal Judiciary and various politicians, while the attorney general set general policy guidelines and criteria, and in some cases got deeply involved with particular nominations, particularly at the Supreme Court level. In addition to this flexibility, there was also a good deal of flux in the department as individuals came into Justice or changed positions.

When Robert Kennedy resigned as attorney general in September 1964, Deputy Attorney General Katzenbach became acting attorney general. For several months, there was no deputy, and with Joseph Dolan's resignation, no assistant deputy, and judicial selection proceeded slowly. Then in February 1965, Johnson appointed Katzenbach attorney general and Ramsey Clark as his deputy.[23] Clark, son of Supreme Court Justice Tom C. Clark, who was a longtime friend of Senator Johnson as well as President Johnson, had been known to Johnson since he was a small child. Ramsey Clark notes that, while serving as assistant attorney general for the Lands Division in the Department of Justice he "had worked extensively on judicial appointments, not just Texas, but many other places, including New York; that was negotiation with senators basically."[24] And because of his Texas background, he was particularly useful as a liaison between the department, Vice President Johnson, and Democratic Senator Ralph Yarborough of Texas concerning judicial appointments in the state. After Johnson's election in November 1964, he also was called over to the White House on "detached duty" to work on various assignments for the president, including analysis of various candidates for judgeships.[25] From that dual position he was promoted to deputy and given the major role in judicial selection. Even before he was confirmed by the Senate, Katzenbach sent a memo to Johnson on 3 February 1965, confirming that role:

> I am asking Ramsey Clark to take prime responsibility for the recommendation of judicial appointments and for staffing the Department. This is traditionally a function of the Deputy Attorney General.
>
> I have also asked him to communicate directly with you and John Macy on appointments. You may rely on the fact that all his recommendations will have been discussed with me and are mine as well.
>
> The formal recommendations for Presidential appointments will be normally submitted over my signature.

And at the bottom of this memo, in the president's handwriting, is "OK, L."[26]

Clark seemed to perform this role with a great deal of attentiveness and concern for quality and competence. These characteristics are evident from the words of Ernest C. Friesen, Clark's assistant deputy attorney general. He wrote:

Ramsey Clark is a special kind of person. He has the courage
to recommend what he believes to be right and the instincts to
know what is right. He is a rare combination of idealist and prag-
matist. Without his constant pressure to seek the most qualified
I doubt that our attempts to hold the line for quality would be
successful. He does all of the negotiating with the political interests with astonishing results.[27]

Clark was involved in checking legal credentials and political clearances, and in some cases, policy attitudes of potential nominees. For
example, a normal product of Clark's work was the following memorandum to the president, which accompanied Attorney General
Katzenbach's formal recommendation:

RE: United States Court of Appeals for the Fifth Circuit
Enclosed are the nomination papers on John Cooper Godbold . . .
—Mr. Godbold is 46 years of age and is presently a partner in [a]
law firm in Montgomery, Alabama. [Here is a summary of Godbold's education and armed services experience.] We recommend
Mr. Godbold's nomination for the following reasons:
    1. His long experience as a general practitioner indicates he is
fully qualified to be United States Circuit Judge.
    2. The American Bar Association has made inquiry into his
capabilities and has found him well qualified to be United States
Circuit Judge.
    3. He has the strong recommendation of Senators [Lister] Hill
and [John] Sparkman [of Alabama].
    4. The Federal Bureau of Investigation discloses no information
to bar Mr. Godbold's nomination.
    5. The Internal Revenue Service advises Mr. Godbold's income
tax returns have been timely filed.[28]

Clark's policy role as investigator of certain philosophies, particularly in the civil rights area, becomes clear in a directive by Johnson
written on a memorandum by Macy attached to recommendations
by Katzenbach and Clark. Johnson dictated: "Call Ramsey. Check to
be sure he [the prospective nominee] is all right on the Civil Rights
question. I'll approve him if he is."[29] Clark did check, the candidate
was acceptable, and thus David W. Dyer was nominated to be judge
for the Fifth Circuit Court of Appeals. And a Louisiana state judge
was nominated to a district judgeship after Clark's assurances that
"we have inquired extensively about Judge [Frederick J. R.] Heebe's

record on matters dealing with civil rights and believe him to be a liberal who would follow the law as a U.S. District Judge."[30]

Attorney General Katzenbach resigned after eighteen months to take a position as undersecretary of state and Clark, after six months in an acting role, succeeded him in March 1967.[31] During his acting stage when there was no deputy, and even after one was appointed, Clark was involved in judicial selection more closely than Katzenbach as attorney general had been. Illustrative is a memo Clark wrote in January 1967, while acting attorney general, which concerned several pending nominations and showed a grasp of the political realities: "As usual, Wisconsin is divided politically and emotionally over this vacancy. . . . [Myron L.] Gordon, according to Cliff Carter, is clearly the Johnson man."[32] Because of his close previous relationship with Johnson, the White House depended upon Clark's judgment in making judicial appointments.

After Clark was confirmed as attorney general, Warren M. Christopher, a distinguished Los Angeles attorney, was appointed as deputy attorney general in June 1967. Although by then the White House staff was exercising more power than before over judicial selections, the position of deputy attorney general was still the focal point of judicial selection. As Christopher has noted, an "area where the Deputy Attorney General has by tradition and custom a large responsibility is in the matter of judicial appointments which are all processed in the Deputy Attorney General's office."[33] The process was carried out in cooperation with the attorney general, particularly when controversial and significant positions were involved. Christopher commented on this cooperative effort after Chief Justice Earl Warren decided to retire:

> As with other appointments, we drew up lists of names for both of the spots and talked about them back and forth, got out their biographies, the things they had written, tried to assess the possible shortcomings and possible handicaps from the standpoint of confirmation and tried to assess what this would mean in a historical sense to the Court.[34]

Obviously, the attorney general would not play such a prominent role in nominations for lower courts; in those, the deputy attorney general would predominate. However, Christopher did not seem to be as involved in the political aspect of selection as Clark had been, and left those considerations to others—either Clark or the White House staff.[35] There was also a slight change in the formal procedure: rather than writing an accompanying memo to the president along with the attorney general's formal recommendation, Christopher would send his memo on the candidate to members of the White House staff (either Temple or Sanders).[36]

The last major position in the Department of Justice team was the assistant deputy attorney general. Dolan, who filled this position under Robert Kennedy and Katzenbach, had a great deal of influence until he resigned. He was replaced in April of 1965 by Friesen, who was "uniquely equipped" for his new role by his prior experience as dean of the National College of State Trial Judges. Friesen took over Dolan's responsibilities of obtaining and screening names of possible nominees and negotiating with the other actors in the selection process, particularly the ABA (although he was skeptical of the ABA ratings).[37] Friesen appears to have had a good working relationship with Deputy Attorney General Clark, which led to considerable responsibility in the process. As liaison with political leaders and the ABA, Friesen attempted to get information and persuade others to accept the department's view. As Friesen explained to Harold Chase:

He [Ramsey Clark] deals occasionally with Mr. [Albert] Jenner [the chairman of the ABA Committee on Federal Judiciary], but more important, I do my best to convey his ideas and represent his special point of view to the committee (though not necessarily attributing the point of view to him).[38]

First sharing duties with and then succeeding Friesen, who was promoted to assistant attorney general for administration (and then became director of the Administrative Office of the United States Courts in December 1967) was Barefoot Sanders, a Texan who served as assistant deputy from February 1965 to November 1966. Sanders had been United States Attorney for the Northern District of Texas from 1961 to 1965, an appointment pushed by Vice President Johnson and made part of a multiappointment deal with Texas Senator Yarborough. As assistant deputy attorney general, Sanders worked closely with Deputy Attorney General Clark and acted as legislative liaison for the Department of Justice with Congress. In 1966, he was promoted to the post of assistant attorney general in charge of the Civil Division, but he continued to perform many of the same tasks, including a role in judicial selection. Sanders had the confidence and increasingly the ear of Johnson and White House aide Watson. Watson, in a memo to the president in 1966 concerning Sanders' promotion to assistant attorney general, wrote, "I have found Barefoot to be 1000% loyal to the President."[39] Sanders was very concerned with the political and personal loyalty aspects of selection. He seemed to be much involved in the increasingly important Watson–White House clearance responsibility (to be discussed later), even when he was serving as assistant attorney general for the Civil Division. By early 1967, Sanders seemed to have gained a great deal of input into Justice Department appointments, as seen in this memo to Watson from Assistant Attorney General Sanders:

SUBJECT: Justice Department Nomination
I have initialed the attached 21 Justice Department nomination recommendations (13 judges, 5 U.S. Attorneys, 3 U.S. Marshals) to indicate my approval. . . .
On the judges I have stayed in touch with Ramsey as he considered the nominations. . . .
Each of these men is qualified. Each will be grateful for his appointment and will appreciate the fact that the President has honored him and shown confidence in him by appointment. Each will serve with distinction and reflect credit on the Administration. . . .
With judges, who after this lifetime appointment are removed from the political arena, appreciation for the appointment and outstanding service on the bench are most important. These nominees come out strong on these counts.
I am attaching some comments on particular individuals:
. . . He is committed to the Administration's programs, I know that he will be everlasting grateful for the appointment.
. . . is a Republican, well qualified, and we very much need some Republican judicial appointments . . . He . . . will . . . appreciate the appointment.[40]

Twelve of the judges were nominated, but next to one name was the note "Send back to Barefoot Sanders." Sanders initialed several of Clark's memorandums to the president indicating his agreement with the attorney general's recommendations.[41] And in another memorandum to the president concerning a district judgeship Macy wrote "Barefoot Sanders advises me that he has discussed all aspects of this appointment with you on several occasions, and that you are thoroughly familiar with the political situation regarding it."[42] These memorandums were written in a period when there was no deputy attorney general, and it appears that Sanders took on that position's selection responsibilities.[43] His influence seems impressive and his ties seemed closer to the White House than to the Department of Justice.

In May 1967 that relationship was formalized, as Sanders moved to the White House Office as legislative counsel to the president. He continued to play a role in judicial selection, passing on the recommendations of nominations that came from the Justice Department until Temple took over.

After Christopher's appointment as deputy attorney general in the middle of 1967, there appeared to be a reorganization of the office. Christopher had assistant deputies for litigation and administration, but none played Dolan's or Friesen's role. Instead, a unit in Christopher's office, supervised by John Duffner, administered the paperwork of listing vacancies, preparing draft replies to letters of resignation, and writing the formal letters of recommendation.[44]

In sum, although the Department of Justice, particularly in the later years when Watson and the White House staff took over much of the political clearance, did not have the almost exclusive executive control over judicial selection that it had had during the Kennedy administration, it nevertheless retained a great responsibility in the process. Katzenbach, Christopher, and especially Clark—in all three roles as deputy attorney general, acting attorney general, and attorney general—continued to influence the appointment of federal judges in the Johnson administration. The power of the Department of Justice and the relationship between the president and Attorney General Clark are indicated clearly by a comment Johnson made to his close friend, Senator Richard B. Russell (D-Ga.), who was pushing a candidate that Clark found unacceptable. According to Temple, "the President said that he had never nominated anyone that had not been recommended by the Attorney General, and didn't think he could or would."[45]

The White House Staff

The White House Office, which had played a relatively minor role in judicial selection during Kennedy's presidency, slowly developed to become an important part of the Johnson selection process. As noted earlier, remaining Kennedy aides (particularly Kenneth O'Donnell and to a lesser extent Walter Jenkins, Jack Valenti, and Bill Moyers) shared in the information the Justice Department received about possible judicial nominees. As the conduit of information between the president and the department, those aides obviously served an important role. Deputy Attorney General Katzenbach recognized this role several times in a memo in early 1964 to O'Donnell. In discussing various judicial vacancies, Katzenbach stated at different

times, "I cannot take any steps to fill this vacancy without some further guidance from you," and "I can do nothing on the Third Circuit
without further guidance from the White House."[46] Although the
staff did perform this function of transmitting Justice Department
information and presidential preferences, it did not seem to have a
major role in decisionmaking during the transition year. In the next
year the Macy operation, which worked out of the White House
Office, was begun, but it exercised largely formal and nonpolitical
responsibilities in judicial appointments. The White House aides
still did not seem to have a great deal of input, only transmitting information and bringing names to the attention of the president and
the department.[47]

But this situation shortly underwent a change, and the leading
edge of that change was Marvin Watson, who assumed Valenti's position as appointments secretary to the president in February 1965,
and who also was liaison to the political committees and the Democratic National Committee. Watson, a Texan, was a close and trusted
aide whose role in the selection process became increasingly significant in the next few years.[48] This was caused by or accompanied by
several factors. One was the president's increasing aversion to criticism, particularly from within the administration, and his demand
for personal loyalty. Another was the requirement for agreement
with Vietnam policy from all appointees. And the third was Johnson's dissatisfaction, by 1966, with the political nonattentiveness of
the Macy operation. Macy comments that the president's grant to
Watson of certain responsibility in the appointments process "was a
vote of no confidence in our review. . . . [Watson's] standards were
quite different from mine. He felt that membership in most liberal
organizations was potentially subversive."[49]

It was to this advice that Johnson seemed increasingly to turn. In
the last several years of his administration, Watson was granted or
took greater responsibilities in screening the political and personal
loyalty of candidates for appointment. Moyers believes that Watson came to dominate the political selection process in the White
House and that Johnson "tolerated at first, and then encouraged, the
winnowing and narrowing of the [appointments] process into a far
more parochial operation than Macy [or other White House aides]
represented."[50]

By the middle of 1966, the Justice Department was funneling its
recommendations through Watson and by the middle of 1967, Watson seemed to be the central point of the information flow to and
from Johnson for almost all input concerning judicial selection.[51]
The Macy operation no longer cleared judicial nominations.[52] Wat-

son's influence had increased as Johnson's attitude toward dissent hardened.

The best example of this particular attitude is in a file concerning the appointment of a U.S. attorney. The Justice Department and Clark recommended an individual highly and wished to move forward with the nomination. On the bottom of a recommendation from Clark, the president had penned a note to Watson. It reads "M—See if he is all the way—always—no maybes—."[53] Watson's assistants ran political checks on the candidate, who was brought to Washington for personal interviews at the Justice Department and apparently with Watson himself before the nomination went through.

Watson continued in this influential role of political clearance through early 1968. In November 1967 he sent a memorandum to the president concerning possible nominees for judgeships: they "are strong in support of President Johnson." What is interesting is that the supporters of these nominees were also rated: the "Westchester County Leader, is strong for [the nominee] and, as we know, he has given strong support to the President," while another nominee is "strongly supported by Mayor [Frank A.] Sedita [of Buffalo] who is publicly supporting the President 100%."[54] And on at least some occasions, Watson initiated the selection process by informing certain individuals of upcoming vacancies and suggesting that they begin to build political support.[55] A January 1968 memo transmits the information Watson requested about the attitude of the California delegation and other politicians (such as Edmund G. "Pat" Brown, Jesse M. Unruh, and Sam Yorty) toward a proposed nominee for a district judgeship in California.[56] Watson was assisted in this role by several subordinates such as James R. Jones and Douglas Nobles, and by Barefoot Sanders, who came to the White House as legislative counsel. For example, in November of 1967 Sanders was making recommendations based on political reasons to the president and by February 1968 the Department of Justice was channeling at least some of its formal recommendations through Sanders.[57] A few other aides, such as Joseph A. Califano, Jr. and Harry McPherson, also played a limited role in the selection process.[58] Mike N. Manatos, who was Johnson's liaison to the Senate, played an important communications role, transmitting information on senatorial preferences and confirmation voting to the White House and the Justice Department.

In April of 1968, Watson was appointed postmaster general as a reward for his loyalty and dedication. By this time much of his role in the judicial selection process had been shared with or taken over by Larry Temple, although Watson still retained at least some overall control over the process until he left. For example, a memo to the president from Sanders in March reads, "At Marvin's request, Larry and I have talked to the attorney general and the deputy attorney general about existing judicial vacancies on the Federal Circuit and District Courts."[59] Temple, who was also a Texan, had been law clerk to Justice Tom Clark and executive assistant to Governor John B. Connally of Texas before coming to the White House as special counsel to the president for the last year of the Johnson administration in late 1967. One of Temple's major responsibilities was his role as liaison with the Department of Justice (and Tom Clark's son Ramsey), which of course involved him in the judicial selection process. In his oral history, Temple described his role in the process:

> [Appointments] related to the legal end in any way or form—obviously all the Judicial appointments . . . —originated with the Department of Justice. Those came through me, and I usually had a considerable number of discussions with people at the Department of Justice about the appointments and about the people involved before we got to the posture of a memo recommending people.[60]

It is interesting that Temple was granted a role in the selection process almost from the start of his tenure in the White House. Temple states that, "beginning probably after I'd been there 30 or 60 days, if they were processing appointments of federal judges, the paperwork process came through me."[61] Even before Watson left, Temple was playing a major role, probably the major role among White House officials. He too was concerned with the political aspects, but did not seem to place the same heavy emphasis on personal loyalty as Watson had. By early February, he was suggesting names of possible candidates to the attorney general, and within a few months he was the primary White House actor in the selection process, coordinating political strategy for appointments for the president and making recommendations to Johnson on judgeships.[62] Temple commented that

> when the President and the Attorney General met in their office, at least during 1968, the president almost always had me in there . . . since I was handling liaison with the Department of Justice he wanted me to know what was transpiring so he wouldn't have to tell me about it and re-educate me at a later time.[63]

Temple's role is seen in memos to the president in July and August describing Temple's discussions with senators on judicial vacancies and giving his recommendations on circuit and district judgeships.[64] Temple played a major role in the Fortas-Thornberry nominating attempt and the 1968 postelection nominations to be discussed later.

The role of the White House Office in the last three years of Johnson's presidency was an interesting one. Watson, Sanders, and Temple had a good deal of input into judicial selection and shared with the Department of Justice the task of screening nominees. The White House screening was largely political, and especially during the Watson era was to determine political and personal loyalty to the president and his policies in areas often removed from the judicial or legal sphere, such as foreign policy. White House aides were responsible as well for the strategy of appointments in two aspects. One was that they, along with the attorney general and assistant attorney general, carried out negotiations with senators and planned the timing of nominations. For example, in a June 1968 memo to Christopher concerning the "New Jersey judgeship situation," Sanders reported: "Larry [Temple] and I met today, and subject to further discussion with you and Ramsey, thought we might proceed as follows" and described a strategy to satisfy various interests by sending several nominations to the White House while holding two other vacancies.[65]

The other aspect was handled largely by the congressional liaison staff, particularly the primary Senate liaison, Manatos. That was the responsibility of securing confirmation of those nominees submitted by the president. Obviously the Justice Department worked closely in most cases with the senators involved, but when the nomination was controversial, as were the second Fortas nomination and others, Manatos kept busy trying to assess probable votes and trying to maintain cordial relationships with essential senators. In those instances Manatos worked closely with Watson or Temple or with the president personally.

The President

The White House Office is obviously a reflection of the occupant of the White House, as is the judicial selection process itself. Of course the president is limited in that selection by tradition and politics and is guided by his own values. As was noted, history affected the process because the Johnson administration in its first year held a caretaker status. Political considerations are always important in selection. What is remarkable is how much the president's values affected judicial selection, partly through the Watson political clearance operation, and partly through the person of the president himself. Johnson, to a greater degree than perhaps any president before him except William Howard Taft, was concerned and personally involved in the selection of judges to all levels of the federal judiciary.[66] Most presidents are attentive to Supreme Court appointments, but Johnson also was interested in appointments to courts of appeals and district courts.

This personal interest in appointments has been attested to by close observers. Macy commented on Johnson's interest in and enjoyment of appointments, and observed that the president

> was deeply involved in a large number of appointments. He had a fantastic memory and he could recall some detail on a summary that we would send him, months and months afterwards, and would frequently enjoy challenging me on whether I could remember as well as he could what those particular details were.[67]

The ABA Committee on Federal Judiciary, in a report on its meeting with the president concerning its role in the judicial selection process, observed that "President Johnson not only took a lively interest in the work and procedures of your Committee but evidenced a knowledge and alertness of its work and activities that thoroughly gratified all of us."[68]

This personal concern with federal judicial selection is apparent in the records at the Johnson Library. In 1965 Valenti asked in a memo if he should contact Clark to pass on a recommendation for a circuit judgeship. The president checked "No" and wrote "I'm committed—L."[69] In a 1966 memorandum to the president, Watson asked "Do you want FBI's run on anybody you may be considering during the next two weeks?" The "Yes" box was checked. Watson continued, "If Yes, we will need any names you may wish to furnish for this purpose." At the bottom, Johnson had written, "I talked to Ramsey and ask [sic] him to get busy on all 6 Judges at once. Hurry— L."[70] In another memo, Watson asked if he should call Louisiana Senators Russell B. Long and Allen Ellender concerning one of "their" candidates if the president decided to sign the nomination. Johnson checked "Yes" and wrote: "Let's send it up with a half dozen other judges. Hurry up Ramsey—."[71] After Senator Wayne L. Morse (D-Ore.) lost his race for reelection, he wrote a letter to Johnson regarding his interest in a judicial appointment. Johnson directed Manatos to "give to Ramsey and say Pres. inclined to do it."[72] In a memo to the president, Clark recommended the elevation of a district judge to the court of appeals. Johnson wrote, "Do not proceed—Put on my desk—L."[73] When Senators B. Everett Jordon (D-N.C.) and Sam J. Ervin (D-N.C.) requested to see the president on a circuit judgeship, Johnson checked "Yes" and wrote "See A G first, then OK."[74] And in a memo to Johnson in March 1968, Sanders commented that "Larry [Temple] and I are to meet with Warren Christopher later this week to re-emphasize your interest in moving as promptly as possible to fill these judicial vacancies."[75] Johnson rejected a recommendation by the Department of Justice and Sanders about two vacancies on the Customs Court and wrote, "Barefoot, show me the provision of the law that says the . . . appointment must be a Republican woman. Also I don't want all these appointments out of the Department."[76]

Johnson was personally much involved in the political aspect of selection. Watson, in a memo to the president, reported that Senator John Stennis (D-Miss.) "thinks everyone in all groups have cleared Governor [James P.] Coleman and that you should send the nomination up." But Johnson believed otherwise and noted some political strategy which he wished the Justice Department to pursue: "Ramsey—haven't done all their work with C.R. [civil rights] groups— [see] Dick Goodwin—."[77] Johnson was right in that Coleman had a good deal of opposition from civil-rights groups during confirmation hearings. But Coleman was confirmed, partly because Johnson sent Attorney General Katzenbach to testify in favor of Coleman at the hearings. Johnson also was often politicking on the phone or in meetings with senators and others who were interested in judicial appointments. An interesting memo from Valenti reads:

> As you know, Senator [Everett M.] Dirksen [R-Ill.] wants to be able to name a District or Circuit Court Judge in Illinois. You said you would talk to Senator [Paul] Douglas [D-Ill.] about this. Do you want me to bring Douglas in or will you call him?

Johnson checked "I will call Douglas" and added "When bill is passed notify me—L."[78] On 18 September 1968, Aide James Jones sent the following memo to the president:

> Mike Manatos got a call from Senator [Edward L.] Bartlett [D-Alaska] asking if the President would call Bartlett. Mike says Bartlett has now agreed to be present for the vote for cloture [on Fortas' nomination?]. Mike said it would be very helpful if the President would talk to Bartlett by phone today. All Bartlett wants to do is recommend a man for the Federal Circuit Judgeship and Bartlett has admitted he already knows the man cannot be appointed but Bartlett wants to be able to say he talked to the President about it.

Later that evening, Jones notified Manatos, "For your information, the call was completed to Senator Bartlett tonight as you suggested."[79] On a letter from a Democratic National committeeman opposing a possible nomination, Johnson wrote "Put on my desk—L."[80]

Johnson's concern also touched on the policy aspect, as will be discussed further in the section on criteria for nomination. It is enough to note here a few of the president's personal inputs concerning nominees' policy orientations. Watson forwarded the two Florida senators' recommendations on a possible nominee for a federal judgeship. Johnson asked on the memo if he was all right on the civil rights issue and stated that he wanted that information on all other candidates.[81] Before announcing some judicial nominations in mid-1967, the president had the nominees in for a visit and stressed to them his civil rights position and the fact that they were Johnson nominees.[82]

In addition to these higher-level political and policy matters, Johnson evidenced some attentiveness to the more mundane aspects of the appointment process. As noted before, he was knowledgeable about the ABA's role in judicial selection. He would sometimes meet with prospective nominees before their nominations were sent to the Senate. A mid-1967 Sanders memo notes: "I strongly urge that before announcing these nominations you have these men in for a visit similar to the one you had with prospective nominees two weeks ago. That was very good session."[83] Johnson even wished on occasion to see the thank-you letters that appointees wrote; on a memo Watson wrote noting that such letters had been received, Johnson asked, "Where are the letters?—L"[84] On the same memo, Johnson agreed to see one of the appointees who wished to thank the president in person. This was not an unusual occurrence, for Johnson visited with several judges who requested a visit for the purpose of expressing their appreciation for the appointment.[85] Sometimes these visits would last thirty minutes.[86] At one of these meetings, according to a report by aide Douglass Cater, Jr., Johnson made some interesting comments that may shed some light on his attitude toward judges:

> The President was in a relaxed, jovial mood. He said he wanted to give [Thomas] Masterson two pieces of advice: (1) Don't get arrogant, (2) Get off the bench when you reach retirement age. The President said that he had detected a tendency toward arrogance among those whom he had helped appoint to judgeships over the years. There is something about the nature of the job

with everybody saying "Your Honor" which seems to cause this. Masterson promised to take this advice to heart [and resigned in 1973, while still in his forties].[87]

Senators

Senators exercised the most influence of any actors outside of the executive branch in the process of judicial selection. Often it was a senator who first suggested a nominee and was the motivating force behind a nomination. In some cases senatorial influence overrode Justice Department hesitance about a particular nominee. In almost every case senators were consulted and played a role in the process.[88]

The usual process was that one or both senators from a state would send their recommendations for a district court nominee to the president. In many instances, although the senator might have one real recommendation he would submit several names either because it was good politics or because in the later years Johnson told the Senate that he wanted more than one name from which to choose.[89] Johnson would acknowledge the senator's interest and have the name sent to the Justice Department (and earlier, the Macy office) flagged with the fact that senators had recommended the person and the president was interested.[90] If the candidate was found qualified after informal Justice Department, ABA, and FBI checks, Justice would often make the person the recommended nominee and send the preliminary nomination to the White House with the notation that the person was sponsored or recommended by a senator.[91] And in the formal documents transmitting the nomination to the White House, the memo usually had as one of the reasons for recommendation: "He has the recommendation of Senator ___."[92]

The senatorial role was often determining in district court vacancies. It was a significant one in vacancies on the courts of appeals, as many circuit vacancies were "reserved" for a particular state and senators from that state played a major role in initiating nominations.[93] However, vacancies on the very important District of Columbia District Court and Court of Appeals were usually controlled by the Department of Justice, because no senator could claim state prerogative.[94]

The Department of Justice sometimes tried to make nominations to District of Columbia courts before senators were aware of the vacancies. This strategy of preempting senatorial initiative and therefore saving hurt feelings was discussed by Deputy Attorney General Katzenbach:

> We have a vacancy, as yet not public information, on the Court of
> Appeals for the District of Columbia to replace Judge [Walter M.]
> Bastian, a Republican.
>
> I have asked him not to publicize it because I think if he does
> we will be flooded by recommendations from a variety of people
> whose candidates are likely unacceptable; for example, Senator
> Eastland and Senator [Hubert H.] Humphrey.[95]

And of course the Senate played a minimal role in choosing nominees to the Supreme Court.

In addition to this variance by level of the court, the role of the
Senate varied with the individual, for the president gave greater
weight to certain senators' recommendations and less to others. But
even then, in the first few years all senators' choices were given priority. Although not to the same extent, this deference to senatorial
prerogative continued throughout the Johnson years. In August 1965,
in response to a recommendation from the editor of a newspaper,
the president snapped "Senators make the choice—L."[96] As Warren
Christopher noted in a memo in late 1968, senators were a prime
source of recommendations and major actors in the initial screening
process:

> Recommendations of a Senator of the President's Party from the
> state where a vacancy exists are very important. Moreover, the
> views of any Senator, whatever his Party, from the state where
> the vacancy exists cannot be ignored, for Senate tradition gives
> them a virtual right of veto.[97]

Johnson was very much aware of this tradition, and on a memorandum from Clark asking if he should proceed with a candidate,
Johnson wrote yes, "if both sitting Senators can & will confirm
him—L."[98] After Johnson received a letter from Secretary of Agriculture Orville L. Freeman asking for consideration of a Minnesota candidate for a circuit judgeship, Johnson directed Clark "to talk to
Minn. Senators—L."[99]

Traditionally, and during the Johnson years as well, it is usually
the senators of the president's party who have this power over judicial selection. Usually the Democratic senators from a state would
cooperate and either trade off vacancies or make joint recommendations.[100] Republican senators had much less of a role. For example,
because California had two Republican senators during the Johnson
presidency, in that state it was the congressional delegation and
Democratic state leaders who were consulted and in most cases the

senators were excluded.[101] But there were also cases in which Republican senators exercised a good deal of influence. In some instances this was because both senators from the state were Republican or because the other Democratic senator was willing to share the power. In other cases it was because the Republican senator used political ploys or political cajolery or appeals to Johnson to gain that influence. For instance, Republican Senator Hugh Scott from Pennsylvania appealed to the president to appoint a Republican judge instead of a Democrat recommended by Democratic Senator Joseph S. Clark of that state.[102]

> [Scott] points out his support of the President not only on Viet Nam (as opposed to Clark's harassment) but on gut issues such as Rent Supplements, Model Cities, Teachers' Corps, etc. He stated he would still support the President in all these areas because he believes the President is right, but claims he has been promised a Republican judgeship under President Kennedy (by Bob Kennedy) and under President Johnson (by Katzenbach).[103]

A Republican judge was indeed nominated and the deadlock broken. And finally, a Republican who enjoyed a special influence in judicial selection was Senator Everett M. Dirksen of Illinois. Perhaps because of his position as Senate minority leader or because of his long working relationship with Majority Leader and then President Johnson, Dirksen's wishes on judicial selection were listened to attentively. For example, on a memo asking if the president wanted a recommendation from Dirksen followed up, Johnson checked "Yes" and wrote, "Nick [Katzenbach]—work out with [Democratic Senator Paul] Douglas—Dirksen, L."[104] And in a memo dealing with the district judgeship for southern Illinois, Watson reported that "Dirksen said he just had to have this one and he would appreciate this one very much. He said he . . . really needed this appointment."[105] He got it.

The relationship between the administration and senators concerning judicial selection involved a great deal of politicking and negotiating. Johnson was not unaware of the bargaining leverage afforded by his power to nominate candidates desired by senators or to delay such nominations. Judicial nominations were entangled in political strategy and became part of deals involving diverse policies. For example, in late 1963, White House adviser Cliff Carter discussed in a memo to Johnson the possibility of such a political bargain with then-Democratic Senator Strom Thurmond over South Carolina vacancies:

> Strom Thurmond is holding out . . . for a former law partner of
> his. . . . It is said Thurmond wants this badly and probably could
> be used as trade bait on Civil Rights, endorsement by the South
> Carolina Democratic Convention, and insurance against un-
> pledged electors.[106]

Another such bargain involved the fact that North Carolina Senators
Sam Ervin and Everett Jordan were extended so far in pushing a candidate for district judge that they had to accept "losing" a court of
appeals position that went to Virginia.[107]

Johnson and the Justice Department recognized that if a senator
registered a "personally obnoxious" vote by the blue-slip device,
most other senators would back him up and the nominee would not
be confirmed. A senator's threat to use the blue slip against a candidate from his state was usually enough to prevent the administration
from going ahead with the nomination. This happened with a candidate for a judgeship in Oregon who was opposed by Democratic
Senator Wayne Morse. The White House sent out emissaries to
Morse to find out the depth of his opposition. Watson reported to
Johnson that Morse "reassured me that he would just lose the blue
card and never find it" if the name were sent forward to fill the vacancy. Justice William O. Douglas reported the same message from
Morse: "He told me he would not 'pick up the blue card.'"[108] The
administration, in light of this threat, nominated another candidate
not opposed by the senator.

Senators, even Republican senators, were able to use Senate procedures to delay confirmation in order to express pique, defeat the
nomination, embarrass the nominee, or exact concessions from the
administration on other judicial nominations. For example, Judiciary Committee delays and a filibuster were used to defeat the Fortas nomination for chief justice. Delays were used to prevent several
nominations from coming up for a vote before the Senate adjourned
in late 1968.[109] Senator Thurmond placed a temporary hold on the
nomination of Shirley Hufstedler, even though she was from a different state, and joined with California Republican Senator George
Murphy in placing a hold on California district judge candidate
Cecil Poole, who would have been the first black judge appointed
west of the Mississippi.[110] Poole was never confirmed.[111] Democratic
Senator James Eastland, Judiciary Committee chairman from Mississippi, apparently deliberately delayed confirmation hearings of
several black nominees.[112] Republican senators sometimes put holds
on Democratic nominees for judgeships in their states in an attempt

to force the administration to agree to nominate some Republicans. Deputy Attorney General Warren Christopher reported to Larry Temple on such a situation:

> You will recall the "hold" placed by Senator [Jacob] Javits [R-N.Y.] on the nomination last fall of Morris Lasker to be a United States District Judge for New York, Southern District. That action was taken because of Senator Javits' desire to have a Republican, Mr. [Orrin G.] Judd, receive one of the Eastern District nominations. Senator Javits has continued his "hold" on Lasker into this session of Congress.[113]

The hold was effectuated by the withholding of the blue slip. Lasker was confirmed only after the administration agreed to nominate the Republican, Judd, and Javits dropped his hold. A similar situation, but one made even more complicated by senatorial rivalry, took place concerning some 1967 Pennsylvania judicial vacancies. Sanders reported to the president that Republican Senator Scott of Pennsylvania was withholding Judiciary Committee approval of Thomas Masterson, a Democratic nominee for the district court in the state, until a Republican was nominated. Democratic Senator Clark, in turn, was blocking the appointment of Francis Van Dusen, a Republican nominee for a circuit court vacancy due to Pennsylvania, until Scott released his hold on Masterson.[114] The administration acceded to Scott's demand for a Republican nominee to the district court for Pennsylvania and both Masterson and Van Dusen were confirmed.

In some instances, rather than agreeing on certain future judicial nominations, the White House sometimes had to give concessions to senators on various other policy areas in order to gain their support of the president's judicial nominations. Temple reports that the White House and the Justice Department, despite Ramsey Clark's hesitance, had to preserve the Subversive Activities Control Board in order to get Senator Dirksen's assistance with appointments:

> Ramsey, frankly, wanted the subversive activities control board to go out of existence. He didn't want to [save] it and I think very frankly would have declined to have referred any business to them, except we needed Dirksen's help on some judge appointments and . . . unless Ramsey referred a case we weren't going to get Dirksen's help, and the balancing of the equities was that Dirksen's help on the judge appointments was more important than letting the subversive activities control board go out of existence.[115]

The administration was not without resources of its own in this relationship with the Senate over confirmation. Since the president has the formal power to nominate, he actually has the trump card in the entire process. There are various strategies he can pursue. He can make appointments when the Congress is in recess, which usually adds to pressure to confirm the candidate. As noted before, President Johnson, although he made a few early recess appointments, did not make any in the last several years.[116] The president could delay making any nominations, thus putting pressure on the senators from the state where the vacancy existed as the judicial work went uncompleted and dockets became more and more crowded and the local bar complained. For example, New York Senator Jacob Javits, although upset about the lack of Republican nominees, did not place a hold on a candidate for the Western District of the state because of a "pressing need for Judicial manpower."[117] Johnson used delays on many occasions to persuade senators to accept candidates.[118]

The administration also sought to foster good relationships with the Senate. Manatos headed a Senate liaison effort that was designed to open communications and ease tensions. The Justice Department also tried to maintain good relationships and the attorney general and deputy attorney general were constantly in touch with senators. Katzenbach claims that "I had the Judiciary Committee in my pocket on both Republican and Democrat. . . . I had an absolutely great relationship [with the Senate]."[119] And of course the administration could and did negotiate with various senators and got them to accept certain candidates in return for promises of "their" nominations in the future. The White House apparently kept its promises, as indicated by a note Johnson wrote to Watson when he signed formal nomination papers for John Reynolds for a Wisconsin district judgeship: "Marvin—notify both senators and tell them this is in accordance with our agreement—L."[120] The confirmation process was an essential element of the Johnson appointment process. The relationship between Senate and administration was a dynamic one, with both sides possessing resources to assist them in the sometimes controversial process of confirming the nominees to the federal bench.

The ABA Committee on Federal Judiciary

The American Bar Association's Standing Committee on Federal Judiciary exercised the greatest continuing influence over the judicial selection process of any actor outside of the federal government during the Johnson presidency. In almost every memo transmitting the

Justice Department's recommendation to the White House, the department noted the rating the committee had given the nominee as a factor in its choice. The rating also affected the negotiations between administration and Senate. If the ABA report were unfavorable to a senator's candidate, that gave the White House and the Department of Justice leverage to convince the senator to accept another, better qualified candidate and also gave the senator an excuse back home for abandoning that candidate.[121]

The ABA Committee enjoyed a good relationship with Johnson during his last two-and-a-half years, but before that the relationship was often stormy, as has been the case with most presidents.[122] Johnson had disagreements with the ABA Committee even before he became president. As vice president he pushed for the appointment of Sarah T. Hughes as a Texas district judge, even though the ABA had rated her unqualified because of her age. The vice president won that battle, but had other less successful bouts with the committee.[123] With this as a background, when Johnson became president there was already tension between him and the ABA Committee. And the relationship between the new president and the ABA Committee got off to a rather bad start with the David Rabinovitz controversy. Even though Johnson pushed him hard in spite of the ABA's rating of "unqualified," Rabinovitz was a Kennedy nominee and thus direct conflict was avoided for the moment. But several of the non-Kennedy nominees in 1964 were also attacked by the ABA as being unqualified. In its 1964 *Annual Report,* the Committee on Federal Judiciary noted:

> Last year's annual report started off with the statement that, during the period covered by it, there had been no nomination for lifetime judicial office submitted to the United States Senate of any person who had been previously reported by this Committee to the Attorney General as "not qualified." We are told that "pride goeth before a fall." Any feeling of satisfaction which your Committee may have then had in the practical agreement between its conclusions and those of the appointing authority has surely been lessened by the nominations submitted since last July. . . . Of the nominations in question, the substantial majority (18) were made by President Johnson, and, of the number nominated (whether or not confirmed) in the entire year, three, as noted, were found "not qualified" comprising, therefore, almost an eighth of the whole. Of the other 20, on the other hand, 9, or nearly half, were found by the committee to be "well qualified" or "exceptionally well qualified."[124]

Strains were developing in the administration–ABA Committee relationship. Johnson was not one who liked giving up power, but in February 1964 the ABA demanded "a greater voice in selecting the federal judiciary through its federal judiciary committee."[125] The ABA's House of Delegates adopted a resolution authorizing ABA officials to ask each candidate for the presidency to agree in writing to give "substantial weight" to association views. The relationship between the president and the ABA, although strained, was still correct as of September 1964, as is seen by a letter from the president of the ABA, Lewis F. Powell, Jr., to Johnson. His letter stated that it "would give me much pleasure" if he could announce to the association Johnson's confirmation of his willingness, if elected, to work with the Committee on Federal Judiciary. Johnson's reply to Powell on 1 October was proper but rather noncommittal:

> I share the views expressed in the resolution adopted by the House of Delegates of the American Bar Association in February 1964 concerning the Federal judiciary. Since assuming the office of President, I have continued the practice of my predecessors, Presidents Kennedy and Eisenhower, in referring to the American Bar Association the names of persons under consideration for appointment to the Federal judiciary. I have found this practice most helpful in the discharge of my constitutional duty of appointing Federal judges and intend to continue it. I have given and will continue to give substantial weight to the recommendations of the Federal Judiciary Committee of your association.[126]

But this proper if not cordial relationship was not to last. Tensions between the Johnson administration and the ABA increased. In April of 1965 Friesen came in as assistant deputy attorney general with a large role in judicial selection and a great deal of skepticism concerning the ABA Committee and its ratings.[127] Professor Henry Abraham noted Johnson's "wheeling-dealings" with the committee's ratings about this time period.[128] Even more dramatic was the battle in late 1965 over the candidacy for district judge in Massachusetts of Francis X. Morrissey, who was rated "not qualified" by the ABA. Pressured by the Kennedy family, Johnson stood behind Morrissey even in light of the hostile testimony before the Senate Judiciary Committee of the last three chairmen of the ABA Committee.[129] Although Morrissey was a "Kennedy legacy" nominee, Johnson and the ABA Committee (as well as Edward Kennedy) had been bruised by the confrontation. In its 1966 *Report,* the committee commented:

Your Committee must regretfully if not dejectedly report that various additional factors other than judicial qualifications have, unfortunately, continued to play a part in the Federal judgeship selection, nomination, confirmation and appointment process. Without going into detail, these factors embrace personal friendship with one or more of those taking part in the process of preliminary consideration and ultimate appointment by the President, and confirmation by the Senate of the United States; "cronyism"; performance of service to political party organizations or to the United States Senators, or others in high public office, state and federal; ethnic origin; religious faith of the candidate; vigorous personal campaign by the candidate himself; current or prior holding of high public office, state and federal on the part of the candidate or his personal or political friend or sponsor; and other like considerations wholly irrelevant to the matter of judicial qualification.[130]

But relations were destined to improve from this low point. In May 1966, rather than the traditional meeting of the ABA Board of Governors with the president, the ABA Committee on Federal Judiciary received an audience with Johnson.[131] The committee made a very favorable report of that meeting to the ABA:

The procedures and work of the Committee were explained to President Johnson and we expounded upon the ideals and objectives of the organized bar, as represented by the American Bar Association, in respect of the need that only qualified members of the bench and bar serve as judges of the courts of the United States. We were at pains to emphasize with the President that the American Bar Association welcomed and sincerely appreciated the opportunity that had been accorded us by him and his predecessors, Presidents Kennedy, Eisenhower and Truman, and by Attorney General Katzenbach and his predecessors, Messrs. Kennedy (Robert), [Tom C.] Clark, and [Herbert] Brownell, to assist the President in the discharge of what the bar of this nation and, in our opinion, the public as well, regards to be as important a duty, responsibility and privilege as any devolving upon the President. President Johnson not only took a lively interest in the work and procedures of your Committee but evidenced a knowledge of alertness of its work and activities that thoroughly gratified all of us.

There was a healthy exchange of views as to problems which
faced the President from time to time as respects the exercise of
his important constitutional function, political niceties that relate thereto and, on the other hand, the work problems and objectives of your committee.[132]

This meeting, or the aftermath of the Morrissey case, seems to be
a turning point in ABA Committee–Johnson relations. Although
there was no apparent change in the selection process itself in regard
to the valuation of the ABA's ratings,

the administration apparently was concerned about the need to
make appointments which would deserve high ratings from the
committee. Understandably stung by the criticism which had
been heaped upon it as a result of the . . . Morrissey nomination,
the administration had good reason to seek to regain the confidence of the press and public, if not the committee.[133]

Perhaps the ABA Committee was also more cautious about assign-
ing "unqualified" ratings. Perhaps the administration and the committee cooperated in having nominees "put their best foot forward,"
as is indicated in a letter from a prospective nominee who told
Temple that John Duffner had called to offer help in filling out the
Personal Data Questionnaire and that "Further, I received a letter
from Mr. [Albert] Jenner [chairman of the ABA Committee] making
suggestions as to the format of my response to the questionnaire."[134]
For whatever reasons, later Johnson appointees were much more
highly rated by the ABA Committee and President Johnson "never
again nominated a candidate who had not been sanctioned by the
ABA Committee, and from 1966 to 1968 he sent 128 nominations to
the Senate."[135]
In February 1967, Chairman Jenner of the ABA Committee transmitted the praise for the administration contained in the committee's report to the ABA:

President Johnson appointed 63 lifetime federal judges in 1966.
This was the largest number of appointments made by any President in any one year in the history of the nation. Especially note-
worthy was the fact that all appointees had been rated "Qualified"
or better by your Committee and, what is more, the percentage
of appointees in the superior range of "Well Qualified" and "Exceptionally Well Qualified" was the greatest of any President of

the United States in the history of your Committee, which came into existence in 1946.

The Committee is pleased wholeheartedly to commend President Johnson, former Attorney General Katzenbach, Deputy (now Acting) Attorney General Ramsey Clark, the United States Senate Committee on the Judiciary and the United States Senate itself, as well as Ernest C. Friesen, Jr., Assistant Attorney General in Charge of Administration for the historical accomplishment in 1966.[136]

President Johnson seemed pleased and suggested to his press secretary, George E. Christian, that he might want to show these statements to the press. He had Clark reply to Jenner, and Clark wrote:

It is the desire of the President and this Department to appoint to the Federal Bench those best qualified for the particular vacancy, and we appreciate the interest and cooperation of your organization in helping to make this desire a reality.[137]

In a report a year later, Jenner repeated the praises for the selection process:

Your Committee is privileged and pleased to report that the quality of lawyers and judges appointed by President Lyndon B. Johnson to lifetime federal judgeships . . . continues to be at an encouraging high level. We unreservedly commend President Johnson, the Senate of the United States and Attorney General Ramsey Clark. . . . President Johnson's record since October 1965 approaches the remarkable. During that period he has made 104 appointments. Your Committee found 60% of those appointees "Well Qualified" or "Exceptionally Well Qualified" and 40% "Qualified."[138]

The good relationship that developed is also seen by the fact that the president asked Jenner on at least two occasions to bypass or supplement the regular committee process and personally conduct the investigation of prospective nominees. Jenner did so in the cases of Alexander Lawrence of Georgia (to be discussed later) and Cecil Poole of California, on whom Jenner submitted a favorable eighty-seven-page report.[139] Also, sometimes officials of the Department of Justice would discuss a vacancy with Jenner even before an informal report was requested.[140]

United States Representatives

As has already been noted, on some occasions a United States representative or a group of representatives made recommendations or were consulted about a prospective nominee.[141] Although not nearly as influential as senators, House members sometimes had a major impact on the selection, particularly when there was no Democratic senator from that state. This was particularly true of the congressional delegation from California, which had no Democratic senator for most of the Johnson years.[142]

Unlike Senate liaison Mike Manatos, the name of Henry H. Wilson, the president's liaison with the House, seldom appears in the files dealing with judicial selection. As Wilson himself noted: "As you know, it is not often that I get into judgeships, because most House Members figure judgeships to be the prerogatives of the Senators."[143] But that same memo discussed the overriding concern about a district judgeship possessed by Representative Porter Hardy (D-Va.), who occupied important positions on several committees. Wilson reported that "I have had a minimum of 50 conversations with him over [the appointment] ranging over the past six months, and his concern and anguish are mounting daily." Although the Justice Department and Johnson had already agreed on a nominee, the president directed, "Ask Ramsey about the possibility of [the original nominee] and Hardy's man." Because of the rather unusual concern of this representative and his powerful position, his candidate (and the other as well) were appointed to the federal court. Representative Adam Clayton Powell (D-N.Y.) recommended Thurgood Marshall as Justice of the Supreme Court in 1965.[144] Sometimes an entire delegation would endorse a candidate, as the South Carolina Democratic delegation did for a circuit judge candidate.[145]

Sitting Judges

A sitting judge might be asked to comment on a prospective or current member of his court, or might come forward on his own with a name.[146] Supreme Court justices suggested nominees to lower federal courts, and occasionally to the Supreme Court itself. The president often asked for justices' views on specific candidates.[147]

Some judges refused to make suggestions, perhaps considering it improper. For example, Chief Justice Earl Warren reported that when he notified Johnson of his intention to retire, the president asked him if he had any candidates. Warren responded "No, Mr. President, that's your problem."[148]

But most justices did respond to Johnson's requests or even initiated recommendations. Among those most active were Justices William O. Douglas, Tom C. Clark, and Hugo Black.[149] Abe Fortas, who was a very influential adviser to Johnson before he was appointed to the Supreme Court, continued and increased that advisory role while on the Court. In a letter thanking Johnson for nominating him to the Supreme Court, Fortas wrote "I can only hope that you will continue to see me and to call upon me for anything that I can do to help."[150] Fortas, soon after his appointment, informed the president of his private direct telephone number at the Court. (Johnson said, "Keep this number for me.")[151] He continued to advise the president on various matters, including Vietnam and the Kennedy Center, as well as serving as a major adviser on judicial nominees.[152] Just after he took his seat on the Court he noted that he would report on suggested judgeships proposed by Ramsey Clark.[153] He endorsed Allan Hart for a judgeship in Oregon as "a most qualified man, as well as a good Johnson Democrat" and then discussed the senatorial politics of the appointment.[154] In January of 1967 he sent a note through Watson to the president discussing the won-lost record of Solicitor General Marshall, presumably as part of the consideration of Marshall as a new justice.[155] In April 1968, Temple wrote to the president, "Based upon . . . the checking we have done with Justice Abe Fortas . . . we are satisfied that [two candidates] possess the ability and loyalty requirements to be appointed to these posts."[156]

Douglas' numerous recommendations also went to the president, but were not given the same weight as Fortas'. Douglas wrote to the president after Warren decided to retire:

> I hope you make Abe our new Chief. He'd be superb. And may I suggest that for his present position you name Warren Christopher? He's fine California—young—progressive—no leftist—no rightist—level-headed and as good a lawyer as I have known. He was my law clerk 20 years ago; and on his own reached the top of law practice in Los Angeles.[157]

Other Actors

A variety of other actors played a secondary role. A memo by Christopher suggests the diversity of actors who were involved in the judicial selection process:

> Sources of recommendations are . . . diverse [and come from a wide variety of sources]—the White House, Department of Jus-

tice officials, Senators, Representatives, Governors, state and
local bar associations, individuals wanting to be considered, and
individuals recommending others.[158]

Some of those and others were also periodically involved in other
phases of the process.

State party officials sometimes gave their opinion of the political
repercussions of a particular appointment.[159] Ambassadors, including United Nations Ambassador Adlai Stevenson, sometimes made
recommendations, as did governors.[160] Mayors of large cities, particularly Richard J. Daley of Chicago and Joseph M. Barr of Pittsburgh,
were often listened to carefully about possible nominees from their
areas.[161] And periodically members of the Cabinet would recommend
someone.[162] Infrequently, ex-presidents would suggest a name; both
Truman and Eisenhower recommended individuals. (Interestingly on
one occasion they recommended competing candidates for one vacancy. Truman's won.)[163] Vice President Hubert Humphrey was hesitant to get involved in judicial selection outside of Minnesota (as
vice president, Johnson had remained directly involved in Texas judicial appointments) but a few times did pass on recommendations.
For example, in 1967 Humphrey passed on the name of California
Justice Stanley Mosk for a Supreme Court vacancy and a year earlier
had recommended the promotion of District Judge Spottswood Robinson to a court of appeals vacancy.[164] In some cases, law professors
and newspaper editors were either asked for or put forward recommendations or judgments about nominees.[165] And various officials in
the Department of Justice suggested names at different times.

Those people discussed above made periodic contributions to the
process; however, several categories of actors were more significant
either because their input was more continual or because their recommendations were given greater weight. The president had confi-
dantes outside of government whom he sometimes asked for advice
on appointments to the courts. These included Abe Fortas, Edwin
Weisl, Sr., James Rowe, Clark Clifford, and Leon Jaworski.[166] Fortas
was consulted on all sorts of problems, including foreign policy and
cultural affairs, as well as personnel matters in and out of the judiciary, both before and after he was appointed to the Supreme Court.[167]
Weisl, an old friend of Johnson's from the New Deal years, had a great
influence over candidates from New York. Most New York state candidates had to be cleared with Weisl before the president would make
the nomination.[168] And Jaworski was consulted on a variety of legal
matters, including nominations of judges in Texas and other states,

even while Jaworski was serving on the ABA Committee on Federal Judiciary.[169]

Also involved on a continuing basis in judicial selection were the FBI, the IRS, and the Democratic National Committee. These organizations ran checks on most prospective nominees to screen out any national security, financial, or political problems.[170] Their approvals were noted in the memorandums sent to the president by the Justice Department and by the Macy operation accompanying each formal nomination. Also apparent in many cases were the requests by those who wished to be considered for a judgeship.[171] Unless they already had sponsorship from senators or were known to Justice, most of these appeals were unsuccessful.[172] On occasion, wives and mothers, fathers and brothers would also write.[173] Finally, a wide range of individuals, from the obscure to the famous, would make recommendations for particular vacancies or simply put forward candidates' names. Obviously many recommendations would go to the senators, but the presidential files are also filled with such messages. They came from noted attorneys and statesmen (such as Thurmond Arnold and Dean Acheson);[174] from labor and civil rights leaders (such as Walter Reuther and A. Phillip Randolph);[175] from prominent journalists (such as Drew Pearson and Anthony Lewis);[176] from famous show-business names (such as Jack Benny and Danny Thomas);[177] and from other famous people (such as Billy Graham and Stanley Marcus of Neiman-Marcus).[178]

It is not clear what, if any, effect these outside sources had on selection. It does seem that beyond the White House, the Department of Justice, the ABA, and the Senate, the level of efficacy went down considerably. In certain instances some input from elsewhere may have been influential and certainly other voices were listened to attentively by the major actors, but their influence was sporadic, not continuing, as was that of the major actors.

The process of judicial selection during the Johnson administration was not an exact one. There were many actors involved and at various times their influence was greater or lesser. Chance played a role in many nominations as a vacancy appeared at the right time for a particular candidate (from a particular party or from a particular area) whose name was known to and accepted by the right actors. What were those right actors looking for in their choices? The next chapter considers that.

5. The Criteria of Choice

In Chapter 2 we suggested that each administration has a set of criteria, explicit or implicit, to guide the selection of judicial candidates. Those criteria usually acknowledge the desire for quality or competence; that standard, however, may have different definitions in different administrations. One administration may emphasize ABA rankings, another may stress policy views, and a third may require appropriate prior experience. The criteria may never be explicitly listed, or if listed, may not completely describe the desired qualities. An analysis of the characteristics of those actually nominated as well as an examination of the announced criteria are necessary to get an accurate perception of the criteria that really guide the process of judicial selection and appointment.

What were the criteria for selection of the Johnson administration? What philosophy guided the Johnson selection process in its search for the right nominee? Obviously, it is impossible to catalogue exactly the qualities sought in candidates because different actors had differing goals and differing standards. It is doubtful that the Justice Department and the Senate had the same goals, or that the ABA Committee had the same criteria as did the White House staff. It has been suggested that the qualities looked for by the ABA Committee match those of the traditional corporate attorney and that senators are often more concerned with political effects than legal competence.[1] This chapter will discuss the philosophy that seemed to guide the Johnson administration—the president, White House assistants, Justice Department, and Macy operation—in its search for judicial nominees with appropriate qualities. Those searched-for qualities seemed to change over time, to some extent, but certain elements remained constant.

It is probably erroneous to state that there was a guiding philosophy behind the judicial selection process. It is doubtful that President Johnson ever brought together the attorney general, Macy, and the White House staff members involved and laid out specific guidelines. Nevertheless, the actors in the Johnson administration's selection process appear to have operated from a shared consensus on the general types of nominees to be chosen. Although there were certainly some disagreements over particular candidates, all of the team followed the general guidelines.

Those general guidelines were largely set forth by the president, although of course his options were constrained by history, tradition, and political forces. But within those parameters, Johnson's wishes set the tone and direction of selection. Macy, in interviews and his book, *Public Service,* and Richard Schott and Dagmar Hamilton in their study describe the general criteria Johnson desired in all presidential appointees.[2] These include an emphasis on high intellectual attainment, as measured by academic credentials and by success in the profession. Related to that was proven competence in the individual's field. There was an emphasis on seeking women, minorities, individuals from various areas and ethnic groups, and relatively younger people, in an attempt to bring diversity and vitality into the administration. Previous experience and success in government, which was related to a commitment to social progress and an activist temperament, were also valued highly.[3] Loyalty was important. This did not necessarily mean partisan loyalty (for Johnson stressed party identification less than many presidents) but rather programmatic and personal loyalty. In the first several years the concern was with commitment to general Great Society policies, particularly civil rights, but later the attention turned to loyalty to Lyndon Johnson, in regard particularly to Vietnam. Merit, then, was the general goal, but the search for merit was complicated by several other considerations.

These general criteria also applied to the selection process for federal judges, with some variations. Because of the impact that senators had on the process, the administration was constrained by political and partisan considerations and usually tried to abide by their reasonable wishes. But even so, the White House, the Justice Department, and the Macy operation used these criteria to make final decisions and often to make preliminary decisions as well where circumstances left them discretion.

Merit

The first criteron was quality or merit or competence or intellectual attainment. Merit is of course hard to define and hard to measure but evidence of intelligence such as a Phi Beta Kappa key or ranking in a law school class or editorship of a law review was valued.[4] Such credentials were always brought to the president's attention in memorandums from the Justice Department or Macy. In a memorandum to the president endorsing the nomination of James E. Doyle to a district judgeship, Macy emphasized the criterion of merit: "Mr. Doyle's appointment would be in keeping with the merit standard which you have applied in other appointments."[5] The Justice Department was particularly concerned with the need for legal quality, as Assistant Deputy Attorney General Ernest C. Friesen, Jr. noted: "Without [Ramsey Clark's] constant pressure to seek the most qualified I doubt that our [the Department's] attempts to hold the line for quality would be successful. He does all of the negotiating with the political interests with astonishing results."[6] Members of the White House staff, too, joined in the department's desire for merit. Larry Temple commented that

> occasionally [a senator] would come up with someone and
> Ramsey and [Deputy Attorney General] Warren Christopher . . .
> might conclude after a conversation with me that maybe there
> were more talented, more able, more qualified people than the
> one the particular Senator recommended. . . . we'd go back and
> usually encourage the Senator to decide this was his nominee if
> we had an especially talented guy.[7]

Although it is difficult to measure merit, some indices might be quality of education or at least reputation of educational institutions and rating of the ABA's Committee on Federal Judiciary. It is interesting to note that in spite of, or perhaps because of, Johnson's perceived or actual hostility to and from Ivy League thinkers, more of his judicial appointees received undergraduate and especially legal education from Ivy League and private schools than did the appointees of John F. Kennedy or almost any other recent president. This is particularly true of district court appointments.[8]

Another index of merit may be the ratings provided by the ABA; in this area the Johnson appointees also come out very well. Seventy-five percent of the appointees to courts of appeals and almost 50 percent of the district court appointees were rated "exceptionally well qualified" or "well qualified," while only 2.5 percent of both groups (or four judges total) were rated "not qualified." This compares quite favorably with Johnson's successors and especially his predecessors. And if one takes into account the relatively low rankings of Johnson's first-year appointees, several of whom were Kennedy legacies, the ratings are even more impressive. (Three of the four ratings of "not qualified" came from that period.)

Table 1. ABA Ratings of Judicial Appointees, Eisenhower through Reagan Administrations

District Court Appointees

ABA Ratings	Eisenhower N = 125	Kennedy N = 103	Johnson N = 122*	Nixon N = 179	Ford N = 52	Carter N = 202	Reagan (First Term) N = 129
Exceptionally well qualified (%)	17.1	10.6	7.4	4.8	—	4.0	6.9
Well qualified (%)	44.6	45.6	40.9	40.4	46.1	47.0	43.4
Qualified (%)	32.6	31.5	49.2	54.8	53.8	47.5	49.6
Not qualified (%)	5.7	6.3	2.5	—	—	1.5	—

Court of Appeals Appointees

ABA Ratings	Eisenhower N = 45	Kennedy N = 21	Johnson N = 40*	Nixon N = 45	Ford N = 12	Carter N = 56	Reagan (First Term) N = 31
Exceptionally well qualified (%)	—	—	27.5	15.6	16.7	16.1	22.6
Well qualified (%)	—	—	47.5	57.8	41.7	58.9	41.9
Qualified (%)	—	—	20.0	26.7	33.3	25.0	35.5
Not qualified (%)	—	—	2.5	—	8.3	—	—
No report requested? (%)	—	—	2.5	—	—	—	—

Note: The Eisenhower and Kennedy percentages are the total number of judges not divided into district courts and courts of appeals. These data come from Harold W. Chase, Federal Judges: The Appointing Process (Minneapolis: University of Minnesota Press, 1972), p. 168.

*The Johnson totals, which are Goldman's, differ slightly from mine. His district court totals exclude the five Kennedy-initiated appointees (Davis, Higginbotham, S. Robinson, Tenney, and Thornberry) and include the two lifetime judgeships from Puerto Rico (Cancio and Fernández-Badillo). Goldman thus counts two fewer blacks and two more Hispanics than I do. He also excludes the Kennedy-initiated appointment of George Edwards to the court of appeals.

Table 2. *Percentage of Judges Appointed during the First Year of the Johnson Administration in Each of the ABA Rating Classifications (N = 18)*

Rating	%
Exceptionally well qualified	5.6
Well qualified	22.2
Qualified	55.5
Not qualified	16.7

Experience

Another characteristic stressed by the Johnson selection process was that of prior governmental experience, which perhaps indicated political support and a willingness to serve. Of district court appointees, 80.1 percent had had judicial and/or prosecutorial experience; for court of appeals appointments, only 20 percent had neither. Almost every file stresses this previous experience (in the legislative and executive as well as judicial branches), and very few attorneys with no governmental experience were nominated.[9] This is particularly true of the nominees to the courts of appeals, where it seems that experience as a judge in a state court or federal district court was almost a prerequisite to nomination.[10] The office of United States attorney seemed to be a frequent stepping-stone to a district judgeship, and over 45 percent of district court appointees had prosecutorial experience of some kind.[11]

Women

For whatever reasons—for political advantage or because of a commitment to equality—Johnson did try to attract a diversity of groups to his administration. The concern for female appointments generally surfaced early. When asked if Johnson ever said that he wanted more women appointed, Ralph A. Dungan, who served as special assistant during the first year of the Johnson presidency, replied, "Oh yes, oh yes, he was very strong on the women's side and I used to have to keep a tabulation of how many women he had appointed."[12] Macy claims that Johnson emphasized the appointment of women so much that the recruitment theme became "Every Day is Ladies' Day with Me" and that the president requested statistics on the number of women appointed.[13]

Table 3. Previous Experience of Judicial Appointees, Eisenhower through Reagan Administrations

District Court Appointees

Experience	Eisenhower	Kennedy	Johnson	Nixon	Ford	Carter	Reagan (First Term)
Judicial (%)	26.4	33.0	34.3	35.1	42.3	54.5	50.4
Prosecutorial (%)			45.8	41.9	50.0	38.6	43.4
Neither (%)			33.6	36.3	30.8	28.2	28.7

Court of Appeals Appointees

Experience	Eisenhower	Kennedy	Johnson	Nixon	Ford	Carter	Reagan (First Term)
Judicial (%)	62.2	52.4	65.0	57.8	75.0	53.6	70.9
Prosecutorial (%)			47.5	46.7	25.0	32.1	19.3
Neither (%)			20.0	17.8	25.0	37.5	25.8

Table 4. *Previous Judicial Experience of Court of Appeals Appointees, Truman through Johnson Administrations*

Administration	Appoint- ments (N)	Those Who Had Been Federal District Judges		Those with Judicial Experience at Federal or State Level	
		N	%	N	%
Truman	26			16	62
Eisenhower	45	18	40	28	62
Kennedy	21	8	38	11	52
Johnson	40	19	48	24	60

Source: Harold W. Chase, *Federal Judges: The Appointing Process* (Minneapolis: University of Minnesota Press, 1972), pp. 179 and 111.

The statistics for female judges—four appointments—were not spectacular, but several points do stand out. The first is that the president did alert the members of the selection team to be concerned with women. Temple wrote in an early 1968 memo to the president that "[Justice Abe] Fortas, [James] Rowe, [Judge Gerhardt A.] Gesell, Christopher, and I all agree that it would be advisable to name a woman to one of these Judgeships in light of [the circumstances that one of the vacancies] was created by the retirement of a woman. . . . Moreover, in the over four years of your presidency, only one woman has been named to a lifetime federal judicial post."[14] Deputy Attorney General Christopher had strongly recommended the nomination of this woman, June L. Green.[15] It was Christopher who in 1968 wrote a memo to Temple emphasizing that

the President has now made 169 lifetime judicial appointments. Only two of them have been women. There are approximately 7,500 women lawyers in the United States and it would be a great encouragement for them if the President would appoint a woman to the Court of Appeals. If he does so, it would be only the second time in history that a woman has been named to the Court of Appeals.[16]

And it was Temple of the White House who made a strong recommendation to the president that

because of the statistical figures Warren points out in his memo, I recommend that either Mrs. [Shirley M.] Hufstedler or Mrs.

[Mildred] Lillie be appointed to one of the judicial vacancies. . . .
But the fact that Mrs. Florence Allen—appointed 6th Circuit—
1934, is the only woman who has served on the Court of Appeals
. . . leads me to the belief that one of these women should be
appointed to the Court of Appeals. . . . I recommend Mrs. Hufstedler's appointment.[17]

And, indeed, President Johnson did nominate Hufstedler to the Court
of Appeals for the Ninth Circuit. She became the first woman nominated for a circuit judgeship since Franklin D. Roosevelt nominated
Allen thirty-four years before, and only the second female court
of appeals judge in history. Besides that appointment, President
Johnson also appointed two women (Constance Baker Motley and
June L. Green) to the district courts. These two constituted one-
third of the total female district judges ever appointed up to that
time. Every day may not have been ladies' day for judicial appointments, but at least a few were (and certainly more than in previous
presidencies.)[18]

Age

Johnson was also interested in bringing in younger people as judges.
This was partly because he felt "that there was need to have the vitality of the younger generation in these appointments" and perhaps
partly because younger appointees to lifetime federal judgeships
could leave more of a Johnson mark than older appointees who
might go off the bench within a few years.[19] In this latter aspect
Johnson was remarkably successful. In 1986, many Johnson judicial
appointees were still active on the federal bench. Thurgood Marshall
remained on the Supreme Court and 19 Johnson appointees served
on the courts of appeals. (This number includes 7 whom Johnson appointed to the district courts and who were subsequently promoted,
usually by the Carter administration, to the appeals level.) In addition, 16 served as senior circuit or partially retired judges, many
quite actively. Nine of Johnson's 12 appointees to the Customs Court,
Court of Claims, or Court of Customs and Patent Appeals continued
to serve in some capacity. And 29 of Johnson's district court appointees remained on the bench. That means that one quarter of Johnson's 125 appointees were active as district judges almost two decades after he left office. Combining that number with the 7 then on
the courts of appeals and the 58 then on senior district judge status,
94, or 75 percent, of Johnson's appointees to the district courts continued on the federal bench.

The chairman of the ABA Committee on Federal Judiciary reported to the ABA House of Delegates that "President Johnson has expressed to us the desirability that younger men be appointed to lifetime federal judgeships and both he and Attorney General Clark have had this factor in mind."[20] Indeed, one of the reasons Hufstedler was recommended by Temple and appointed was that she was "ten years younger than Mrs. Lillie and offers the probability of a longer judicial career as a Johnson appointee."[21] Whatever the reason, the president constantly inquired about ages of appointees and publicized the youthfulness of his judicial nominees.[22] Those nominees were younger as a whole than the nominees of his two predecessors.

Besides Johnson's interest in the lower end of the age spectrum, he had a real concern about superannuated judges. This is apparent by the fact that less than 10 percent of his appointees were sixty years old or older. Only 8 percent of his courts of appeals appointees were sixty or over, which is in striking contrast to the Kennedy and Eisenhower appointees. Johnson's concern in this area is also shown in his comments to newly appointed federal judges. One such episode occurred all the way back in 1961, when he was speaking to Adrian A. Spears, a close friend whom Vice President Johnson had been instrumental in getting appointed to the District Court of Texas. Spears reports that soon after he was appointed, Johnson met with him and said:

> I want you to make me one promise. . . . The only thing I would like for you to do is to keep in mind the problem that we have with judges when they get too old. When you've served your time and have gotten to the point where you should retire, retire and let some younger man have the job. That's the best way to keep the judiciary functioning properly.[23]

And in 1967, as president, Johnson said almost the same thing to an individual he had just nominated to the federal court. Johnson's advice was "get off the bench when you reach retirement age."[24] And a newly-appointed judge reported about Johnson's comments at a reception for judicial nominees that "nothing could more emphatically call to their attention the necessity for allowing younger men to succeed them when they reach retirement age."[25]

But Johnson would occasionally push for individuals who were older, even those whom the ABA Committee had rated "Unqualified Because of Age." The ABA would not rate anyone qualified if he or she were older than sixty-three. But sixty-four-year-old Sarah T. Hughes of Texas was nominated to the federal district court by Presi-

Table 5. Percentage of District and Circuit Court Appointees in Various Age Groups in the Eisenhower, Kennedy, and Johnson Administrations

Administration	District Judges				Circuit Court Judges			
	60+	50–59	40–49	30–39	60+	50–59	40–49	30–39
Eisenhower (%)	10	56	31	3	33	52	13	2
Kennedy (%)	8	54	34	4	19	62	19	0
Johnson (%)	9	49	39	3	8	57	33	2

Source: Harold W. Chase, *Federal Judges: The Appointing Process* (Minneapolis: University of Minnesota Press, 1972), p. 179.

dent Kennedy in spite of her age, partly because of the urgings of Vice President Johnson.[26] And as president, Johnson nominated at least one person to a judgeship despite the ABA's rating of "not qualified because of age."[27]

Race

Johnson tried to bring more minorities, especially blacks, into the federal judiciary. Again, perhaps this was for political advantage, but more important, it reflected his concern for equal opportunity and for the appointment of role models for younger blacks. Certainly Johnson was not unmindful of seeking whatever political benefits he could obtain from any act. This is evident in a memo in the file of a Negro nominee to a district court in Michigan. The memo, dictated by Johnson for Press Secretary George E. Reedy, says:

> Find out how many Negro judges I have named. Have a planted question—each time one is announced—ask if this is a Negro judge. All of every kind—and tell the number—7 or 8—more than any other President.[28]

And this political astuteness is also evident in a Johnson directive to Marvin Watson on the occasion of Thurgood Marshall's nomination to the Supreme Court. After seeing an article in a Negro newspaper which praised the president's action, Johnson directed Watson to "get it out to every leading negro in the country."[29]

But the article itself illustrates the other aspects of Johnson's desire to appoint blacks to judgeships. The article notes the very significant symbolic aspect of the appointment and commends Johnson for appointing a role model for black children:

> It sure is important, too, that he is a black man. I think thousands and millions of black kids dig this country a little bit more right now.
>
> 'Cause they got a powerful piece of evidence—right under their nose—that the sun do move. These kids got a little more to work for, to be proud of. They need this, Mr. President. They need to know that the bad happenings in the South [are] not the only happenings in America.[30]

The role model aspect was one of the reasons Johnson had chosen Marshall to be his solicitor general. In Marshall's words:

He wanted people—young people—of both races to come into the Supreme Court Room . . . and somebody to say, "Who is that man up there with that swallow tail coat on arguing," and somebody to say, "He's the Solicitor General of the United States." Somebody will say, "But he's a Negro!" He wanted that image.[31]

Johnson was concerned with equalizing opportunity, and he was interested in statistics on the number of black judges. His actions in this area of appointments often meant a loss of political power in order to get blacks through the Senate. As Bill Moyers points out:

And he would often trade power, he would often give up some of his [political advantage] . . . in order to get [Senator Everett] Dirksen to accept a Black or [Senator Richard] Russell to go along with it.[32]

Johnson seemed particularly concerned that blacks were nominated to positions vacated by blacks, perhaps to keep the number of black judges from declining or perhaps because the political struggle would be less in appointing a black for a seat held by a black.[33]

The Johnson record in this area was summarized by Attorney General Clark: "In the judiciary he appointed more Negro judges than all the preceding presidents combined."[34] The appointment of Thurgood Marshall to the Supreme Court was a major groundbreaking step. Johnson appointed two blacks to the courts of appeals and one to the Customs Court. He also appointed seven blacks to the district courts.[35] Included was Constance Baker Motley of the Southern District of New York in 1966, the first black woman to be given a lifetime appointment to the federal judiciary.[36]

Ethnicity and Religion

Somewhat related to this search for black nominees was a concern for ethnic and religious representation on the bench. This was not the major consideration in most cases, but it sometimes played a role. On several occasions members of Congress contacted the White House concerning the request for the nomination of federal judges of ethnic extraction. For example, Representatives Dan Rostenkowski (D-Ill.) and John C. Kluczynski (D-Ill.) wished to tell the president that they believed, "as Mayor [Richard J.] Daley does, that the appointment of a person of Polish decent [sic] to this job [federal district judge] is most important."[37] And Congressman Frank Annunzio

(D-Ill.) wrote to Joseph A. Califano, Jr., to which Califano replied, "Many thanks for your letter . . . concerning the appointment of Italo-Americans to Federal judicial positions. As you know, this is a problem of great concern to me."[38] And Congressman Peter W. Rodino, Jr. (D-N.J.) passed on to Califano a letter from a state judge urging the creation of a "Paisano Chair" on the Supreme Court and later talked at great length to Barefoot Sanders about his interest in a judicial appointment for Edward D. Re as well as "his great concern that the Administration has not been making enough appointments of Italo-Americans."[39] Early on, Joseph Dolan reported that Senator Thomas J. Dodd (D-Conn.) "said that it will be difficult politically for him to recommend, between now and the election, an appointee for the District Court other than a lawyer of Italian descent" and recommended two names, including Robert C. Zampano.[40] And Congressman John H. Dent (D-Pa.) in a confidential letter to the president said that "many of my friends of Italian origin are interested in the vacancy in the Third Circuit Court of Appeals in Pennsylvania. Unanimously, they seem to be supporting the selection of Judge Ruggero J. Aldisert."[41]

The Johnson administration followed some of those recommendations and appointed several ethnic Americans. Congressman Annunzio informed Califano that the appointment of an Italian judge "has really electrified our community."[42] Aide James Falcon sent a memo commenting that Johnson's choice of Thomas D. Lambros for a district judgeship in Ohio is "as far as I know, . . . the first appointment of a Greek-American to the Federal judiciary."[43] And Zampano and Aldisert received appointments to the federal bench. Ethnic and religious politics also apparently influenced the selection of Irish and Jewish judges, as seen in the nomination of Francis X. Morrissey and Arthur Garrity in Boston and the nomination of Fortas to replace Arthur J. Goldberg and continue the "Jewish seat" tradition on the Supreme Court. Johnson appointed large numbers of Catholics and Jews to the judiciary, which reflects both "ethnic" politics and the makeup of the Democratic party. And Johnson nominated only the second Hispanic to the federal bench.[44]

Party Politics

A major factor in the selection process was party politics. As J. Woodford Howard notes, "Judgeships normally are rewards for political service."[45] This service may be to the senator involved, to the president, or to the party. Joel B. Grossman reports that since "the first administration of Grover Cleveland, no president has made less than 82.2 percent of his judicial appointments from the ranks of his own party."[46] And since 94.8 percent of the Johnson appointees to the district courts and 95 percent of his appointees to the courts of appeals were Democrats, certainly the Johnson administration did not reverse this trend.

Johnson's and Macy's oft-repeated claim of unconcern with *party* loyalty (as compared to policy or personal loyalty) may be valid. Richard Schott and Dagmar Hamilton report that their data suggest that party identification was not especially salient in other presidential appointments.[47] Sheldon Goldman categorized appointees on the basis of their previous participation in party work or party office-holding; his data indicate that Johnson's appointees were less active in a partisan manner than other recent presidential appointees. Large percentages of Johnson's political activists had been involved in elective politics, rather than just party work.[48]

Macy points out that the president was pleased when Macy reported to him that the sixteen Republicans selected to federal judgeships (along with seven nonpartisans) were "the largest number of appointees from an opposing party in the last six presidencies."[49] On several occasions the selection team sought a Republican for a vacancy because there was a perceived need for more Republican nominees. This is demonstrated in a memo from Macy to the president in which Macy notes that Johnson had previously "indicated that, if a more qualified Republican were available, you preferred to nominate him" as well as memos between Watson and Sanders concerning attempts to recruit Republican Congressman William T. Cahill of New Jersey for a judgeship.[50] This search for Republicans occurred even when there was no particular pressure from Republican senators, and even in the face of some Democratic party opposition.[51] But Johnson was aware of political advantages and political trade-offs in judicial selection, as evidenced by an arrangement involving Mayor Daley and Senator Dirksen. Because Johnson wanted "to get Dirksen's help on the tax bill," he nominated a Republican and Daley was promised a Democrat for the next vacancy.[52] The selection team was constantly aware of the need to maintain good relations with all senators, no matter what party, by being attentive to their thoughts on judicial selection. Politics was a major part of the Johnson persona, and it was part of the Johnson judicial selection process as well.

Personal Loyalty

All presidents want to appoint people loyal to them. Johnson was no different in this regard, except that he inherited an administration largely made up of "Kennedy men." Perhaps this enhanced the natural tendency to desire loyalty, but Johnson had always valued it.[53] As vice president he was responsible for placing old friends and political allies Sarah Hughes, Homer Thornberry, and Adrian Spears on the federal bench. His first nominee to the Supreme Court was his long-time adviser and crony Fortas. He nominated as federal judge the brother of Tom Corcoran, an old acquaintance and New Dealer. And one of his last actions as president was to renominate his close aide, Barefoot Sanders, to a court of appeals position. And of course there were many such appointments of allies to nonjudicial positions.

An examination of loyalty to President Johnson was always a part of the judicial selection process. In the first few years of the administration, this was generally represented by adherence to progressive ideals and the Johnson-Humphrey ticket (or even the 1960 Johnson for President attempt).[54] But in the later years, particularly in 1967 and 1968, the criterion of loyalty screened out those who did not fully support the president, particularly on his Vietnam policy. Watson, who in those years had the primary responsibility for screening candidates for the White House, interpreted the criterion to mean personal and political loyalty.

On a memo in late 1966 from Watson concerning a candidate, Johnson wrote, "Will he be an all out J-man?—L"[55] Apparently Watson found that the candidate would, because he was soon nominated. Clark submitted a recommendation of Charles D. Scott accompanied by a report that "there was an allegation that Scott had supported Goldwater. We have checked this out thoroughly and find that it has no basis."[56] With this assurance, Scott was nominated. Watson pushed forward a nomination for a U.S. attorney in response to Sanders' assurance that the candidate was a Johnson man after the president had directed Watson to check on the candidate's loyalty.[57] And two nominations went through after Watson assured the president that the candidates believe "in the principles of President Johnson's program and believe in the President personally."[58] There were also some personal interviews for political loyalty checks. On one occasion, Temple recommended to Johnson that he sign two nomination papers. "Then Barefoot and I can meet with both of them and be sure of their loyalty before their appointments are announced." The two nominations were sent to the Senate a few days after Temple reported that "Barefoot and I met with the two candidates. Based upon

Table 6. Party Activism of Judicial Appointees, Eisenhower through Reagan Administrations

			District Court Appointees				
	Eisenhower	*Kennedy*	*Johnson*	*Nixon*	*Ford*	*Carter*	*Reagan (First Term)*
Past party activism (%)	—	—	48.4	48.6	50.0	60.4	61.2

			Court of Appeals Appointees				
	Eisenhower	*Kennedy*	*Johnson*	*Nixon*	*Ford*	*Carter*	*Reagan (First Term)*
Past party activism (%)	66.7	81.0	52.5	60.0	58.3	73.2	58.1

Note: The Eisenhower and Kennedy percentages are the total number of judges not divided into district courts and courts of appeals.

these meetings . . . we are satisfied that both possess the . . . loyalty requirements to be appointed to these posts. Both meet all of the requirements that we look for in the appointment of Judges." [59] Aspects of this loyalty program included the desirability of not being supported by Robert Kennedy and the requirement that a candidate's endorsers be pro-Johnson. [60]

Vietnam loyalty was essential. [61] Harry C. McPherson, Jr. suggests that it became the most important criterion: "What you felt about the war was more important than what you felt about anything else. I think you could even dislike Lyndon Johnson and support the war and that would be fine. You'd be on his 'A' list." [62] Again, Watson attempted to screen out those candidates who did not fully support the war effort.

Professors Robert A. Carp and Claude K. Rowland's cohort analysis reveals that the appointees of 1967 were markedly less liberal than other Johnson appointees. [63] This was the year that Watson's "loyalty program" was in high gear, rejecting those candidates who were not "all-out J-men" and did not support Johnson's Vietnam actions. The Carp-Rowland analysis seems to strengthen the argument that loyalty to Johnson became a major criterion of selection in 1967. It might be noted, however, that during the last several months of the Johnson presidency (especially after Watson left the White House) the loyalty program mellowed and merit and the desire to reward old friends became the major criteria for judicial selection. But even then loyalty remained a significant element. [64]

Domestic Policy Concerns

In addition to personal loyalty, the selection process examined policy loyalty. Those who subscribed to the ideology of the Great Society were favored. [65]

One of the major issues of both the Great Society and the judicial selection process was civil rights, especially racial justice. This was particularly salient for judges because so much civil rights litigation was proceeding, especially in the courts of the southern circuits, that is, the Fourth and Fifth. Clark was particularly attentive to and adamant about candidates' attitudes toward the racial justice issue. He stated in an interview:

> I had a rule that a person with a history of neutrality on the race issue is not enough. We've been through so many times a person that had never done anything either way, turn[s] out to be a racist. [66]

This civil rights policy aspect of the selection process can be seen in a letter from White House aide Lee C. White to Aaron F. Henry of the National Association for the Advancement of Colored People (NAACP). White wrote: "Let me assure you of the importance attached to the attitude of any potential candidate on the extremely important subject of civil rights. This is one of the key factors considered in connection with any court vacancy."[67]

Perhaps the best evidence of the concern for the "correct" views on civil rights comes from a handwritten note from the president himself. On a memo in June 1966 discussing the Florida senators' views on a potential nominee, Johnson had written:

> How is he on Civil Rights? Ask Ramsey to thoroughly explore background—prior associations in cases, etc., and give me memo before I act. I want this on every Judge.[68]

From that point on, almost all nominees, at least in the South, were investigated respecting their positions on civil rights.[69] In the few instances that this did not occur prior to the president receiving the recommendation from the Justice Department, Johnson would direct that the investigation be made. For example, attached to a recommendation for a judgeship on the Fifth Circuit that did not include the civil rights portion, there is a directive from the president: "Call Ramsey. Check to be sure he is all right on the Civil Rights question. I'll approve him if he is."[70]

The correct civil rights position became such a prerequisite for Southern judicial candidates that internal pre-investigation checks were institutionalized in the Department of Justice. In an early 1967 memo, then-Assistant Attorney General Sanders wrote to Friesen:

> So that we may have a system about southern judges selection I suggest that before we request an FBI check or begin the FBI on any judgeship in the South that we first check with John [M.] Doar [who was in charge of the Civil Rights Division and was familiar with the attitudes and records of many southern lawyers] to see if he can get us a brief run-down. I know this has been done in some instances in the past but I don't find that we have done it uniformly.[71]

Such concern is indicated by memos from Clark and Macy to the president concerning a Louisiana judge considered for a district judgeship. They report that the Justice Department has "inquired extensively about Judge [Frederick J. B.] Heebe's record on matters dealing with civil rights and believe him to be a liberal who would follow the law as a U.S. District Judge."[72] Heebe was nominated. So too were William C. Keady of Mississippi and James A. Comiskey of Louisiana after civil rights groups described them as moderates on the issue.[73] The checks were very rigorous. Sanders reported to the president that "Ramsey has checked carefully to determine [Claude F. Clayton's] attitude on civil rights and he's concluded that he has been fair and just and that he has and would follow the law in handling such cases." The checks included a reference from the director-counsel of the NAACP and a report of Clayton's handling of a case as a state judge in 1939 where he tried a white man accused of the murder of a Negro.[74]

These checks sometimes included questioning other federal judges. When, for example, another district judge was being considered for elevation to the Fifth Circuit, judges on that circuit were asked to evaluate the district judge's performance on civil rights.[75] And, as noted before, the president agreed "to lean hard on [Woodrow W. Jones, a prospective nominee to a North Carolina district court] whose nomination . . . is opposed by civil rights groups. [He] needs a good talking to on civil rights." Johnson did meet with the nominee and indeed gave him a "good talking to." (See the discussion of the events surrounding the Fourth Circuit appointment in Chapter 6.) On another occasion, Johnson met with several prospective judicial nominees and "stressed the importance of equal justice for all regardless of race, economic condition or social status."[76]

President Johnson was very much concerned with the policy views and personal inclinations of his judicial appointees. A number of recent studies have found that personal attributes are related to judicial decisionmaking propensities and that there are linkages between appointing presidents and judicial policymaking.[77] Although the relationships may not be causal, certainly the associations are significant. "Given the role of the president in judicial selection and the centrality of ideological criteria in judicial recruitment it is not surprising that substantial differences occur among appointing-president cohorts."[78]

C. Neal Tate measured the voting behavior of Supreme Court justices on nonunanimous cases involving civil rights and liberties and economics cases between 1946 and 1978. He found that a combination of personal attributes, including party identification, appointing president, educational institution, and experience accounted for 70 to 90 percent of the variance in nonunanimous votes. He concluded that one major attribute that correlated closely with voting behavior was the judge's "appointing president": in civil rights and liberties cases the "influence of the appointing presidents' presumed concern with the values of their appointees is clearly documented" and in economics cases the "influence of appointing presidents is again revealed."[79]

More specifically, Tate found that Johnson's appointees differed from other presidents' appointees, particularly Truman's and Nixon's. Johnson's appointees were more liberal, especially in the civil rights and civil liberties area, where Tate's model predicts the "most liberal score for the . . . justice . . . who is a Democrat appointed . . . by Lyndon Johnson."[80] This point is reemphasized in a table accompanying the Tate article that lists the justices and their scores on the two types of cases. There is an almost incredible correlation between the scores of Justices Fortas and Marshall, President Johnson's justices, on the hundreds of cases in both the civil rights and civil liberties area and the economics area. In the first area, Justice Fortas scored 84.3 percent liberal and Justice Marshall scored 84.2 percent liberal; in the economics area, Fortas scored 67.6 percent liberal and Marshall scored 67.5 percent liberal! In both areas the justices were separated by one-tenth of a percentage point.[81]

The scores and the Fortas-Marshall correlation are even more impressive when compared to the differences between Johnson appointees and other presidents' appointees and within other presidents' cohorts (see Table 5.7). On economics cases, the Johnson appointees were 4.5 percentage points more liberal than the next leading group (Roosevelt's), 7 percentage points more liberal than the average of all justices, and 35 points more liberal than the Nixon appointees. On civil rights and liberties cases, the differences are even more striking. Fortas and Marshall are 19 percentage points more liberal than the next group (Kennedy's), 33.6 points more liberal than the average, and 65 percentage points more liberal than the Nixon and the Truman appointees. And where Fortas and Marshall differed only .1 percentage point on both economics and civil liberties areas, some of Roosevelt's appointees differed some 83 points, and the closest non-Johnson correlation is 7.6 points difference on economics for Kennedy's appointees and 9.3 points difference on civil liberties for Truman's appointees. If, as this chapter has suggested and as Laurence Tribe has argued, presidents are very aware of the policy role of justices and desire to appoint justices with ideologies to make the right constitutional choices, then President Johnson succeeded very well in his appointments to the Supreme Court.[82] Fred P. Graham phrased this well in a summation of Fortas' first term on the Supreme Court:

Table 7. Civil Rights, Civil Liberties, and Economics Decisions in the U.S. Supreme Court, 1946–1978

Appointing President	Justice	Civil Rights and Liberties Cases				Economics Cases			
		Votes (N)	Greatest Difference within Cohorts*	% Liberal	Average Score*	Votes (N)	Greatest Difference within Cohorts*	% Liberal	Average Score*
Roosevelt	Black	1,044		73.3		740		85.4	
	Reed	282		11.0		350		45.2	
	Frankfurter	487		46.6		452		21.0	
	Douglas	1,230	83.3	94.4	62.3	772	82.6	82.1	62.9
	Murphy	87		94.3		110		96.4	
	Jackson	218		36.7		208		13.9	
	Rutledge	89		80.9		113		96.5	
Truman	Burton	367		20.4		373		30.3	
	Vinson	208		17.3		217		41.5	
	Clark	685	9.3	25.3	19.8	532	34.9	65.2	47.3
	Minton	181		16.0		177		52.0	
Eisenhower	Warren	743		79.1		510		82.0	
	Harlan	795		23.3		477		23.3	
	Brennan	1,120	58.1	81.4	51.2	553	64.8	74.5	46.5
	Whitaker	195		26.3		169		17.2	
	Stewart	1,038		45.8		464		35.6	
Kennedy	White	884		41.5		346		58.4	
	Goldberg	167	47.7	89.2	65.35	100	7.6	66.0	62.2
Johnson	Fortas	248	.1	84.3	84.25	102	.1	67.6	67.5
	Marshall	569		84.2		154		67.5	

	Cases (N)				Cases (N)			
… (cut off)			18.2		120		20.0	
Blackmun	420		26.0		109		32.1	
Powell	351		30.8		93		36.6	
Rabuquist	352	26.3	4.5	19.37	96	21.0	15.6	32.7
Stevens		—	54.7	—	39	—	48.7	—
Ford	148							
COURT	1,452		50.6		875		60.5	
Mean (25 justices)			48.1				50.9	
Standard deviation			30.2				26.3	

Source: C. Neal Tate, "Personal Attribute Models of the Voting Behavior of U.S. Supreme Court Justices: Liberalism in Civil Liberties and Economic Decisions, 1946–1978," *American Political Science Review* 75 (June 1981): 357.

* Computed by the author.

When President Johnson appointed Abe Fortas to the Supreme Court, it was widely predicted that he would be a liberal Justice. Now, after Justice Fortas' first term on the Court, it appears that the word "liberal" is not sufficiently precise. He is a Great Society liberal.[83]

This description could apply to Marshall's term as well.

Carp and Rowland's major empirical study of the effects of appointing presidents on federal district judges' policy decisions presents information on the "Johnson effect" at the other end of the federal judicial system. Their conclusions are similar to Tate's: there is a definite link between appointing presidents and their appointees' policy decisions, and Johnson's appointees were more liberal as a group than other presidents' appointees. They state:

> The appointing President is a variable of considerable importance in influencing the behavior of trial judges. For example, the percentage of Johnson appointees voting on the liberal side of judicial questions is some 21 points higher than for Nixon appointees for the same years. Our investigation further suggests that the variables of political party affiliation and appointing President are not entirely synonymous. That is, some Presidents have obviously selected (or been able to select) district court judges with greater ideological care than others. . . . Thus . . . to a fair degree, Presidents tend to get out of their judicial appointees the kind of decisions they want from them.[84]

Carp and Rowland compared the liberalism of different appointing president cohorts on several different policy areas and found that Johnson's appointees on the district courts were generally more liberal than those of other recent presidents. In criminal justice cases between 1960 and 1977, Johnson appointees, more than other appointees, tended to support the defendant: "their decisions reflect President Johnson's liberal selection criteria."[85] In the economic policy area, Carp and Rowland found that "presidents can affect judicial policy making" and that the Johnson cohort group was more liberal than any other recent group and was particularly distinguishable from the Nixon appointees.[86] It is interesting to note that the 67 percent liberalism score of the Johnson district court appointees is extremely close to the 67.55 score in Tate's study of Johnson's Supreme Court appointees.

Table 8. *Differences in Support for Criminal Defendants among District Judge Cohorts Defined by Appointing President, 1960–1977*

Appointing President	Opinions Supporting Criminal Defendant	
	%	N
Eisenhower	20	1,486
Kennedy	25	2,066
Johnson	35	2,326
Nixon	26	1,210
Overall	28	7,088

Table 9. *Differences in Economic Liberalism among District Judge Cohorts Defined by Appointing President, 1961–1977*

Appointing President	% Liberal Opinions (N = 3,917)
Eisenhower	61
Kennedy	64
Johnson	67
Nixon	48

Conclusion

The Johnson judicial selection process was guided by several criteria, criteria often specified personally by President Johnson. The desire for merit and competence was always present, especially in the Department of Justice and the Macy operation. The selection process attempted to bring in individuals with diverse backgrounds, particularly minorities and younger persons, and it also recruited those with prior governmental experience. In the later years especially, the desire for loyalty was important and sometimes came into conflict with the other criteria. The policy stand of candidates was a major element in the selection process.

Criteria changed at least somewhat over time. And within the Johnson selection team, different actors stressed different standards. So there was no single standard or even set of standards against which prospective nominees were judged, although certain criteria did guide the process. Furthermore, as Moyers observed in an interview in the Schott and Hamilton work, Lyndon Johnson also brought a strong element of intuition to his personal involvement in the process.[87] That intuition was backed up by what McPherson termed an impressive capacity to judge people: "He is the fastest learner of personality that I have ever encountered in my life." And Fortas reportedly stated that Johnson was the best judge of character he had ever seen.[88]

This interplay of intuition and criteria, especially loyalty, experience, merit, policy stands, can be seen in Johnson's explanation of why he selected certain individuals for nomination to the Supreme Court: "[Fortas] was the most experienced, compassionate, articulate, and intelligent lawyer I knew, and . . . I was certain that he would carry on in the Court's liberal tradition. . . . [Thornberry], a former . . . U.S. Congressman, and then a Federal Judge, had been a close friend of mine for many years. He was one of the most competent, fairminded, and progressive jurists in the entire South."[89] This mixture of elements and, of course, politics guided not only President Johnson's selection of Supreme Court nominees but also that of all federal judges and determined the characteristics and values of those selected. In turn, those characteristics and values influenced the decisions the Johnson judges made. Studies have concluded that Johnson appointees on all levels of the federal judiciary tended to make liberal decisions in civil rights and liberties, economics, and criminal justice. President Johnson was very much aware of the policy importance of his judicial appointments and seems to have succeeded in selecting judges who reflected his views of the Great Society.

6. Case Studies in Judicial Appointment

The preceding chapters have described the general process of judicial selection during the Johnson administration, the major participants in the process, and the criteria used by those participants to choose appropriate candidates. We have identified many common elements in each selection and shown the factors that tended to be dominant generally in the process.

Case studies furnish a method to point out specific or unique aspects while also taking note of the general process. This chapter presents several case studies of judicial selection in order to illustrate the complex interplay of participants and philosophy in the process. The case studies are taken from the three levels of the federal judiciary and also from different time periods of the Johnson presidency. We can see how senators' roles were primary in district court selection, while the Department of Justice played a major role in choosing appellate judges and the president took the leading role in Supreme Court selection. Other participants were involved in all case studies. We can see how the process developed as time passed and the Kennedy process was replaced by the people and criteria of the Johnson process, although it too changed.

District Court

The appointment of Judge Ray McNichols of Idaho is an illustration of the typical process of appointment of a district judge in the early months of the Johnson presidency. The process is a rather straightforward one, but it contained several interesting elements.

McNichols was an attorney in a small town in Idaho and was very active in Democratic party politics in the 1950s. In 1960 he was a delegate to the Democratic National Convention in Los Angeles and supported Kennedy there even though Lyndon Johnson personally tried to get his support. McNichols was also a friend and supporter of Frank Church, the only Democratic senator from Idaho.

After Kennedy's election, it was understood that McNichols would receive the next appointment to the federal bench. Church made it known that McNichols was his choice to succeed the incumbent judge. Other potential hopefuls, seeing no possibilities for appointment, did not mobilize any campaigns. And President Kennedy, in recognition of McNichols' support for his nomination in 1960, promised to appoint McNichols to the bench.[1] Judge Chase Clark informed Senator Church that he was ready to retire in the near future. Church submitted his formal recommendation of McNichols to the Department of Justice, which began its informal investigations. The department was satisfied, as was the ABA, and on 14 November 1963 the department forwarded this information and its recommendation of McNichols to the White House in preparation for Clark's retirement.[2] There was thus understanding that McNichols would soon become a district judge.

Of course this understanding was disrupted by the assassination of John Kennedy. It was unclear if Johnson would support McNichols in light of his 1960 position. Nevertheless, in 1964 Senator Church again informed the Department of Justice that McNichols was his choice, and when Clark submitted his resignation, Church publicly announced his support for McNichols.

There did not seem to be any opposition from the White House. As noted in Chapter 4, particularly in the early years of the Johnson administration, the choice of district judge was largely left to the Democratic senator. If there was no real opposition from politicians or other attorneys in the state, as was the case in Idaho, the administration usually went along with that choice; the process was simply one of checking out and validating the selection. After Church had informed the White House and specifically the Department of Justice, the formal process began. A Macy operation file on McNichols was instituted.[3] FBI and IRS checks were done and a thorough ABA investigation, including a lengthy personal interview, was initiated. Once these were successfully completed, the formal nomination was sent to the Senate and McNichols received a telegram in April 1964 signed by President Johnson informing him of the nomination.[4]

The nomination came during the battle over the passage of the Civil Rights Act of 1964, legislation pressed by Johnson and opposed by many Southern legislators including Senator James Eastland (D-Miss.). Eastland was chairman of the Senate Judiciary Committee and attempted to use his control over judicial confirmation hearings to extract compromises from the administration or at least to delay Johnson's appointments. The McNichols nomination, among others, would have been one of these attempts but Johnson, who according to McNichols was "two jumps ahead of everybody in that kind of machination," had a strategy to deal with the Eastland delays.[5] He would send a series of names to the committee; among those names was usually that of a nominee endorsed by one of Eastland's fellow Southerners. That senator would urge Eastland to move on the confirmation hearings, and usually the hearings would be held relatively quickly. This occurred with the McNichols nomination: his name was sent to the Senate with a few others, including one from the South. Eastland had a subcommittee chaired by Senator Olin D. Johnston (D-S.C.) conduct the hearings. Subcommittee hearings were usually pro forma, and they were in McNichols' case; Senator Church, Senator Len Jordan (R-Id.), and the two Idaho representatives (both Democrats) endorsed the nomination and the brief hearing was, in McNichols' words, a "love feast." McNichols was confirmed and took his place on the bench in Idaho.

The McNichols appointment illustrates the early district court selection process. The actual selection was made by the Democratic senator; the individual was checked by the Department of Justice procedures, and if no problems appeared, the name was approved and sent to the White House for final approval. The name was transmitted to the Senate, a Judiciary Committee staff member informed the nominee of the date of the hearing, and confirmation followed. This appointment illustrates also Johnson's ability to use the appropriate tactics to get the Senate to follow his will. But the president did not play a very active role in the selection of judges in those early months.

This case study also illustrates the selection criteria used by the administration at that time. McNichols was a Democrat and a successful attorney. He was highly regarded by his peers and was rated "qualified" by the ABA. He was relatively young when appointed and would serve some twenty more years. Other criteria, such as policy stands and personal loyalty, had not yet been developed and thus were not utilized in the McNichols selection. The major criterion was simply the endorsement of a Democratic senator for a qualified candidate.

The McNichols appointment is interesting for its unusual aspects. Most notable is the politics of the situation—the Kennedy support and the Kennedy promise of a nomination for McNichols. Yet Johnson, known for his loyalty to supporters and enmity to others, nevertheless appointed McNichols. It might be that Johnson simply did not notice or remember the Idaho nominee (which is unlikely in light of Johnson's long political memory) because so many district judge nominations came to his office. It might also be that in those early years Johnson attempted to fulfill the Kennedy pledges on judicial appointments. The most likely explanation is that Democratic senators initiated the selection process for district judges particularly in the early years and that their choices were generally accepted unless they were unqualified or politically offensive. McNichols was neither, and with Senator Church's strong support was nominated and appointed to the district judgeship, where he served until his death in 1985.

A relatively conventional nomination for a district judgeship (except for the fact that the nominee was the first black woman ever appointed to a federal court) was that of Constance Baker Motley in January 1966.[6] Because of Mrs. Motley's background as associate counsel for the NAACP Legal Defense and Educational Fund, she came to the attention of the Macy operation in early 1964 as a possibility in civil rights appointments. Active consideration of her as a judge began when Senator Robert Kennedy recommended her to the Justice Department for a vacancy on the District Court for the Southern District of New York caused by the death of the incumbent in early 1965. Motley, who by this time was a New York state senator and soon to be elected as Manhattan Borough president, had come to Kennedy's attention when he was attorney general. The Justice Department, after checking with the White House, made some preliminary investigations and by July 1965 had run FBI and IRS checks, begun informal ABA investigation, and checked with the Democratic National Committee, which rated her "very good." It received tentative approval from the New York congressional delegation, especially Republican Senator Jacob Javits.[7]

On 14 July Attorney General Nicholas Katzenbach sent a memorandum to the president describing a discussion he had had with Senator Kennedy concerning the replacement for Thurgood Marshall, newly appointed solicitor general, as judge on the Second Circuit. Kennedy suggested that they still put Motley on the district bench, "assuming that we could get the American Bar Association to certify her 'qualified'; but perhaps even if we could not" and appoint another district judge to the circuit vacancy, because "he believed that the replacement of one Negro by another on the Circuit Court underlined by the fact that both Marshall and Motley were primarily NAACP civil rights lawyers would get some adverse reaction and would appear to be too political." Katzenbach commented to the president that "I think there is merit in Senator Kennedy's assessment and that it is worthy of consideration." This indicates that the president had been thinking about Motley for the circuit judgeship and certainly proves that he was knowledgeable about the Motley candidacy. For whatever reasons, the decision was made to go forward with Motley's nomination to the district court. On 14 September 1965 Katzenbach and Deputy Attorney General Ramsey Clark prepared their formal memorandums for transmittal of the nomination of Motley to the president. Katzenbach formally described her background in law and politics and officially recommended the nomination. Clark enclosed the nomination papers and set forth the reasons for the Justice Department's recommendation:

1. Her extensive experience as a general practitioner, as a legislator, and as a litigator for the Legal Defense and Education Fund indicate that she is fully qualified by experience and temperament to serve as a United States District Judge.
2. The American Bar Association has made inquiry into her capabilities and has found her qualified to be a United States District Judge.
3. She is strongly recommended by Senator Robert F. Kennedy.
4. The Federal Bureau of Investigation discloses no information to bar Mrs. Motley's nomination.
5. The Internal Revenue Service advises that Mrs. Motley's income tax returns have been timely filed.

These papers were forwarded to Macy's office, but New York state politics had intervened and the nomination was delayed. Clifford L. Alexander, deputy special assistant to the president, reported to Bill Moyers, John Macy, and Marvin Watson in a memorandum on 20 July that several New York Democratic leaders who had been alerted to the possibility of a Motley nomination by the FBI checks asked that the nomination be delayed until after the City of New York elections of November, in which Motley was a candidate. J. Raymond Jones, New York County Democratic leader, explained that any earlier nomination

would ruin the chances of the Democratic slate in New York. Motley has already received the endorsement of the Liberal Party and probably will also be selected on the Republican line. . . . The ensuing chaos [if Motley were to be appointed and resign from the Borough Presidency race] would have disastrous results for the Party in New York.

And Louis Martin of the Democratic National Committee raised the same objection: "Please," he said, "don't touch Motley until *after* the election." Apparently this concern reached Senator Kennedy, because he asked that the nomination be postponed unil January. The president informed Macy, who asked, "Is the Attorney general aware this decision?—JWM." Katzenbach was aware and all agreed to delay the nomination.

Finally, on 17 January 1966, Macy sent the papers to the White House. In a memorandum for the president, Macy wrote:

> In the attached memorandum, the Attorney General and Deputy Attorney General recommend the nomination of Mrs. Constance B. Motley to the United States District Court for the Southern District of New York. I concur in this recommendation.
>
> Mrs. Motley has the strong recommendation of Senator Robert Kennedy.
>
> The FBI investigation and the IRS check have been completed, and National Committee and Congressional clearances have been obtained.

On the bottom, where there were lines designated "Approve", "Disapprove," and "See Me," the president had checked "Approve."[8] Macy was informed on 19 January of the president's decision. On 25 January, the nomination was announced to the press by the president with Motley present at the White House for photographers.[9] It was sent to the Senate the next day and then to the Judiciary Committee. Chairman Eastland took some time to schedule subcommittee hearings, but on 4 April, with the strong endorsements of New York Senators Kennedy and Javits, the subcommittee unanimously approved the appointment. Again after more delays and administration pressure, the full committee voted 12 to 2 on 24 August to approve Motley.[10] Senators James Eastland and John L. McClellan (D-Ark.) voted against the appointment (Senators George A. Smathers, D-Fla., and Sam Ervin, D-N.C., abstained), and Eastland fought the appointment on the floor, alleging that Motley had been active in the Young Communist League twenty years earlier. However, the Senate confirmed the nomination at the end of August and President Johnson formally made the appointment. On 9 September Motley was sworn in and took her seat.[11]

This appointment illustrates several of the criteria used to select judges. Motley's competence was proven: she was a graduate of Columbia Law School and had been a leading attorney for major desegregation cases sponsored by the NAACP. Certainly an activist temperament and great experience were demonstrated by her NAACP work and her success in politics. She was also a Democrat and, more important, supported the Great Society social programs, especially civil rights. It did not hurt her chances to be black, a woman, and young (forty-four years old), as these were several of the characteristics Johnson valued. And the recommendation and support of the Democratic senator from the state of the district court vacancy was a major factor in her nomination.

The nomination and appointment of Motley illustrates judicial selection in the early years of the Johnson presidency. The early standards of merit, experience, demographic characteristics, and loyalty to a progressive ideology were met. The judicial selection team was the early Johnson team with Katzenbach and Clark at Justice and Macy taking leading roles. The White House staff was concerned with the political aspects and the president took personal interest in the nomination. Politics was involved in the beginning of the initiation of the process on Kennedy's recommendation, in the timing because of state politics, and in the public announcement so that the president could extract political benefit. Politics, process, and philosophy for selection were intertwined to produce the Motley nomination for a seat on the district court.

Courts of Appeals

The Johnson process, philosophy, and politics of nomination to the courts of appeals were similar to those for district courts in many respects, but differences were apparent. The major general difference is that because a circuit encompasses more than one state, senators share their power over appointments with the administration more than with district judgeships. In the Johnson years, prior judicial experience seemed to be an essential prerequisite for appointment to the appellate court. Merit was stressed highly and competence on the lower court was the evidence most sought to prove merit. Yet politics remained a significant element in these appointments also.

These points are illustrated by the nomination of John Butzner to the Court of Appeals for the Fourth Circuit in 1967. This was during the mature Johnson selection process, when Clark was attorney general and Watson dominated the political side of selection from the White House. After a vacancy occurred upon the death of a judge from Virginia, Senator Harry F. Byrd (D-Va.) recommended Butzner, who was a district judge in the Eastern District of Virginia.[12] After receiving the go-ahead from the White House and the standard clearances (the ABA Committee rated Butzner "exceptionally well qualified"), the Justice Department submitted the formal recommendation to the president through Attorney General Clark's memorandum of 15 May. Accompanying that was a memorandum from Barefoot Sanders (who was then assistant attorney general for the civil division, but as noted earlier continued to play a role in judicial selection as the "White House's man in the Department") that seconded the recommendation, noting that "Butzner is a Democrat and his nomination is recommended by Senator Byrd." By this time the Macy operation had lost much of its role in judicial selection, and Macy does not appear to have been asked for approval. After receiving the president's signature, the nomination was sent to the Senate. Hearings were soon held and Butzner was confirmed. Butzner wrote a thank-you letter to the president.[13]

What is not apparent from this description of the process is the political maneuvering that accompanied Butzner's nomination. That process involved Democratic senators, district court vacancies, and Johnson's political abilities. The players included senators, congressmen, Watson and others in the White House Office (including congressional liaison aides Manatos and Wilson), Clark, Sanders, and others in the Justice Department, the ABA, the NAACP, and Johnson himself. A superficial description of this is related by Donald D. Jackson in *Judges.* Jackson quotes a "Washington lawyer" about the somewhat complex political-judicial situation in Virginia preceding the Court of Appeals vacancy:

> There were two District Court vacancies in Virginia. . . . Senator [Harry] Byrd was backing Richard Kellam, Senator [William] Spong was behind John MacKenzie, and Robert Merhige had the support of Reynolds Metal Company in Virginia, which was a big donor to the Johnson campaign. So he had three men for two spots. Johnson's contribution to the workings of democracy was to elevate Judge John Butzner to the Fourth Circuit Court of Appeals, which gave him three openings in Virginia. Everybody was happy. Voila, eh?[14]

In reality the situation was much more complex and involved considerations of geography and merit as well as the politics of district court selection. Before the vacancy on the Fourth Circuit occurred, there were two existing vacancies on the Virginia Eastern District Court; and the competition for those was fierce. In early- and mid-1966, several recommendations were submitted to the White House and the Department of Justice. James Rowe, a Johnson adviser, wrote to the president recommending Merhige of Richmond and noting that Merhige had suported Johnson in 1964, and in 1964 in Virginia that "took courage." He also noted that there were several other candidates from Norfolk, but that there had been no judge appointed from Richmond in thirty years and that "there are enough vacancies to go around."[15] Senate liaison Mike Manatos and House Liaison Henry Wilson also received recommendations and passed these on to Watson in the White House and Clark or Sanders in Justice.[16] By now newly elected Senator Spong and Congressman Porter Hardy (D-Va.) were backing MacKenzie, Senator Byrd was backing Kellam (who was the brother of Sidney Kellam of the Democratic National Committee), and Rowe and Reynolds Metal Company supported Merhige. There were two vacancies and three qualified candidates with strong political backing; neither the White House nor the Justice Department could come to a conclusion.

By early 1967 two new elements came into the situation. Circuit Judge J. Spencer Bell of North Carolina died. There was also a vacancy on the North Carolina District Court. Senators Sam Ervin and Everett Jordan of North Carolina were pushing Woodrow Wilson Jones for that district court vacancy, but Jones had received a good deal of opposition from civil rights groups for his previous conservative stands. In March, Sanders reported to Attorney General Clark that Manatos had called to say that Senator Byrd of Virginia "had suggested to him that Judge John Butzner of Richmond be promoted to the Fourth Circuit and that all three Virginia Eastern candidates be put on the District Bench."[17] At the same time, the North Carolina senators were moving to claim the Bell vacancy on the Court of Appeals for their state. Senator Ervin submitted several names to the Justice Department for the Fourth Circuit vacancy and told Justice that he wanted them to know that "he is submitting six names because the President has told him he would like to have more than one name from which to choose; that the fact he is submitting six names does not in any way indicate that he is any the less interested in having a North Carolina man appointed to the vacancy."[18] The department was considering the North Carolina claim; Sanders concluded that on the "basis of the attached caseload statistics it looks to me like Virginia is entitled to a second circuit judge rather than North Carolina." At the time North Carolina and Virginia each had one judge but the Virginia caseload was larger.[19]

In April, Sanders reported on the situation to Clark and made some recommendations:

We have four vacancies which should probably be resolved at one time:

North Carolina Western—for which Senators Jordan and Ervin are pushing Woodrow Wilson Jones very strongly. I believe we should go with Jones.

Two Virginia Eastern with three candidates—John A. Mac-Kenzie, Richard B. Kellam, and Robert Merhige. MacKenzie and Kellam are from the Tidewater area. Spong wants MacKenzie very badly as does Porter Hardy. I think we should recommend MacKenzie and Merhige who are relatively young and have prepared nomination papers on them.

The Fourth Circuit vacancy created by the death of Judge Bell of North Carolina. Senator Ervin has submitted six names for consideration and we are asking the ABA for informals on all six, but I have told . . . Ervin's staff man that the choice is between North Carolina and Virginia and North Carolina should not figure that the Bell vacancy belongs to it.

I recommend that the situation be resolved by appointment of: Kellam to the Fourth Circuit or promoting Butzner to the Fourth Circuit and naming Kellam as his replacement. Butzner is 49 years old, a Kennedy appointee, and John Duffner says he has been a good District Judge. If we decide to go with Butzner we will need an ABA report.[20]

Clark seems to have accepted Sanders' recommendations, for within a few days the nomination papers for Jones (with the comment that it would be a controversial appointment because "Jones is conservative on race"), MacKenzie, and Merhige were sent to the president.[21] Sanders' memos described the complex Virginia–North Carolina situation and commented: "Jordan and Ervin are extended so far in pushing Jones that we are in a fairly good position to go ahead with Jones and give the Fourth Circuit vacancy to Virginia. There are distinct advantages to this." The advantages included the opening up of another vacancy (either the Fourth Circuit or Butzner's vacancy) in Virginia for the third contender, Kellam. "Either solution would resolve our problem in Virginia Eastern. On balance we recommend promotion of Butzner and appointment of Kellam as his replacement, at the same time going ahead with Jones in North Carolina Western." Sanders recommended that the president should go ahead and immediately nominate MacKenzie and Merhige; however, Johnson apparently wanted the entire situation resolved at one time and the nomination papers were returned to the Justice Department.

In the middle of May, Attorney General Clark sent a memo to Johnson that included nomination papers on all five and repeated

Sanders' suggestion: "Promotion of Butzner to the Fourth Circuit would resolve the very difficult problem of picking two of the three." Clark also commented on the North Carolina vacancy: "The nomination of Jones will be regarded in North Carolina as a defeat of the NAACP and a victory for Jordan, Ervin, and North Carolina conservatives. On the other hand, failure to nominate Jones will be regarded by Jordan and Ervin as a slap and as a victory for the NAACP."[22] In the interim, Ervin had continued to push for Jones in the Justice Department.[23] Johnson seems to have accepted the department's recommendations: a few weeks later he held an hour-long, informal meeting with the five prospective nominees. The president presented his customary views on arrogant and superannuated judges and, in light of the controversy surrounding Jones and in response to the Sanders memo urging Johnson to "lean hard" on Jones and give him a "good talking to on civil rights" "stressed his interest in equal justice and equal rights for all and told those present that they should always strive not only to be fair but to be sure that all who appeared before them thought they were being treated fairly and impartially." He concluded that they should remember that they were to be Johnson nominees and that senators, representatives, the Justice Department, and he personally "had reviewed their qualifications and that he was personally satisfied that they were the best men available."[24]

But Johnson clearly did not want to take hasty action on this complex matter because the nomination papers were held in the White House for six weeks. On 26 June, Sanders (who was not officially a member of the White House staff) urged action in a memo to Watson:

> It is very important that the North Carolina–Virginia–nominations be sent to the Senate today. You have the papers on these
> . . . . Senators Eastland, Ervin and Mike Mansfield [D-Mont.] have the Judiciary committee and Senate schedule so arranged that these nominations can be heard this week, and confirmed. If we wait until after the July 4 recess we may run into strong NAACP opposition on Jones because the NAACP convention beginning July 10 is apt to discuss the subject. If the nomination is already an accomplished fact it is unlikely that the subject will come before the NAACP convention.[25]

Apparently that memo prompted rapid action—later that day Sanders sent a memo to press secretary George Christian noting that "Marvin tells me that the President will announce" the Virginia–

North Carolina nominations that day and instructing Christian how to describe the nominees.[26] Thus Butzner and the others were nominated; however, their nominations were not submitted to the Senate until mid-July. Part of the delay was because the Virginia election of Senator Spong was held and it would have been "too obvious" to send up the nominations to the Senate immediately after the election.[27] Once the nominations were received by the Senate, they were promptly confirmed and Butzner took his seat on the Court of Appeals for the Fourth Circuit.[28]

The Butzner nomination illustrates the workings of the process in 1966 and 1967, the mature Johnson judicial selection period. A number of actors played important roles. Senators and a few representatives were the initiators of the nominations of district judges and, to a lesser extent, judges of the courts of appeals. The Department of Justice sought out qualified nominees who would also be politically acceptable. Clark and Sanders were the primary movers in the Justice Department. A positive rating from the ABA was a necessity, as was clearance from the FBI and IRS. The White House Office played a major role. Congressional liaison officers Manatos and Wilson served as a conduit of information on the preferences of key members of the Senate and House. Watson was very much concerned with and influenced the politics of selection. President Johnson was also involved: he set the general criteria, personally approved the nominees, and hosted a reception for the candidates in which he set forth his views on judging.

The Butzner and related nominations also illustrate the criteria used in selection. Obviously, politics was of significance. The views of Democratic officeholders were given great weight, even when their candidates may not have been the first choice of the administration (because of civil-rights stands, for instance). Prior experience, especially judicial experience, was valued in promotion to the court of appeals. Geographic equity considerations were important in the district court choice and in the decision to award Virginia rather than North Carolina the position on the Fourth Circuit. The policy position concerning civil rights was also considered, even though in the Jones nomination it was outweighed by political considerations. The civil rights criterion was stressed, however, in Johnson's talk with the prospective judges. And finally, merit played a major part in the selection of Butzner for the court of appeals, as illustrated by the Justice Department's statement that Butzner had "been a good District Judge."

Supreme Court

The selection of nominees for the Supreme Court is very different from that for lower court judgeships. The president plays a primary role and may be the major actor in the process. That is, presidents, recognizing the long-lasting significance of their Supreme Court appointments, may make the initial decision on a candidate from personal knowledge about the individual, simply have the Justice Department take the necessary steps (ABA, FBI, and IRS checks) to validate the person the president wants. For example, Chief Justice Earl Warren reports in his oral history that when he went to the White House to tell President Johnson of his intention to retire and to tender the letter of resignation, Johnson asked if he had any candidates to replace him. Warren told him no, that it was Johnson's problem. But Warren also notes: "And he thought a moment and he said 'What do you think of Abe Fortas?' And I said, 'I think Abe would be a good Chief Justice.'"[29] This indicates that the president chose a candidate and then had Justice and the White House staff proceed from there. And Christopher comments that "the nominations at the Supreme Court level are considered a good deal by the President on his own and in his private conversations with the Attorney General."[30] Christopher goes on to note that in the Fortas-Thornberry nomination, he and the attorney general were the only two involved at the Justice Department as they considered various names and noted any possible problems with confirmation.

Although the formal process of selecting a Supreme Court justice is the same for lower courts (ABA investigation, formal Justice Department recommendation, etc.), each individual nomination to the Court is so unique that case studies cannot present an accurate picture of the general process. Further, it is difficult to describe patterns of nomination to the Supreme Court because of the few such nominations most presidents are able to make. Nevertheless, Johnson's role in his Supreme Court nominations is illustrative of his judicial concerns and his personal attentiveness to the judicial selection process. This section describes that role, emphasizing the aspects not revealed by prior research on the nominations.[31]

Johnson submitted four nominations to the Senate. In 1965 he nominated Fortas and in 1967 he nominated Marshall; both were confirmed. However, in mid-1968, after he announced that he would not seek reelection, he submitted the nomination of Fortas to be chief justice and of Homer Thornberry to fill Fortas' seat as associate justice. These nominations failed to come to a Senate vote because of a filibuster, and the nominations were withdrawn. A common element in all of these was the president's primary role in choosing men whose capabilities and political and policy positions he was very well aware of and with whom he was intimately acquainted.

The first vacancy on the Supreme Court during Johnson's presidency was in great part the result of Johnson's actions. Adlai Stevenson, ambassador to the United Nations, died on 14 July 1965, and Johnson wished a replacement of stature. He wanted Arthur Goldberg, who had been appointed by John Kennedy in 1962 to the Supreme Court, and he used his considerable talents to persuade the reportedly unwilling Goldberg to give up his position on the Court to assume what Johnson promised was to be a policymaking, peacemaking role as United Nations ambassador.[32] Chief Justice Warren provides an enlightening picture of the situation in his oral history as he describes his conversation with Goldberg the day before the announcement of his resignation:

> Goldberg came from Washington with the President. I was out in California, and I went to Illinois to the funeral of Adlai Stevenson and I saw Arthur there. And Arthur told me then that there was talk of his going to the United Nations, but that he was rather inclined against it. I told him that I would have the same feeling because I would hate to see him leave the Court. But he had the misfortune of going back on the plane with the President that night, and the next morning it was announced in the press that he was going to [accept the United Nations position].[33]

Goldberg resigned, but not without regret. At the public announcement, Goldberg said, "I shall not, Mr. President, conceal the pain with which I leave the Court after three years of service. It has been the richest and most satisfying period of my career."[34] That theme was echoed in his formal letter of resignation to the president:

> You are already aware of the reluctance with which I leave the Court. I do so only at your insistence, and in the belief that no American citizen could in good conscience refuse the new duty you have requested me to undertake.[35]

Johnson also needed all of his persuasive abilities in the next step of the process. Apparently Johnson was persuaded that Goldberg would step down from the Court while they were still in the air on their return flight from Stevenson's funeral, because Paul Porter, Fortas' law partner, reports that Johnson "called Abe from Air Force

One and said, 'I am arriving and I'm going to announce your appointment to the Supreme Court.' . . . And Abe said, 'God Almighty, Mr. President, you can't do that. I have got to talk to you about it.'"[36] This indicates that either Johnson immediately settled on Fortas as his nominee after he spoke with Goldberg or that he had been planning to persuade Goldberg to accept the U.N. job and therefore had had time to consider a replacement.[37] Or perhaps Johnson had always known that he would appoint his longtime friend and close adviser to the first Supreme Court vacancy.

The next evening Fortas had dinner with the Johnsons at the White House, where again the president repeated his intention to appoint him.[38] Fortas had been offered the attorney generalship earlier and had turned it down. He now decided against accepting the Supreme Court nomination, and wrote Johnson a handwritten letter thanking him for the chance but turning him down. Fortas was hesitant to refuse the president but felt very stongly that he "did not want to do it."[39] Johnson reports that he continued to talk to Fortas but "could not sway him."[40]

But Johnson was not deterred. Goldberg, who had been the recipient of the Johnson personal persuasion, reportedly told his incoming law clerks, "The President says he's going to appoint Abe and Abe says no. The President won't even consider other names. He's going to wear him down. He'll wait until the end of time."[41] Word of the Fortas possibility had leaked to the press; Press Secretary Moyers commented that he himself had once told the president he did not want a job but had been persuaded to accept.[42] In the interim, Justice William O. Douglas had written the president on 21 July, commenting:

> I need not tell you what a superb choice Abe Fortas would be for Goldberg's vacancy. I hope you feel free to release him for that post. He can still serve you and the Court, too.[43]

About the same time, Douglas reports, the president asked the justice to talk with Fortas about the position. Douglas did so but received a "firm refusal" because Fortas' personal affairs "would not permit him to leave private law practice at that time."[44] Congressman Adam Clayton Powell (D-N.Y.), foreshadowing future developments, suggested that the president consider Marshall for the vacancy, which apparently Johnson had done already.[45]

The President had one more trick up his sleeve for Fortas. On 28 July, Johnson called Fortas and asked him to come over to the White House for a press conference. Porter reports that "Abe said, 'Look, you don't suppose he is going to lean on me some more about this.' I said, 'Oh, I think you are off the hook from what I have heard.'"[46] Unfortunately for Fortas, he accepted this counsel from his partner. In his oral history, Fortas described what happened:

> I got a call from [Johnson] asking me to come over. He was about to have a press conference—a televised press conference. I went over and he said he was signing an order sending men to Viet Nam and he was going to announce at a televised conference that he'd appointed me to the Supreme Court. By that time we were half way down the hall to the press conference. To the best of my knowledge and belief I never said yes.[47]

Johnson described it this way:

> On July 28, I invited Fortas to my office. When he came in, I told him that I was about to go over to the theater in the East Wing of the White House to announce his appointment to the Supreme Court. I said that he could stay in my office or accompany me to the theater, but that since he was the person being appointed, I thought he should go with me. He looked at me in silence for a moment. I waited. Then he said, "I'll accompany you." That was the only way I managed to get him on the Court.[48]

The nomination was announced on 28 July and submitted to the Senate after the Justice Department processed the necessary ABA checks and formal papers. The Judiciary Committee held hearings the next week, and after brief testimony from Fortas, recommended his appointment. The Senate confirmed Fortas on 11 August, with three Republicans dissenting.[49] On 4 October, Associate Justice Fortas was sworn in and took his seat. Johnson's first nomination to the Supreme Court was completed.

The president also was personally involved in the second Johnson nomination to the Supreme Court. Again, he knew the nominee well; this time, however, he did not have to engage in the same persuasion to convince him to accept the nomination. The nominee was, of course, Marshall, who had been successively the chief counsel to the Legal Defense and Education Fund of the NAACP, a judge on the Court of Appeals for the Second Circuit (appointed by Kennedy), and Johnson's solicitor general.

There is the possibility that the appointment of Marshall as solicitor general was Johnson's way of testing him, just as Katzenbach and Clark had undergone testing periods as acting attorneys general before appointment to the attorney generalship. There is no indication of this in Johnson's comments to his solicitor general. According to Marshall:

> The other thing which goes through every conversation we had from then on—he would say at least three or four times, "You know this has nothing to do with any Supreme Court appointment. I want that distinctly understood. There's no quid pro [quo] here at all. You do your job. If you don't do it, you go out. If you do it you stay here. And that's all there is to it.[50]

Marshall also notes that at the announcement of his appointment to be solicitor general, members of the press thought he was being nominated to the Supreme Court and were asking each other, "Who has resigned from the Supreme Court?"

The opportunity to make the appointment came when Justice Tom Clark retired at the end of the Court's term in 1967. Because Clark's resignation was announced in advance, there were a great number of suggestions sent to Johnson about Clark's replacement. Vice President Hubert H. Humphrey passed along the fact that Justice Stanley Mosk of the California Supreme Court was very interested in the appointment.[51] Cliff Carter advised the president that a number of supporters from across the country, and especially from the South, had expressed their views on the vacancy:

> All seem to think that Thurgood Marshall would be a nominee and while they have no objection they feel the adverse impact would be softened if it came simultaneously with your filling a second vacancy on the Court.[52]

Senator Harry Byrd sent his views, as did James Rowe.[53] On 24 May Senator Everett Dirksen, "instead of going through channels and sending it to John Macy," wrote a letter to Watson in which he asked him to pass along his recommendation of Albert Jenner, chairman of the ABA Committee on Federal Judiciary. There is a comment on the letter (probably written by Watson, perhaps after speaking with the president) that reads, "Call Sen. Dirksen. Believe committed."[54]

It seems that the president had been committed to Marshall for some time, although there is no proof. Johnson had repeatedly commented that he wished to appoint a non-white and a non-male to the Court, and Marshall was a non-white who ranked high in the administration.[55] Who actually initiated the Marshall nomination process is unclear, but Abraham reports that "only one other individual had in fact closely participated in the President's selection: his new Attorney General, Ramsey Clark, the son of the retiring Justice, Tom C. Clark."[56] Marshall had proven his competence in his role as solicitor general, and certainly his ideological position on social issues was well known to the president and compatible with his own.

The actual announcement of the nomination on 13 June 1967 came as something of a surprise because very few people except the president and Ramsey Clark had been involved in the decision. Clark had quietly requested and received an informal ABA rating of Marshall—just as with Fortas, the report was positive. Marshall reports that although he had hopes, he had no knowledge of the nomination.

> We had a party the night before for Tom Clark because he resigned that day. All of us were chatting around, and nobody suspected . . . and nobody said a word to me. A lot of people think it was discussed. I didn't know about it. I imagine it was. I know [Justice] Clark must have known, and I know Ramsey knew. But they just don't pass any information.[57]

The next day Ramsey Clark called Marshall at his office and asked him to come see the president (and enter through a private entrance). Clark would not tell him what the meeting was to be about. When Marshall arrived at the White House, Watson brought him into the Oval Office, and after he and the president had talked for a while, the president said, "You know something, Thurgood, I'm going to put you on the Supreme Court." Marshall replied, "Well, thank you sir."[58] They then went out into the Rose Garden, where the president made the dramatic announcement. Johnson said that there had been "very little pressure of any kind" concerning the Court vacancy and that Marshall "is the best qualified by training and by very valuable service to the country. I believe it is the right thing to do, the right time to do it, the right man and the right place."[59] The front page headline of the *New York Times* read "MARSHALL NAMED TO HIGH COURT, ITS FIRST NEGRO." The White House was inundated by telegrams of congratulation from black and white liberal leaders, including Whitney Young, A. Philip Randolph, Norman Vincent Peale, G. Mennen Williams, Walter Reuther, and Jack Greenberg.[60] Albert Jenner, chairman of the Committee on Federal Judiciary, praised Marshall's qualifications for the post.

Some groups and individuals were not as pleased. Most Southern senators made no comment on the nomination; Strom Thurmond (R-S.C.) announced he was opposed to Marshall because it would increase the number of liberals on the Court. Senator Eastland engaged in delaying tactics throughout the confirmation process and did not schedule committee hearings for a month. When the hearings did get underway, the "Marshall nomination ran into considerable and protracted opposition, led by Democratic Senators from the Deep South."[61] Senator McClellan slowed down the process by extensive questioning of Marshall concerning recent Court decisions. Ervin came out against Marshall. Thurmond, to test the nominee's knowledge of the Constitution and to delay the hearings, interrogated Marshall with several dozen questions on the finer points of constitutional law and history. Eastland questioned Marshall about civil rights. On 3 August, nevertheless, the full committee voted 11 – 5 to approve Marshall. However, all five Southern members voted against the nominee and Eastland stated that the nomination would be held from the floor until 21 August in order to allow time for a minority report to be prepared. Finally, on 30 August 1967, after six hours of speeches, the Senate voted 69 – 11 to confirm Marshall. All eleven who were opposed came from the Deep South except for Byrd of West Virginia, and all were Democrats except for Thurmond. On 2 October, in the presence of President Johnson, who paid a surprise visit to the Supreme Court, Marshall was sworn in as the first black Supreme Court justice and the last Johnson appointee to the Supreme Court.[62]

But Johnson tried other appointments to the Court in his last year. On 11 June 1968 James Jones of the White House staff sent a memorandum to the president:

> Justice Abe Fortas called to say that Chief Justice Warren would like to see the President at the President's convenience. Shall I schedule Chief Justice Warren for an appointment later this week . . . .[63]

The president read the memo on 12 June and said "Bring him in tomorrow." Jones reported on that meeting for the record:

> Chief Justice Earl Warren met with the President at 9:25 a.m. today and departed the President's office at 9:45 a.m. He came down to say that because of age, he felt he should retire from the Court and he said he wanted President Johnson to appoint his successor, someone who felt as Justice Warren did.[64]

In a formal letter of resignation dated that day, Warren wrote "I hereby advise you of my intention to retire as Chief Justice of the United States, effective at your pleasure," and also submitted an accompanying letter stating that after fifty years of public service, he still enjoyed the work of the Court; "the problem of age, however, is one that no man can combat."[65] Warren reports in his oral history that he wished to resign effective upon the appointment of a successor so that there could be continuity on the High Court. The wording of the letter is somewhat ambiguous, so President Johnson's return letter tried to be precise: "With your agreement, I will accept your decision to retire effective at such time as a successor is qualified." This wording was decided upon by the attorney general and his deputy as a means to have a chief justice at all times.[66] Nevertheless, it still occasioned a controversy, as some senators opposed to Fortas insisted no vacancy ever existed.

As noted earlier, Chief Justice Warren reported that when he told the president of his intention to resign, Johnson already had Fortas in his mind as a successor. Cyrus Vance's name was tossed around, but Joe Califano reports that Johnson "reached fairly rapidly in his own mind the decision to make Fortas the Chief."[67] It is quite probable that he also quickly decided on Homer Thornberry, a longtime Texas friend and political ally whom Johnson had appointed to the Court of Appeals for the Fifth Circuit, as Fortas' replacement as associate justice. During the subsequent fight over confirmation, the president discussed with Macy how he had decided on Fortas. Macy reported that

> we conversed for several minutes about the process he pursued in selecting a successor to Chief Justice Warren. He explained that he had considered all of the members of the Court and had reviewed the selection process of previous Presidents in making Supreme Court nominations.[68]

Johnson also made a particular point to Macy that President Kennedy had nominated one of his close friends, Byron White, to the Court.

Christopher reports that after the president informed Ramsey Clark of Warren's intention to retire,

> the Attorney General asked me to consider with him the question of a successor to one of the Associate Justices if it would be our recommendation that one of the present sitting Justices would go to the Chief Justiceship. As with other appointments, we drew up lists of names for both of the spots and talked about them back and forth, got out their biographies, the things they had written, tried to assess the possible shortcomings and pos-

sible handicaps from the standpoint of confirmation and tried to assess what this would mean in a historical sense to the court. . . . As far as I know, the Attorney General did not discuss [the] subject with anybody here at the Department other than with me.[69]

Again it seems that Clark and Christopher served largely to endorse Johnson's selections, not really to initiate recommendations. Johnson had also spoken to Larry Temple, Barefoot Sanders, Clark Clifford, and Ed Weisl, Sr., about the nomination and had asked for recommendations, although again it seems he had already made up his mind on Fortas and Thornberry.[70] This seems to be borne out by the fact that Johnson had already asked Albert Jenner, chairman of the ABA Committee, to make an informal and confidential check on Fortas. On 26 June, Jenner sent a confidential letter to Clark that stated:

I am pleased to advise you that as a result of our investigation, our Committee in unanimously of the opinion that Honorable Abe Fortas, of Washington, D.C., presently an Associate Justice of the Supreme Court of the United States, is "highly acceptable from the viewpoint of professional qualifications" for appointment as Chief Justice of the Supreme Court of the United States.[71]

Later Johnson told Larry Temple of the decision on Thornberry, and Temple, joined by Mrs. Johnson, advised that there could be criticisms about cronyism in appointing a close friend. Johnson discounted the warning and continued the process.[72]

The president did not make public Warren's plans until 26 June, although news of the impending resignation had leaked.[73] During the two-week interim, Johnson attempted to arrange confirmation and inform significant parties to the process, including the nominees and important senators. The president acknowledged this during the press conference at which he announced the Fortas and Thornberry nominations. In response to a question of whether he had discussed the matter with Senator Eastland or others on the Judiciary Committee, Johnson replied, "Yes, I have discussed it with the Leadership, with several members of the Senate, the Democratic Leadership and Republican Leadership, and the Leadership of the Committee."[74] He informed Fortas, who stated that there was not much prior consultation but that Johnson "did tell me he was sending my name up and he thought that it would go through all right."[75]

Thornberry reports that he received a call from the president informing him of the nomination and was greatly surprised. During the conversation, Johnson told Thornberry that Senator Richard B. Russell (D-Ga.) was in his office and "he agreed to support both Mr. Justice Fortas and me."[76]

Besides Russell, Johnson apparently also received commitments from Mississippi's Eastland, who chaired the Judiciary Committee, and Minority Leader Dirksen.[77] In addition, to head off problems Johnson foresaw concerning charges of lame-duck appointments, Johnson had aides and Clark prepare memorandums concerning previous lame duck appointments of Supreme Court Justices (including Justice Louis D. Brandeis by President Wilson and Justice William Brennan by President Eisenhower) and the necessity for continuity in the chief justiceship.[78] Armed with those statements and with the assurances from the power in the Senate, Johnson on 26 June made public Warren's letter and his reply and announced his nomination of Fortas and Thornberry.

On 28 June Sanders reported that sixty-seven senators would probably support the nomination of Fortas as opposed to only twenty-eight who would oppose.[79] On 29 June, the Senate liaison Mike Manatos reported that the head count on the nominations in the Senate was sixty-one "solid right" votes and nine "probably right" against twenty "solid wrong" and nine "probably wrong."[80] The president, who knew the Senate and the senators better than his aides, was not convinced that all would go smoothly and continuously attempted to keep his support firm. Johnson recognized that the key was not the vote on confirmation, but that on cloture if a filibuster were organized, and had his congressional liaisons working on that issue with key Southerners and Republicans. He directed Temple and McPherson to pull out favorable extracts from Fortas' book, *Concerning Dissent and Civil Disobedience*, and "show them to Senator Richard Russell."[81] He used this same kind of tactic with several senators by having aides or the Justice Department extract favorable opinions from the cases decided by Fortas and Thornberry.[82]

Johnson was particularly concerned about the commitment from Senator Dirksen and had his aides keep in close contact with the minority leader. After getting Dirksen's commitment, but before announcing the nomination, Johnson got some indication that there might be trouble with Dirksen. Manatos reported that Senator Eastland had told him "that he talked to Roy Cohn today, and that Cohn had seen Senator Dirksen this morning. Cohn reports that Dirksen is opposed to Fortas, contrary to the impression he may be giving."[83] But Dirksen again reassured the White House of his support. On 26

June, Manatos reported that Dirksen is "OK. . . . feels Republican opposition is being chipped away by him. 'Let it simmer a while. We'll take care of it,' [Dirksen commented]."[84] And as late as 2 July, Dirksen continued to assure White House aides that he was for confirmation and saw no problems. Manatos informed the president that "Dirksen reports that in his view there will not be a filibuster. . . . He assured Marvin Watson and me several times, 'We will win this one.'"[85]

Johnson personally kept a very close eye on the confirmation process. The White House did as much as possible to retain support and supply favorable information to the Senate. Attempts were made to persuade certain senators to support or at least not oppose the nominees or to vote for cloture to allow the vote to proceed. But there were charges of lame-duck appointments and cronyism. Senate liaison Manatos contends that Johnson's lame-duck status killed the nominations: "Strom Thurmond and others wanted to hold this vacancy for the new president, hopefully Richard Nixon, and it's nothing more than that."[86] Fortas was alleged to have committed ethical improprieties by accepting honoraria while a justice. During the hearings it was disclosed that he had received $15,000 for teaching a summer course at the American University Law School in 1968. The money had been raised by Porter, his former law partner, from five prominent businessmen, including one whose son was involved in federal criminal litigation.[87] Fortas was also pilloried concerning the liberal decisions of the Warren Court and his role in those decisions.[88] Amid the ignoring of commitments from Dirksen, Russell, and others, Fortas' nominations ran into a filibuster initiated by Republican Senator Robert Griffin, and on 2 October 1968 Fortas asked the president to withdraw his name.[89] Johnson complied with his request "with a heavy heart." Thornberry's nomination became moot and, in Warren's phrase, "Homer just got lost in the whole thing."[90]

There was some quiet but apparently very serious consideration in the White House of attempting another nomination before the Johnson administration ended. It appears that Johnson was thinking about honoring a commitment Goldberg says was made to him to persuade him to give up his seat on the Court in 1965. Indeed, several people had urged Johnson to nominate Goldberg instead of Thornberry to the Fortas vacancy as associate justice.[91]

Immediately after the Fortas nomination was withdrawn, various people suggested the president make another nomination for chief justice. Tommy Corcoran, the old New Dealer, renewed his suggestion that the president nominate James Rowe (who had been Johnson's assistant during his days as majority leader).[92] Old friend Willard Deason suggested Tom Clark and noted that the nation would have a "glow in its heart at the thought of the son now stepping down in deference to the Father."[93] Aide Charles Murphy put forth Solicitor General Erwin N. Griswold's name and Senator Ernest Gruening asked "Why not now appoint Arthur Goldberg to be Chief Justice?"[94]

Apparently the president had already begun to think about the possibility. On 3 October, the day after Fortas asked that his name be withdrawn, the president had already asked several aides not usually close to the judicial selection process their opinions on whether he should send up another name. Murphy replied that after "thinking about whether it would be wise for you to make another nomination for Chief Justice," he had concluded that

> it would be a good idea if, *but only if,* you can find someone who meets the following qualifications:
>   1. He must be qualified to be a good Chief Justice.
>   2. His prestige and reputation must be such that his qualifications will be widely recognized and generally acknowledged.
>   3. His personal relationship with you must be such that there would be no basis for regarding him as a "crony."
> If you nominated such a man and the Senate did not act on his nomination, you could then give him a recess appointment.[95]

Murphy suggested Griswold as the one who met those qualifications.

DeVier Pierson also sent the president a memorandum that day stating, "You asked for my opinion on whether you should send up another name for Chief Justice of the Supreme Court." Assuming a Nixon victory, he went on to say that it was unlikely Nixon (particularly if goaded by a large Wallace vote) would pick a successor in the Warren tradition (which would have a profound social impact over the years) and that there was everything to gain and nothing to lose by making another nomination, whether or not the Senate would confirm. "Even if the Senate shirks its responsibilities, you should not end your term in office leaving vacant the most important appointment a President can make." Pierson suggested the same criteria as Murphy had and added that "he should be a man whose withdrawal by Nixon would be difficult and embarrassing to the new President." He noted the problems with a recess appointment (Warren would have to leave the bench) and suggested that Johnson make the nomination now and if necessary, again in January when the Senate reconvened.[96] Two days later Pierson sent some further reflections, including possibilities for nominees. He mentioned Tom Clark, Justices (and Eisenhower appointees) William Brennan and Potter Stewart, Senators Philip Hart (D-Mich.) and John Pastore (D-R.I.), and administration members Cyrus Vance and Henry Fowler; he also raised the possibility of nominating someone from outside of Washington—either from the law schools or from other parts of the judicial system. He again repeated that he did not believe that the president "should 'toss in the sponge' on the most important appointment he has to make—particularly when he has reason to believe that his successor will materially redirect the court's philosophy" and recommended Hart or the "outsider" as the best possibilities.[97]

The advice was considered by the president; so too was the nomination of Goldberg. This is evident in a "personal and confidential" letter from Drew Pearson to the president on 18 November, which starts out, "Following up our conversation regarding the Chief Justiceship . . . ." In the letter, Pearson reminded Johnson of the pre-1937 anti–New Deal Court and the Nixon-Thurmond views on desegregation and the Court. He continued, "Bearing in mind what you already told me confidentially about Nixon and Arthur Goldberg, it occurs to me that an outgoing President has one request which he can make of an incoming President and which is automatically granted." Pearson suggested that Johnson point out to Nixon the "valiant service Arthur has performed by going off the Court at a time of international U.N. crisis" and Johnson's own cooperation with Nixon in the transition and recommended that Johnson proceed with the nomination of Goldberg.[98]

The president continued to consider that possibility very seriously. On 9 December 1968 Sanders responded to a request from the president on Goldberg's chances of confirmation:

> It seems to me that any nomination by the President would encounter opposition from all 6 of the Republicans on the [Judiciary] Committee. . . . The Republican Senators would maintain that the nomination should be left to Nixon.
>
> The 3 Southern Democrats on the Committee—Eastland, Ervin and McClelland—would probably oppose; I know of no reason why they would rush to support Goldberg after opposing Fortas. . . .
>
> Additionally to be considered is the attitude of Chairman Eastland. . . . I know of no reason why Eastland would be any friendlier to Goldberg than he was to Fortas and he strung the Fortas hearings along for months.

So if a nomination were submitted I think it unlikely that it could be confirmed. To reject Goldberg might prove slightly embarrassing for the Republicans but to be repudiated again by the Senate on a Chief Justice nomination would also be embarrassing to the President.

I would recommend against the nomination of a Chief Justice either in a special session or in the 91st Congress.[99]

Apparently that memorandum persuaded the president to drop the idea of nominating Goldberg for chief justice. Nothing further was done by the Johnson administration. Chief Justice Warren reports that Johnson did not ask him to stay on after Fortas was defeated, but that president-elect Nixon called him a few days before he took office and asked the chief justice to stay on the Court for the sake of continuity until a successor was named.[100] Warren did so.

Lyndon Johnson recognized that his nominations to the Supreme Court were the most important of any he would make. Therefore, he took a very intense personal interest in the selection of his nominees, so much so that it may be said that it was he alone, possibly with the help of the attorney general, who made the actual choice. He wanted to be sure of the qualifications of his nominees; he therefore relied on personal knowledge of individuals who were close to him and who shared his views on important legal and social questions. Johnson appointed the first black to the Supreme Court and attempted to appoint the first Jewish chief justice. His first two nominations went through to general acclaim. But the last two nominations failed to be confirmed by the Senate and Johnson's Supreme Court nomination process concluded on a rather sour note. Rather than ending his presidency with the chief justice and two associate justices being his appointees, Johnson left with two appointees as associate justices, one of whom (Fortas) had a cloud over his head and was soon to resign.

Conclusion

The case studies confirm the general process set forth in earlier chapters. They also show differences in the process of selection at each level of the judiciary.

The district court case studies illustrate the primary role of Democratic senators from the state in which the vacancy existed. Certainly the Department of Justice and the White House carefully screened the candidates' legal and political credentials and had the final authority over nomination, but in most district court appointments the senator initiated the selection and was consulted by the administration. The case studies suggest that at the beginning of the Johnson presidency, the input by senators was seldom questioned, but that later in the presidency the Justice Department and the White House took a more active role, and the Macy operation also participated.

The courts of appeals case studies illustrate that the administration, while adhering generally to geographic representation, nevertheless had more leeway in choosing candidates. The Department of Justice often initiated the search, guided by the Johnson criteria, and cleared the candidates with senators and the ABA Committee. In district court and even more in courts of appeals nominations, it is apparent that the White House was interested and involved in judicial selection. Close presidential advisers and/or the president himself oversaw the process and checked that the proper criteria had been met. Those criteria included merit (and ABA rating), experience (particularly prior judicial experience for courts of appeals), activist temperament, correct policy stands, party affiliation in many instances, and personal loyalty at certain times, as well as considerations of geography, age, sex, and race. In all the case studies, politics was a major factor in selection and sometimes in confirmation as well.

The case studies of the Supreme Court nominations illustrate the unique nature of those important choices. Johnson recognized the significance of his Supreme Court legacy and was personally and intensely involved in every phase of the process, from initial choice through Senate confirmation. He may have consulted with his attorney general, but in all four instances he had apparently already decided whom he would nominate. Johnson knew what he was looking for in a Supreme Court justice and matched those requirements with individuals whom he personally knew and trusted to further the policy goals of the Great Society.

Perhaps it is appropriate to conclude this section with Chief Justice Warren's response to the question, "Is the separation of powers solid enough that it doesn't make much difference to the Court who is President, what Administration is in?" Warren answered:

No, I don't think we can say that. I think it made some difference in the Court to have Nixon and Agnew out whipping up people against the Supreme Court in order to get into office, and carry on a vendetta against the courts from the time they do get into office up to the present time. I think it all hurts the Courts, because you see the Courts can't fight back.[101]

7. The Last Year and the Transition

In the last year of the Johnson administration, a number of controversies arose over judicial nominations; a transfer of power was also underway. Traditionally, transitions between presidential administrations, particularly of differing parties, have been haphazard and often hostile. (John Adams refused to attend Thomas Jefferson's inauguration and Andrew Johnson held a cabinet meeting during U.S. Grant's inauguration.[1]) The "transition" between John F. Kennedy and Lyndon B. Johnson was of course a traumatic and difficult one, and perhaps as a result of that experience, Johnson wished to make the transfer of power to his successor as orderly as possible. This chapter will explore one part of the transition—judicial selection during the last six months of the Johnson administration.

While President Johnson was officially a lame duck after his 31 March 1968 speech in which he declined to run again, and while he desired to have a smooth transition, he nevertheless had political and personal goals he wished to secure before leaving office. These often competing aspects of the final months were apparent in the judicial selection process. Johnson in his final months as president wished to reward several associates with judgeships and concomitantly wished to appoint as judges those individuals whose policy positions were similar to his own. This was particularly true as prospects for Richard Nixon's election improved. An added incentive was the fact that Congress passed an act in June 1968 that created several new vacancies on the federal courts of appeals. Even before the act was passed, Attorney General Ramsey Clark wrote to the president that "we should plan now for nominations to these positions since time will be very short within which to secure ABA and FBI reports and confirmations. The bill will provide an important opportunity to appoint some outstanding people."[2] The judicial selection team attempted to appoint people to those and other vacancies during the last several months in 1968 and even through January 1969. Those months were marked with controversy and ended in frustration for the Johnson selection team and for Johnson personally.

One of the most frustrating episodes involved Richard Russell, the Democratic senator from Georgia and also Johnson's mentor and most respected friend. Before it was over, the selection and nomination of a district court judge in Georgia would become mixed up with the Abe Fortas–Homer Thornberry confirmation battle.

In March 1967, the incumbent judge, who had originally been recommended by Russell (in 1946) and who was characterized by Clark in 1968 as "one of the most difficult and unyielding of southern judges in civil rights cases," submitted his resignation.[3] Russell, splitting the patronage in the state with Senator Herman Talmadge, submitted to the White House the name of Alexander Lawrence as his only choice.[4] The Justice Department initiated preliminary checks by February 1968; those checks, besides finding Lawrence to be an exceptionally competent attorney, turned up a 1958 speech that was anti-desegregation and anti–federal judicial desegregation decisions.[5] Because of this, several civil rights groups opposed the nomination of Lawrence, and Clark agreed.[6]

In early May 1968, Senator Russell asked to see Johnson to discuss the nomination. On 4 May he met privately with the president and explained his personal interest in and endorsement of Lawrence. Johnson called for the voluminous file on Lawrence and apparently promised to talk with Clark about it.[7] Yet Clark remained opposed; on 11 May he so informed Russell and on 13 May wrote the president that "I would recommend you not make this appointment" at that time.[8] Perhaps prodded by a lengthy and strongly anti-Clark letter from Russell on 20 May that concluded "I feel justified in insisting most respectfully that you send Mr. Lawrence's nomination to the Senate," Johnson on 22 May directed that Clark institute a further investigation. One of the more fascinating aspects of this complex situation, which came to involve the downfall of the Fortas nomination, is contained in a 20 May memo from Larry Temple to the president.[9] One of the reasons that Johnson apparently pushed Clark to reconsider his position was that Fortas had said he saw nothing wrong with the Lawrence nomination if it would "keep the good will of Senator Russell." And a month later Fortas repeated," I think we should go ahead on this now for sure."[10] Johnson would not overrule Clark and stated that he would do nothing to undermine the federal judiciary, particularly where civil rights matters were concerned, but he highly valued Russell's friendship and hoped that Lawrence could be appointed.[11] He continued to bombard Clark with information favorable to Lawrence and even asked Albert Jenner, the chairman of the ABA Committee on Federal Judiciary, to go to Georgia and rate Lawrence personally.[12]

During this period the president made the nominations of Fortas and Thornberry to the Supreme Court. Johnson, before making the announcement, had cleared the nominations with Senator Russell, who had a great deal of influence over the all-important Southern senators and was thus a key to the confirmation. To shore up that support, on 31 June the president sent Temple to Russell's office to provide Russell with positive information on Fortas.[13] At the end of the meeting Russell asked if Temple knew anything about "his" judgeship—the Lawrence nomination. Temple replied that Johnson had recently had a conversation with Clark about it and Russell said to tell the president that he was still very interested.[14] Temple reported this and Johnson again prodded the attorney general to expedite the matter (which Clark was apparently delaying in hopes of killing the nomination).

On 1 July Russell sent a long letter to the president. It discussed the history of the Lawrence nomination and went on:

> To be perfectly frank, even after so many years in the Senate, I was so naive I had not even suspected that this man's nomination was being withheld from the Senate due to the changes expected on the Supreme Court of the United States until you sent in the nomination of Fortas and Thornberry while still holding the recommendations for the nomination of Mr. Lawrence either in your office or in the Department of Justice.
> . . . This is, therefore, to advise you that, in view of the long delay in handling and the juggling of this nomination, I consider myself released from any statements that I may have made to you with respect to your nominations, and you are at liberty to deal with the recommendations as to Mr. Lawrence in any way you see fit.[15]

Russell had already called or was just about to call Robert Griffin, the leader of the Republican Senate opposition to Fortas, to offer him his support against confirmation.[16]

Johnson was amazed, hurt, and angry about the letter. Temple reports that the president immediately called Clark and chewed him out, saying that his foot-dragging on the Lawrence nomination had destroyed his relationship with Russell.[17] (He also said he still had a commitment to nominate Lawrence, if Clark could recommend him.) He immediately had his staff begin to draft a letter to Russell. After numerous revisions by Temple, Sanders, McPherson, and Johnson, the final letter refutes Russell's conclusions about a trade, noting that the Lawrence process started months before Chief Justice Earl Warren notified Johnson of his intention to retire.[18] Johnson stated that the Lawrence and Fortas matters were entirely separate and concluded:

> I am frankly surprised and deeply disappointed that a contrary inference would be suggested. Both my own standards of public administration, and my knowledge of your character, would deny such an inference.[19]

In addition, Johnson sent emissaries to Russell and the senator's staff to try to reestablish relations. Tom Johnson, a White House aide, was told by the staff that Russell very strongly believed he had been duped by the president. The aide suggested that the president call Russell, quoting Russell's executive assistant as saying, "This matter is now between the President and the Senator."[20] The president followed the suggestion and called Russell, explaining that he had been distressed by the letter, the basis of which Johnson said was untrue. But apparently the close relationship between Russell and Johnson never was the same.[21]

Senator Russell did not vote to end the anti-Fortas filibuster and the Fortas nomination attempt ended in failure. But Johnson intended to keep his commitment to Russell. The ABA report was completed by Jenner and it rated Lawrence "well qualified," concluding that the candidate had changed since his 1958 speech.[22] Civil rights groups' opposition died down as Lawrence's record of the preceding ten years was publicized. And Clark, although he continued to voice some doubts, made the recommendation to the president on 12 July 1968 (while Johnson was considering talking to Russell).[23] The president submitted the nomination to the Senate on 17 July, and Lawrence became a federal district judge. Yet the controversy over his nomination, by "releasing" Russell from his commitment, which was the key to the Southern Democrat's support, may have helped defeat the nominations of Fortas and Thornberry and thus altered the entire complexion of the Supreme Court in the 1970s.

Even before this episode ended, President Johnson was beginning to plan for the transition of power. He was determined to be as helpful as possible and even before the election invited the candidates to name representatives to deal with transition matters.[24] As his representative, Johnson named Charles Murphy, who directed each cabinet member to plan for the transition.[25] That, of course, included Attorney General Clark, who became the target of the Nixon law-and-order campaign against crime and lax law enforcement. Yet in 1969 the new attorney general, John Mitchell, said "Ramsey Clark has been extremely conscientious about his responsibilities in the transition. He did everything he could to make it as smooth as possible for us."[26] Included in the discussions was information on the judicial selection process from the Justice Department's perspective.

The White House Office was also included in the transition. Temple reports that the president admonished the staff to leave nothing undone for their Nixon counterparts. Temple's counterpart in the judicial selection process seemed to be John Ehrlichman (whom Temple found to be efficient, knowledgeable, and a cold fish) and Temple offered to put together some information on how the Johnson administration had handled the process. He recalls the offer was accepted very coldly by Ehrlichman.[27] Temple wrote to Ehrlichman on 16 December 1968:

> In accordance with our conversation . . . I am enclosing copies of Warren Christopher's memoranda for his successor on the following subjects: . . . (3) Re: Judicial Appointments. Although these memoranda are drafted from the standpoint of the activities of the Department of Justice, they are instructive on some of the responsibilities within your jurisdiction. Let me know if anything specific comes to your mind that I can assist you on.[28]

Ehrlichman replied: "And thanks for the Christopher materials too. They just arrived and I am very glad to have them."[29] Temple concluded that the transition went smoothly, overall.[30]

Perhaps the procedures did, but several of the substantive matters of judicial nomination during the transition hardly did. Several judicial vacancies, due either to resignation or the creation of new positions by the Congress, remained as of June 1968. As noted earlier, Clark had told the president that this was an opportunity to appoint some outstanding judges; it was also an opportunity for Johnson to reward friends and ensure that judges with his general political views were named. On 10 July 1968, during the battle over the Fortas-Thornberry appointments, Clark sent a memo to the president concerning a dozen individuals (including Shirley Hufstedler, Alexander Lawrence, and Lewis Morgan) selected for lower court nominations:

> I recommend that you send a number of nominations to the Senate this week and all that can be prepared next week.

Clearly our first priority is to secure the confirmation of Justice Fortas and Judge Thornberry. I believe that sending other judicial nominations forward now will not harm and might help the Senate confirmation of the Justices. My reasons are:

(1) It is the orderly and the right thing to do since our position is that vacancies on the judiciary are inimical to justice.

(2) It is consistent with the Supreme Court nominations to send other nominations forward and repudiate the lame-duck argument.

(3) It will bring additional pressures to bear for judicial confirmations.

(4) We risk losing the important opportunity to fill these many vacancies if we wait until after the confirmations of Fortas and Thornberry. Their confirmations can be easily delayed to the week of July 22 if not beyond. Confirmation of later nominations before an early August recess might then be impossible. The charge of midnight nominations will become more substantial later.

Charges that these nominations are made to secure votes on the Justices' confirmations are unavoidable. They can be made if nominations are sent forward after such confirmations as well as before. The fact is that these nominations were prepared without regard to the Supreme Court nominations and for the most part before they were made. Some will be clearly irrelevant to Senators' votes on the Justices' confirmations and some will be to states where the Senators will vote against anyway.[31]

The president agreed, and in the next several months nominated a number of individuals.[32] Most of them were confirmed.

However, by October the judicial appointment process and specific nominees were meeting grave problems. The lame-duck argument was gaining ground, particularly among Republicans who expected patronage rewards in the next administration. On 10 October, Mike Manatos reported to the president a conversation he had had with Senator James Eastland of the Judiciary Committee:

He told me that in his view it would be a mistake to send up any new Judicial appointments. He indicated, for instance, the opposition to Barefoot's nomination went deeper than Strom Thurmond. Apparently, there is a flat Republican policy of opposition for any of these Judicial appointments.[33]

Barefoot Sanders was one of the specific nominees who was meeting problems in the Senate, particularly from Thurmond. As in the

Fortas affair, the charge of cronyism had been raised against Sanders and against longtime associate David Bress, a political protege of Fortas.[34] Thurmond also raised ideological objections to several nominees, including Cecil Poole, a black United States attorney from California.[35]

Partly for these reasons and also because of the Fortas-Thornberry confirmation battle, which delayed consideration of other nominees, when Congress adjourned in October 1968 the nominations of Sanders, Bress, Poole, and two others (James Alger for the Territorial Court of Guam and William M. Byrne for the California District Court) were still pending and therefore lapsed. Johnson had made no recess apointments since the ill-fated David Rabinovitz episode of the early years, and Clark was consistently opposed to them.[36] Johnson, however, strongly considered making such appointments— at least for Sanders. Sanders wrote thanking the president for his support of his nomination and added: "You mentioned to me the possibility of a recess appointment. I do not think that would be wise, but I do appreciate your having considered it."[37] Johnson nonetheless continued to consider it. In a memo to Charles Maguire concerning Sanders' letter, Johnson said, "I am not sure I agree [about the recess appointment]. I want to talk to you about that recess thing." And in his reply letter to Sanders, Johnson wrote: "For now, I would like to give some more thought to a recess appointment. I want to talk it over with you before we make a final decision."[38] Perhaps persuaded by Sanders, Maguire, or Clark, the president finally decided not to make any recess appointments.

Instead he considered resubmitting the nominations when the new Senate convened. It was by then clear that Nixon would be the new president and Mitchell his attorney general. In December the White House made inquiries about existing judicial vacancies. Christopher sent an extensive memo to Temple detailing the vacancies and the history of end-of-term nominations. He noted that there were twenty-five vacancies and that "prospects seem bleak" for any new nominations. He stated, however, that "the fate of end-of-term nominations depends much on the attitude of the incoming Administration." Five of Harry Truman's seven end-of-term nominations had been withdrawn by Eisenhower, but none of Dwight Eisenhower's four January 1961 nominations had been withdrawn by Kennedy. Christopher continued:

> Five nominations were pending when Congress adjourned, and they may merit special consideration. They are Barefoot Sanders for the D.C. Circuit, Byrne and Poole for California District

Courts, Bress for the D.C. District Court, and Alger for the
Guam territorial court. It is notable that all of the end-of-term
nominations by Truman and Eisenhower were drawn from those
nominations pending when the preceding Congress adjourned.
A strong case can by made through resubmitting each of these
nominations *if* the candidate is willing to run the gauntlet and if
our probes indicate that there is a reasonable chance. . . .

It may be that a safe passage for the few nominations could be
worked out through negotiation with the incoming Administration and the Senators concerned. However, unless such nominations can be carefully and successfully explored in advance, my
inclination is that they would risk considerable injury to all
those involved without any compensating likelihood of success.

We may be better able to appraise the possibility after we have
talked more with our successors.[39]

The nominations were still pending after the new year began. On
4 January 1969, Temple wrote a memorandum to the president about
conversations he had had with Clark and Christopher about the possibility of sending to the Senate some judicial nominations. "Both
Ramsey and Warren recommend that the President renew his nominations of the five candidates whose nominations were pending before
the Senate at the time Congress adjourned." Temple asked, "Does the
President want to prepare the nomination papers?" Johnson answered
on the memo, "not until I can get a reading from Justice on what
Senate will do—L."[40] Two days later, Clark renewed his recommendation for resubmission. In a memo to the president, he argued, "We
have a strong obligation to resubmit the five nominations which
were pending when Congress adjourned last October," and concluded that the nominations, if resubmitted, would probably be confirmed. On the memo, Johnson directed Temple, "Check out thoroughly on Hill & report at once to me—L."[41] Temple proceeded to do
so; he had Manatos make inquiries. On 8 January 1969, Manatos
reported on his meeting with Majority Leader Mike Mansfield:
"Mansfield did say he saw Ramsey Clark last night and urged upon
him as strongly as he knew how that the judgeship nominations
which were before the Senate last year before adjournment be resubmitted." Reassured by this word from Mansfield, Johnson noted on
the memo, "Yes I would send them on up—LBJ."[42]

The next day the renominations were announced. The president
told Clark to work with the Judiciary Committee and to call Attorney General–designate Mitchell to inform him of the nominations.[43] Clark called Mitchell and told him the five names had been

sent to the Senate. Clark reported, " I told him that we might not manage to get them through the Senate before inauguration but that we were going to try. He thanked me for letting him know and said he would advise the President-elect."⁴⁴ Shortly after that telephone conversation, Clark called Mitchell back on another matter. During that call, according to Clark, Mitchell mentioned he had told Nixon about the nominations and the president-elect had approved them. Clark immediately called the White House to tell the president the welcome news, but Johnson was taking a nap and instead Clark delivered the message to Temple. Temple transcribed the message:

> Ramsey called Attorney General designate John Mitchell and advised him of the judicial nominations. In a subsequent conversation Mitchell told him:
> "I talked with Dick about those judges. He told me to tell you to tell the President that he understood, that he had no objection, and that he would not withdraw them." Mitchell told President-elect Nixon that there was no necessity for him to go this far. But Nixon replied that while there was no necessity for him to go that far, he wanted to and he wanted that message conveyed to the President.⁴⁵

The message was conveyed and plans were dropped to try to expedite the confirmation hearings in the Senate. Since there was now no fear that the nominations would be withdrawn by the new administration, the Johnson team relaxed and ended its plans to try to get confirmation before Inauguration Day. Johnson's efforts to effect a congenial transfer of power and his directives not to begin any new major projects that would commit the incoming administration had apparently borne fruit.⁴⁶

Three days after his inauguration, Nixon withdrew all five nominations. His press secretary Ron Ziegler reported that Johnson's nominations pending before the Senate had been withdrawn but that they would be reviewed "without prejudice" for possible renomination. The *New York Times* reported that there "was no comment from Mr. Johnson on whether the withdrawals had been expected," but added that:

> President Johnson had sent the most important names to the Senate so late in his Administration that it was widely assumed most of them would be acceptable to the incoming Republicans.
> There were reports of intense pressure from leading Republican

figures who wanted to replace the nominees with men of their own. Spokesmen for the new Administration declined comment on this aspect of the case.[47]

Former Attorney General Clark, however, did have some comments. Clark was outraged. He first called Johnson in Texas to explain why he had not made an all-out effort to get confirmation earlier, and then went public with his wrath.[48] He issued a public statement describing the 9 January conversations with Mitchell and the firm commitment Nixon had made, and accused the new president of political maneuvering. Clark concluded: "Recognizing the strains of the transition and the immense burdens borne by President Nixon, I can readily understand if the nominations were withdrawn by mistake and are to be resubmitted. Otherwise, a serious question is raised: Not whether these five men should be judges, but whether Mr. Nixon keeps his word."[49]

The Nixon administration's response was quick: the only mistake was Clark's in misunderstanding what had been agreed upon. Attorney General Mitchell's statement characterized his predecessor's version as "far beyond the facts and the bounds of propriety" and added that Clark had "failed to understand that definitive approval of the nominations was not expressed during the telephone conversation."[50] President Nixon, who remarked that he remembered "exactly what did occur," in his first news conference gave his view of the controversy:

What happened was that Ramsey Clark discussed this matter during the period between the election and the inauguration with Attorney General Mitchell. He asked Attorney General Mitchell to ask me whether I would object to action on the part of President Johnson in the event that he did submit these appointments to the Senate.

My reply was that I would not object to President Johnson's submitting such—submitting names to the Senate. . . . As you ladies and gentlemen are quite aware, I have scrupulously followed the line we have one President at a time and that he must continue to be President until he leaves office on January the 20th.

However, I did not have any understanding with the President directly and no one including Attorney General Mitchell as far as I was concerned had any discretion to agree to a deal that those nominations having been made would be approved by me.

I have withdrawn them and now I'm going to examine each one of them, and as I've already indicated I have decided that in at least some instances some of the names will be resubmitted.[51]

Clark contended that the Nixon statement was a series of half-truths adding up to a misrepresentation of the situation.[52] If his reporting of the conversation with Mitchell that he described to Temple was true, the memorandum of 9 January 1969 backs up his claim. The *New York Times* commented that in his reply, the "President thus sought to establish that his commitment went no further than a pro forma one of acceding to something the Johnson administration could do anyway."[53] Only one of the judicial nominations, that of Byrne, was resubmitted by the Nixon administration.

Just as his first judicial nominations had been mired in controversy, so too were the final judicial nominations of President Johnson. The judicial selections process in the last year of the Johnson administration did not go smoothly; although the president and the Justice Department had attempted to ensure an orderly transition period and in great part the procedural transition did go well, the substance of judicial appointment during the transition resulted in controversy and anger.

8. Conclusion

One of the many responsibilities of a president is to nominate and appoint judges to the federal courts. The Constitution assigns the responsibility, but it does not define how the task is to be carried out. Nor does it describe the characteristics nominees for federal judgeships should possess. The Constitution also grants to the Senate the role of advising and consenting to the president's judicial nominations, but it does not specify either the advisory process or the grounds on which the Senate is to base its consent. The Constitution provides that both the president and the Senate shall have powerful roles, but it does not specify how they are to coexist or how political conflicts are to be resolved. Neither does the Constitution specify what, if any, other actors are to participate in the selection of nominees. Instead, each president, guided by past practice and his own objectives, develops and manages a judicial selection process and provides, implicitly or explicitly, a set of criteria for choice. Each president chooses how to practice the politics of selection.

In the last decade, we have seen different methods of practicing these politics. Jimmy Carter attempted to institute a commission form of selection in order to choose candidates on the basis of merit and affirmative action. Although the commissions were not always welcomed by senators who feared their power would be circumscribed, particularly in circuit judge selection, the commissions were successful in achieving Carter's aims. They also chose candidates who tended to agree with Carter's ideology.

Ronald Reagan's selection process in some aspects returned to the traditional methods—granting individual Republican senators a major role in selecting candidates—but also centralized the process in the White House staff. This centralization contributed to the Reagan administration's self-conscious attempt to transform the federal judiciary from a perceived liberal bench to one more compatible with the conservative ideology of the president. Although Reagan himself was not personally involved in the choice of candidates, except in the case of Supreme Court selection, his staff has ensured that the criteria embraced by Reagan for eligibility to become a judicial candidate have been met. The White House staff has played the major role in checking on the ideological purity of candidates for federal courts, including a separate investigation of candidates by the president's personnel office. The Reagan administration's efforts have been very successful in selecting judges that are competent and conservative. Reagan's choice of how to practice the politics of selection—a mixture of deference to Republican senators and centralization of ideological oversight in the White House staff—has borne fruit.

This volume has detailed the process that resulted from the choices made by Lyndon Johnson. Johnson, whose political career had been affected by the federal judiciary, was perhaps more than most presidents aware of the significance of those choices. As president, he translated that awareness into a personal concern with managing the selection process and controlling the results of that process. Not only did he direct the selection of nominees to the Supreme Court, but he also was personally involved in many lower court nominations. He participated in many of the political negotiations and accommodations between the administration and senators or other politically powerful forces. He set the criteria that guided the members of the selection team and constantly checked to see if those criteria were being followed. Most importantly Johnson was able to structure the selection process so that relevant information flowed to him and his directives were communicated to selection team members. Thus, to a great extent, the president was able to retain his options and reserve his control over the judicial selection process. As a result, most of his objectives were achieved.

Because no president can devote his complete attention and energies to judicial selection or any other single responsibility, he must design structures to carry out his duties. These structures, referred to as subpresidencies, are active in various tasks and aid the president from a presidential perspective. The judicial selection subpresidency also took this presidential perspective and included several departmental officials and a nonofficial organization (the ABA Committee on Federal Judiciary) as regular parts of the process. Johnson's management of these diverse actors and the criteria he set forth have been the focus of this book.

The tasks of a subpresidency include providing information and advice to the president based on analysis of the subject matter as well as transmitting and putting into effect presidential directives.

The judicial selection subpresidency was very effective in those tasks. The Johnson archives reveal a constant two-way stream of communications concerning the choice of judicial nominees. Data from the members of the selection subpresidency were used to inform and guide presidential decisions which, in turn, were transmitted to those making the day-to-day judgments. Johnson seemed to be generally satisfied with the options presented to him and with the overall performance of the selection process.

Although there were some changes in the process over time, there was a general selection process throughout the Johnson years. It began with a search for appropriate candidates. Often an attorney would initiate a campaign for judicial office by writing letters to the Department of Justice or the White House or by soliciting recommendations from individuals in influential positions. In most cases, especially at the district court level, the Democratic senator from the state in which the vacancy existed was the major initiator of a candidacy, and the Johnson selection team often went along with the recommendation. In other cases, the Justice Department, White House staff, or other advisers suggested names of potential nominees. The candidates were evaluated by the Department of Justice under the criteria set by the White House and were also evaluated by the ABA Committee on Federal Judiciary in a preliminary informal and then a final formal report. The FBI and IRS also screened candidates. If the Justice Department was satisfied, it would transmit its recommendation to the White House, where Johnson's assistants and the Macy operation and often the president himself would evaluate the nomination. If it were acceptable, the papers would be signed and delivered to the Senate, where in most cases a pro forma Judiciary Committee hearing and Senate vote would occur. The president would then sign the formal appointment papers and a Johnson judge would take his (or in a few instances her) place on the bench.

The actors in the selection team were several and played different roles. In the Justice Department the attorney general and deputy attorney general and their offices played the major role in screening candidates. In most administrations the attorney general is usually concerned with judicial selection only for the Supreme Court and a few other controversial vacancies, but Ramsey Clark as attorney general apeared to be involved in the entirety of judicial selection. At the White House several aides, many of them Texans, played key roles in selection and clearance of judicial candidates. Marvin Watson, Barefoot Sanders, and Larry Temple were involved with the politics of nomination. The congressional liaison staff served as a conduit of senatorial recommendations and also tried to ensure smooth or at least successful confirmation proceedings. For a while, John Macy's office played a substantive role in judicial selection but later was relegated to record-keeping functions. Lyndon Johnson personally chose his nominees to the Supreme Court. He was also involved in many lower-court nominations and maintained a close control over the general processs. He participated in much of the political negotiating and accommodations. And, of course, he set the criteria that guided the members of his selection team.

Those criteria were diverse. Heading the list was merit or competence as defined by credentials, reputation, and rating by the ABA. Experience was also highly valued, as was diversity. Johnson attempted to bring women, minorities, and younger people into the judiciary. Of major importance was the candidate's political ideology and policy stands; the selection team sought those who shared the Johnson–Great Society views, or who at least were not antagonistic to the basic thrust of the Johnson administration. Especially important was a progressive stand on civil-rights and economic issues. And at least for a few years, the criteria included personal loyalty to Lyndon Johnson and increasingly to Johnson's position on Vietnam. Those criteria and, often, the president's character assessments guided the selection team.

The judicial selection processes of all modern presidents share many of the same elements, since they are all faced with similar challenges and similar political and legal requirements.[1] But procedures do vary and Johnson's process added several new elements and put together traditional elements in a new way as Lyndon Johnson attempted to integrate the various elements and maintain control over selection. Certainly the Macy operation as it existed in its first two years was an innovation in that it brought a greater role to the White House staff, in contrast to the preceding administrations. And, of course, the Johnson White House Office played an even more influential role under Watson, a role that did not seem to be equalled by that office in later administrations until Reagan's presidency.

The role of the ABA Committee on Federal Judiciary changed during the Johnson years. In the first years there were a number of conflicts between the ABA and the administration, as there had been under the Kennedy process. But after that there was generally cooperation, and no more candidates rated "unqualified" by the ABA were nominated. But this cooperation was not the same as the domination exercised by the ABA under the Eisenhower, and to a lesser extent, Nixon administrations.

In the early years Johnson had granted senators of his party the major prerogative in judicial selection, as did Presidents Nixon and

Ford, and to some degree, Reagan, in their administrations. Both Harold Chase and Alan Neff contend that this deference to senatorial preferences continued throughout the entire Johnson presidency, in contrast to Johnson's two immediate predecessors.[2] My research indicates that this is not completely accurate; the Justice Department and White House in the later Johnson administration made independent judgments on nominees and were not bound by senatorial wishes. The Justice Department, and therefore Johnson, did not often accept senatorial candidates if they did not meet the Johnson criteria. Even in district court nominations, where senators exercised the most influence, Johnson often had senators submit several names in order to allow room for maneuvering. Certainly senators were important, but they did not control the selections. This may be contrasted to the Kennedy administration's deference to influential Southern senators and the resulting number of segregationist Kennedy judges.[3]

Perhaps the major difference between the Johnson process and others was the role of Johnson himself. Lyndon Johnson was not a bystander at the selection process, but rather a participant. Other presidents, while engaging in the selection of nominees to the Supreme Court, are often not involved in the choice of nominees to the other federal courts. Johnson participated in selection at all levels of the federal judiciary and his participation was much more than a formality.

Part of the reason for Johnson's personal involvement was because of the political significance of judicial selection. It is a process with high rewards to appointees and to politicians who are in a position to recommend or consider. The framers of the Constitution recognized that politics would affect appointment, but they probably did not foresee the development of senatorial courtesy in judicial selection and thus did not realize what a strategic position the process they mandated would grant to senators. The constitutional requirements create pressure on the president to consider local, state, and regional politics.

There was a constant concern with the views of senators and other influential political figures. Particularly in the first two years, the choice of district court nominees was dominated by senators. In later years the senators' wishes were not always followed, but they were always given consideration. Throughout the Johnson years the administration was attentive to the impact of judicial selection on other political matters and on the president's power stakes. In many cases there was a good deal of political maneuvering and negotiating over candidates, and in all cases political clearance was required for the candidate. Most of the nominees had previously been active in political affairs. Thus politics permeated the process of judicial selection in the Johnson administration.

But the national importance of federal judgeships requires presidential consideration of more than political pressures. A president must balance the politics of judicial selection with his own policy objectives as well as the public interest. Johnson's concern with merit is evidence of this, as is his attentiveness to the Bar Association's ratings. A major task of the judicial selection process was the mediation of politics, merit, and the president's own goals. Of course, these are not mutually exclusive.

It could be argued that considerations of partisanship (excluding only the more blatant uses of it) make a positive contribution to the rationality of the selection process. First, they insure that the selection process will be indirectly responsive to popular sentiment. More important, they insure that the important question of the social and political philosophies of the judicial candidate will be considered.[4]

Lyndon Johnson understood the political aspects of judicial selection. But he also understood the larger legal and policy significance of federal judicial power to the American society and wished to "shape" the judiciary through the selection process.

To a great extent, he was successful in the effort. A significant percentage of the 125 district judges, 41 courts of appeals judges, and 2 Supreme Court justices whom he appointed could be termed "Great Society liberals" on the bench. Several studies support the contention that Johnson's appointees to the lower federal courts and the Supreme Court were more in the Johnson progressive mold than appointees of preceding or succeeding presidents.[5] A large number remained on the bench for several years, and many Johnson judges have continued to affect American law and politics long since Johnson has left office. Arthur Garrity, appointed by Johnson to the District Court in Massachusetts, has been a central figure in the Boston school desegregation controversy. William Wayne Justice, appointed by Johnson to a district court in Texas, has made several major decisions affecting state government, including an order for revamping the entire state penal system. And Thurgood Marshall, the only remaining Johnson appointee to the Supreme Court, remains a continuing voice and vote for liberal social policy. The Johnson administration had a role in beginning the process of opening up the federal judiciary for blacks and women. And the nominees of the Johnson administration were generally rated "qualified," indicating that Johnson's criterion of merit was also met.

Those criteria were met through the judicial selection process. Johnson was able to manage the diverse actors and competing considerations to produce a process generally responsive to his wishes. This study has revealed how he was able to do so and how the process allowed a president with numerous responsibilities to be informed and to accomplish his objectives. The collaborative effort of the actors in the process give validity to the democratic objective of overall direction of governmental responsibilities through decisions made by elective officials.

Appendix: Characteristics of Johnson's Judicial Appointees

SUPREME COURT

Name	Court	Year Appointed	Year of Birth
Fortas, Abe	Supreme Court	1965	1910
Marshall, Thurgood	Supreme Court	1967	1908

COURTS OF APPEALS

Name	Circuit	Year Appointed	Year of Birth
Ainsworth, Robert A.	5	1966	1910
Aldisert, Ruggero J.	3	1968	1919
Anderson, Robert P.	2	1964	1906
Bright, Myron H.	8	1968	1919
Butzner, John D.	4	1967	1917
Carter, James M.	9	1967	1904
Celebreeze, Anthony J.	6	1965	1910
Clayton, Claude F.	5	1967	1909
Coffin, Frank M.	1	1965	1919
Coleman, James P.	5	1965	1914
Combs, Bert. C	6	1967	1911
Craven, James B.	4	1966	1918
Cummings, Walter J.	7	1966	1916
Dyer, David W.	5	1966	1910
Edwards, George C.	6	1963	1914
Ely, Walter R.	9	1964	1913
Fairchild, Thomas E.	7	1966	1912
Feinberg, Wilfred	2	1966	1920
Freedman, Abraham L.	3	1964	1904
Gibson, Floyd R.	8	1965	1910
Godbold, John C.	5	1966	1920
Goldberg, Irving L.	5	1966	1906
Heaney, Gerald W.	8	1966	1918
Hickey, John J.	10	1966	1911
Holloway, William J.	10	1968	1925
Hufstedler, Shirley A.	9	1968	1925
Kerner, Otto	7	1968	1908
Lay, Donald P.	8	1966	1926
Leventhal, Harold	D.C.	1965	1915
McCree, Wade H.	6	1966	1920
McEntee, Edward M.	1	1965	1906
Morgan, Lewis R.	5	1968	1913

Age at Appointment	Party	Religion*	Law School
55	D	J	Yale
59	D	P	Howard

Age at Appointment	Party	Religion	Law School
56	D		Loyola
49	D	RC	Pennsylvania
58	R	P	Yale
49	D	J	Minnesota
50	D		Virginia
63	D		USC
55	D		Ohio Northern
58	D	P	Mississippi
46	D		Harvard
51	D	P	George Washington
56	D	P	Kentucky
48	D	P	Harvard
50	D	RC	Harvard
56	D		Stetson
49	D	P	Detroit
51	D	P	Texas
54	D	P	Wisconsin
46	D		Columbia
60	D		Temple
55	D	RC	Missouri
46	D	P	Harvard
60	D		Texas
48	D	RC	Minnesota
55	D	RC	Wyoming
45	D		Harvard
43	D		Stanford
60	D		Northwestern
40	D	P	Iowa
50	D		Columbia
46	D	P	Harvard
59	D	RC	Boston University
57	D	P	Georgia

COURTS OF APPEALS *(continued)*

Name	Circuit	Year Appointed	Year of Birth
Peck, John W.	6	1966	1913
Robinson, Spottswood W.	D.C.	1966	1916
Seitz, Collins J.	3	1966	1914
Simpson, Bryan	5	1966	1903
Stahl, David	3	1968	1920
Tamm, Edward A.	D.C.	1965	1906
Thornberry, W. Homer	5	1965	1906
Van Dusen, Francis L.	3	1967	1912
Winter, Harrison L.	4	1966	1921

DISTRICT COURTS

Name	District	Year Appointed	Year of Birth
Arnow, Winston E.	Fla.	1967	1911
Atkins, Clyde	Fla.	1966	1914
Belloni, Robert C.	Ore.	1967	1919
Bownes, Hugh H.	N.H.	1968	1920
Boyle, Edward J.	La.	1966	1913
Bratton, Howard C.	N. Mex.	1964	1922
Bryant, William B.	D.C.	1965	1911
Cabot, Ted	Fla.	1966	1917
Cassibry, Fred J.	La.	1966	1918
Christie, Sidney L.	W.Va.	1964	1903
Collinson, William R.	Mo.	1965	1912
Comiskey, James A.	La.	1967	1926
Copple, William P.	Ariz.	1966	1916
Corcoran, Howard F.	D.C.	1965	1906
Curtin, John T.	N.Y.	1967	1921
Davis, John M.	Pa.	1964	1906
Doyle, James E.	Wis.	1965	1915
Eaton, Joe O.	Fla.	1967	1920
Edenfield, Newell	Ga.	1967	1911
Eubanks, Luther B.	Okla.	1965	1917
Ferguson, Warren J.	Calif.	1966	1920
Frankel, Marvin E.	N.Y.	1965	1920
Fullam, John P.	Pa.	1966	1921

Age at appointment	Party	Religion	Law School
53	D		Cincinnati
50			Howard
52	D	RC	Virginia
63	D		Florida
48	D		Pittsburgh
59		RC	Georgetown
59	D	P	Texas
55	R	P	Harvard
45		P	Maryland

Age at appointment	Party	Religion*	Law School
56	D		Florida
52	D		Miami
48	D	P	Oregon
48	D		Columbia
53	D	RC	Loyola
42			Yale
54			Howard
49	D		Miami
48			Tulane
61	D		Cumberland
53	D	P	Missouri
43	D		Loyola
50	D		Berkeley
59		RC	Harvard
46	D		Buffalo
58		P	Pennsylvania
50	D		Columbia
47	D	P	Florida
56			Georgia
48	D		Oklahoma
46	D	RC	USC
45		J	Columbia
45	D		Harvard

DISTRICT COURTS *(continued)*

Name	District	Year Appointed	Year of Birth
Garrity, Arthur	Mass.	1966	1920
Gasch, Oliver	D.C.	1966	1906
Gesell, Gerhard A.	D.C.	1967	1910
Goodwin, William N.	Wash.	1966	1909
Gordon, Eugene A.	N.C.	1964	1917
Gordon, James F.	Ky.	1965	1918
Gordon, Myron L.	Wis.	1967	1918
Gray, William P.	Calif.	1966	1912
Green, June L.	D.C.	1968	1914
Gubow, Lawrence	Mich.	1968	1919
Guinn, Ernest A.	Tex.	1966	1905
Harris, Oren	Ark.	1965	1913
Harvey, Alexander	Md.	1966	1923
Hauk, A. Andrew	Calif.	1966	1912
Heebe, Frederick	La.	1966	1922
Hemphill, Robert W.	S.C.	1964	1915
Henderson, Albert J.	Ga.	1968	1920
Higginbotham, A. Leon	Pa.	1964	1928
Hill, Irving	Calif.	1965	1915
Hogan, Timothy S.	Ohio	1966	1909
Hunter, Elmo B.	Mo.	1965	1915
Jones, Woodrow W.	N.C.	1967	1914
Judd, Orrin G.	N.Y.	1968	1906
Justice, William W.	Tex.	1968	1920
Kaufman, Frank A.	Md.	1966	1916
Keady, William C.	Miss.	1968	1913
Keith, Damon J.	Mich.	1967	1922
Kellam, Richard B.	Va.	1967	1909
Kinneary, Joseph P.	Ohio	1966	1905
Krentzman, Isaac B.	Fla.	1967	1914
Lambros, Thomas D.	Ohio	1967	1930
Langley, Orville E.	Okla.	1965	1908
Lasker, Morris E.	N.Y.	1968	1917
Latchum, James L.	Del.	1968	1918
Lawrence, Alexander A.	Ga.	1968	1906
Leddy, Bernard J.	Vt.	1966	1910
Lord, Miles W.	Minn.	1966	1919
Lynch, William O.	Ill.	1966	1908
MacKenzie, John A.	Va.	1967	1917
Mansfield, Walter R.	N.Y.	1966	1911
Masterson, Thomas A.	Pa.	1967	1927

Age at Appointment	Party	Religion*	Law School
46	D	RC	Harvard
59	R	P	George Washington
57			Yale
57	D		Oregon
47	D		Duke
47	D		Kentucky
49	D		Harvard
54	R		Harvard
54			Washington College
49	D	J	Michigan
61	D		Texas
62		P	Cumberland
43	D	P	Columbia
54	D		Catholic University
44			Tulane
49	D	P	Univ. of South Carolina
47	D		Mercer
36	D		Yale
50	D		Harvard
57	D	RC	Cincinnati
50	D	P	Missouri
53	D	P	Wake Forest
62	R	P	Harvard
48	D	P	Texas
50	D	J	Harvard
55	D	P	Washington University
45	D	P	Howard
58	D	P	
61	D	RC	Cincinnati
53	D		Florida
37	D		Cleveland Marshall
57	D		Tulsa
51	D		Yale
50	D	P	Virginia
62		P	
56	D		Boston College
47	D	P	Minnesota
58	D	RC	Loyola
50	D		Washington & Lee
55	R		Harvard
40	D		Pennsylvania

DISTRICT COURTS *(continued)*

Name	District	Year Appointed	Year of Birth
Maxwell, Robert E.	W.Va.	1965	1924
McMillan, James B.	N.C.	1968	1916
McNichols, Raymond C.	Idaho	1964	1914
McRae, Robert M.	Tenn.	1966	1921
Mehrtens, William O.	Fla.	1965	1906
Merhige, Robert R.	Va.	1957	1919
Mitchell, Lansing L.	La.	1966	1914
Morgan, Robert D.	Ill.	1967	1912
Motley, Constance B.	N.Y.	1966	1921
Muecke, Charles A.	Ariz.	1964	1918
Murray, Frank J.	Mass.	1967	1904
Napoli, Frank	Ill.	1966	
Neville, Philip	Minn.	1967	1909
Nichol, Fred J.	S.Dak.	1965	1912
Nixon, Walter L.	Miss.	1968	1928
Noland, James E.	Ind.	1966	1920
Peckham, Robert F.	Calif.	1966	1920
Pettine, Raymond J.	R.I.	1966	1912
Pittman, T. Virgil	Ala.	1966	1916
Pollack, Milton	N.Y.	1967	1906
Port, Edmund	N.Y.	1964	1906
Porter, David S.	Ohio	1966	1909
Pratt, John H.	D.C.	1968	1910
Pregerson, Harry	Calif.	1967	1923
Real, Manuel	Calif.	1966	1924
Reynolds, John W.	Wis.	1965	1921
Roberts, Jack	Tex.	1966	1910
Robinson, Aubrey E.	D.C.	1966	1922
Robinson, Spottswood W.	D.C.	1964	1916
Rubin, Alvin B.	La.	1966	1920
Russell, Donald S.	S.C.	1966	1906
Russell, Dan M.	Miss.	1965	1913
Schwartz, Edward J.	Calif.	1968	1912
Scott, Charles R.	Fla.	1966	1904
Seals, Woodrow B.	Tex.	1966	1917
Simons, Charles E.	S.C.	1964	1916
Singleton, John V.	Tex.	1966	1918
Smith, John L.	D.C.	1966	1912
Smith, Orma R.	Miss.	1968	1904
Smith, Russell E.	Mont.	1966	1908
Smith, Sidney O.	Ga.	1965	1923

Age at Appointment	Party	Religion*	Law School
41	D		West Virginia
52	D	P	Harvard
50	D	RC	Idaho
45		P	Virginia
59	D		Florida
48	D	RC	Richmond
52			LSU
55	R	P	Chicago
43	D		Columbia
46	D		Arizona
63			Georgetown
58	D	P	Minnesota
43	D	P	S. Dakota
40		RC	Tulane
46			Indiana
46	D		Stanford
54	D		Boston University
50	D	P	Alabama
61	D		Columbia
58	D		Syracuse
57		P	Cincinnati
58	D	RC	Harvard
44	D		Boalt Hall
42	D	RC	Loyola
44			Wisconsin
56	D		Texas
44			Cornell
48			Howard
46	D	J	LSU
60	R	P	Univ. of South Carolina
52	D		Mississippi
56			San Francisco
62	D	P	Valparaiso
49			Texas
48	D	P	Univ. of South Carolina
48	D	P	
54	R	RC	Georgetown
64	D	P	Mississippi
58	D		Montana
42	D	P	Georgia

DISTRICT COURTS *(continued)*

Name	District	Year Appointed	Year of Birth
Suttle, Dorwin W.	Tex.	1964	1906
Taylor, William M.	Tex.	1966	1909
Tenny, Charles H.	N.Y.	1963	1911
Theis, Frank G.	Kans.	1967	1911
Thomas, William K.	Ohio	1968	1911
Thornberry, W. Homer	Tex.	1963	1906
Travia, Anthony J.	N.Y.	1967	1911
Troutman, E. Mac	Pa.	1967	1915
Von der Heydt, James A.	Alaska	1966	1919
Waddy, Joseph C.	D.C.	1967	
Weber, Gerald J.	Pa.	1964	1914
Weiner, Charles R.	Pa.	1967	1922
Weinstein, Jack B.	N.Y.	1967	1920
Whelan, Francis C.	Calif.	1964	1907
Whipple, Lawrence A.	N.J.	1966	1910
Williams, Paul X.	Ark.	1967	1908
Wise, Henry S.	Ill.	1966	1909
Woodward, Halbert O.	Tex.	1968	1918
Young, Don J.	Ohio	1965	1910
Zampano, Robert C.	Conn.	1964	1929

Age at Appointment	Party	Religion*	Law School
58	D	P	Texas
57	D	P	Texas
52	D		Yale
56	D	P	Michigan
55	D	P	Ohio State
57	D	P	Texas
56	D	RC	St. Johns
52	R	P	Dickinson
47			Northwestern
			Howard
50	D	RC	Pennsylvania
45	D		Temple
47		J	Columbia
57	D		California
56	D		John Marshall
59	D		Arkansas
57	D		Washington University
50	D		Texas
55	D	P	Case Western
35			Yale

SPECIAL COURTS

Name	Court	Year Appointed	Year of Birth
Baldwin, Philip B.	CCPA	1968	1924
Beckworth, Lindley	Cust. Ct.	1967	1913
Collins, Linton M.	Ct. Claims	1964	1902
Cowen, A. Wilson	Ct. Claims	1964	1905
Landis, Frederick	CCPA	1965	1912
Maletz, Herbert N.	Cust. Ct.	1967	1913
Newman, Bernard	Cust. Ct.	1968	1907
Nichols, Philip	Ct. Claims;	1966,	
	Cust. Ct.	1964	1907
Re, Edward D.	Cust. Ct.	1968	1920
Rosenstein, Samuel M.	Cust. Ct.	1968	1909
Skelton, Byron G.	Ct. Claims	1966	1905
Watson, James L.	Cust. Ct.	1966	1922
Cancio, Hiram R.	Puerto Rico	1965	1920
Fernandez-Badillo, Juan B.	Puerto Rico	1967	1912

Sources: Stuart Dornett and Robert Cross, *Federal Judiciary Almanac, 1984* (New York: John Wiley & Sons, 1984); Bicentennial Committee of the Judicial Conference of the United States, *Judges of the United States* (Washington, D.C.: Government Printing Office, 1983).

* J = Jewish
P = Protestant
RC = Roman Catholic

Age at Appointment	Party	Religion*	Law School
44	D	P	—
54	D	P	—
62	D		—
59	D	P	Texas
53	R	P	Indiana
54			Harvard
61	R	J	NYU
57	D		Harvard
48	D	RC	St. Johns
59	D	J	Cincinnati
61	D	P	Texas
44	D		Brooklyn
45			Puerto Rico
55			Puerto Rico

Notes

1. Introduction

1. Emmette S. Redford and Marlan Blissett, *Organizing the Executive Branch: The Johnson Presidency* (Chicago: University of Chicago Press, 1981), p. 11.

2. See, for example, Redford and Blissett's "reorganization subpresidency" in ibid., and W. Henry Lambright's "science and technology subpresidency" in *Presidential Management of Science and Technology: The Johnson Presidency* (Austin: University of Texas Press, 1985); pp. 5–6, 13–16.

3. Joel Grossman, *Lawyers and Judges: The ABA and the Politics of Judicial Selection* (New York: John Wiley and Sons, 1965), p. 18. This section draws on this discussion.

4. The first quote is from Franklin D. Roosevelt, *Letters*, ed. Elting E. Morison (Cambridge: Harvard University Press, 1952), vol. 5, p. 396, and the second refers to the *Northern Securities Co. v. United States* case of 1904. (193 U.S. 197).

5. Henry J. Abraham, *Justices and Presidents: A Political History of Appointments to the Supreme Court* (New York: Penguin Books, 1975), p. 246.

6. Merle Miller, *Plain Speaking: An Oral Biography of Harry S. Truman* (New York: G. P. Putnam's Sons, 1973), pp. 225 and 121. Truman continued about Clark, "It isn't so much that he's a bad man. It's just that he's such a dumb son of a bitch."

7. The figures include five district judges and one appeals judge whose nominations had been initiated by the Kennedy administration but whose appointments were made by Johnson. Johnson also made two appointments to the court in Puerto Rico, which, although established by Congress under its authority to govern the territories, is classified as a district court and has the same jurisdiction. Unlike judges in courts in other territories, Puerto Rican judges receive lifetime appointments.

8. Letter, Albert E. Jenner, Jr., to president, 14 February 1967, Ex FG 500, "The Judicial Branch 11/23/63–3/16/67," WHCF, LBJ Library.

9. Jethro Lieberman, *The Litigious Society* (New York: Basic Books, 1981).

10. Merle Miller, *Lyndon: An Oral Biography* (New York: G. P. Putnam's Sons, 1980), p. 60. This discussion of the 1937 election also relies on Rowland Evans and Robert Novak, *Lyndon B. Johnson: The Exercise of Power* (New York: New American Library, 1966), p.8.

11. Evans and Novak, *Lyndon B. Johnson*, p. 9.

12. Abraham, *Justices and Presidents*, especially pp. 259–269; Lawrence Baum, *The Supreme Court* (Washington, D.C.: Congressional Quarterly Press, 1981), ch. 2; John R. Schmidhauser, *Judges and Justices: The Federal Appellate Judiciary* (Boston: Little, Brown and Company, 1979); Robert Shogan, *A Question of Judgment: The Fortas Case and the Struggle for the Supreme Court* (Indianapolis: Bobbs-Merrill Company, 1972).

13. Sheldon Goldman, "Politics, Recruitment, and Decisional Tendencies of the Judges on the United States Courts of Appeals, 1961–4" (unpublished dissertation, Harvard University, 1965), p. 16. From this study also comes his "Judicial Appointments to the United States Courts of Appeals," *Wisconsin Law Review*, Winter 1967, p. 186. See also his articles on judicial backgrounds: "Johnson and Nixon Appointees to the Lower Federal Courts: Some Socio-Political Perspectives," *Journal of Politics* 34 (1972): 935–951; "Judicial Backgrounds, Recruitment, and the Party Variable: The Case of the Johnson and Nixon Appointees to the United States District and Appeals Courts," *Arizona State Law Journal* 1974: 211–222; J. Woodford Howard, *Courts of Appeals in the Federal Judicial System* (Princeton: Princeton University Press, 1981); and Richard J. Richardson and Kenneth N. Vines, *The Politics of Federal Courts: Lower Courts in the United States* (Boston: Little, Brown and Company, 1970).

14. Alan Neff, *The United States District Judge Nominating Commissions: Their Members, Procedures and Candidates* (Chicago: American Judicature Society, 1981), chs. 1–2; Henry J. Abraham, *The Judicial Process: An Introductory Analysis of the United States, England, and France*, 4th ed. (New York: Oxford University Press, 1980), ch. 2; Howard Ball, *Courts and Politics* (Englewood Cliffs, N.J.: Prentice-Hall, 1980), ch. 5; and Sheldon Goldman and Thomas Jahnige, *The Federal Courts as a Political System*, 3d ed. (New York: Harper & Row, 1985), ch. 3. An older study that provides some historical and constitutional perspectives on the role of the Senate in judicial nominations is the classic work by Joseph P. Harris, *The Advice and Consent of the Senate: A Study of the Confirmation of Appointments by the United States Senate* (Berkeley: University of California Press, 1953). See also Joseph C. Goulden, *The Benchwarmers: The Private World of the Powerful Federal Judges* (New York: Weybright and Talley, 1974).

15. Richard L. Schott and Dagmar S. Hamilton, *People, Positions, and Power: The Political Appointments of Lyndon Johnson* (Chicago: University of Chicago Press, 1983), p. 4.

16. Ibid., p. 19, quoting from Jack J. Valenti interview.

17. Goldman, "Judicial Appointments," p. 189.

18. Schott and Hamilton, *People, Positions, and Power*, p. 4.

2. The Historical Development of the Appointments Process

1. Joseph P. Harris, *The Advice and Consent of the Senate* (Berkeley: University of California Press, 1953), p. 21. This work is still the best study of the history of the appointing power.

2. Ibid., p. 21.

3. Ibid., p. 24.

4. Harold W. Chase, *Federal Judges: The Appointing Process* (Minneapolis: University of Minnesota Press, 1972), p. 4, makes this point, relying on Burke Shartel, "Federal Judges—Appointment, Supervision, and Removal—Some Possibilities under the Constitution," *Michigan Law Review* 28 (1930): 485–529.

5. Chase, *Federal Judges*, p. 5.

6. Ibid., p. 15.

7. Howard Ball, *Courts and Politics: The Federal Judicial System* (Englewood Cliffs, N.J.: Prentice-Hall, 1980), p. 169.

8. Ibid., p. 16; Chase, *Federal Judges*, pp. 16, 22–23.

9. Senate Resolution 334, 86th Cong., 2d Session, 1960, and 5 U.S.C.§5503 (1982), noted in Ibid. Chase, *Federal Judges*, p. 15, and in Joel B. Grossman, *Lawyers and Judges* (New York: John Wiley & Sons, 1965, p. 118.

10. *United States* v. *Allocco*, 305 F.2d 704 (1962), *cert. denied*, 371 U.S. 964 (1963), as noted in Chase, *Federal Judges*, p. 15. See also Harris, *Advice and Consent*, pp. 255–257.

11. Sheldon Goldman, "Carter's Judicial Appointments: A Lasting Legacy," *Judicature* 64 (1981): 344, 345.

12. These terms are taken from Richard J. Richardson and Kenneth N. Vines, *The Politics of Federal Courts* (Boston: Little, Brown & Company, 1970), p. 58, and Ball, *Courts and Politics*, p. 177. Ball also includes another role, that of "affirmer," which is handled by the Senate.

13. Henry J. Abraham, *Justices and Presidents: A Political History of Appointments to the Supreme Court* (New York: Penguin Books, 1975), p. 155.

14. William P. Rogers, "Judicial Appointments in the Eisenhower Administration," *Journal of the American Judicature Society* 41 (1957): 40.

15. Grossman, *Lawyers and Judges*, p. 25. This might explain the less-than-liberal votes of several of the Kennedy Southern appointees in racial justice cases. On this point, see Victor Navasky, *Kennedy Justice* (New York: Atheneum Publishers, 1971).

16. Rita Cooley, "The Department of Justice and Judicial Nominations," *Journal of the American Judicature Society* 43 (1958): 86, noted in Grossman, *Lawyers and Judges*, p. 25.

17 Chase, *Federal Judges*, p. 14.

18. Executive Order 12,059, 11 May 1978, 3 C.F.R. 180 (1978); see also Executive Order 12,097, 8 November 1978.

19. Charles E. Rice, "Ronald Reagan and the Supreme Court Issue," *Wall Street Journal*, 23 September 1980, p. 34:4; W. Gary Fowler, "Judicial Selection under Reagan and Carter": "A comparison of Initial Recommendation Procedures: *Yale Law & Policy Review* 1(1983):299–356.

20. Grossman, *Lawyers and Judges*, p. 25.

21. Ibid.

22. Chase, *Federal Judges*, pp. 17, 43–45.

23. Sheldon Goldman, "Judicial Apppointments to the United States Courts of Appeals," *Wisconsin Law Review* (Winter 1967): 186.

24. Sheldon Goldman, "Reaganizing the Judiciary: The First Term Appointments," *Judicature* 68 (1985): 315.

25. Graeme Growning, "Reagan Molds the Federal Court in His Own Image, *ABA Journal* 71(1985): 62.

26. Goldman, "Reaganizing the Judiciary," p. 315.

27. See Alexander Hamilton's argument in *The Federalist* No. 66 and Harris, *Advice and Consent*, pp. 28–38.

28. Evans Haynes argues that the Senate "has appropriated the President's power of nomination so far as it concerns appointments of interest to senators of the party in power" (Haynes, *Selection and Tenure of Judges* [Newark: National Conference of Judicial Councils, 1944], p. 23); see also Harris, *Advice and Consent*, p. 20. Even senators of the opposite party are sometimes able to influence selection.

29. Harold W. Chase, "Federal Judges: The Appointing Process," *Minnesota Law Review* 51 (1966): 185.

30. Bell, who had been a court of appeals judge, noted to the Senate Judiciary Committee that "I wasn't merit selected. I knew two senators and one President, so I was appointed" in 1961. He expanded on this elsewhere: "For me, becoming a federal judge wasn't very difficult. I managed John F. Kennedy's presidential campaign in Georgia. Two of my oldest and closest friends were the two senators from Georgia. And I was campaign manager and special, unpaid counsel for the governor. It doesn't hurt to be a good lawyer" (Nina Totenberg, "Will Judges be Chosen Rationally?" *Judicature* 60 [1976]: 93).

31. See Ball, *Courts and Politics*, p. 172.

32. See the reports of the American Judicature Society on these commissions: Alan Neff, *The United States District Judge Nominating Commissions: Their Members, Procedures and Candidates* (Chicago: American Judicature Society, 1981); Larry Berkson and Susan Carbon, *The United States Circuit Judge Nominating Commission: Its Members, Procedures and Candidates* (Chicago: American Judicature Society, 1980). See also Goldman, "Carter's Judicial Appointments," p. 345; and Elliot E. Slotnick, "Reforms in Judicial Selection: Will They Affect the Senate's Role?" *Judicature* 64 (1980): 60–73, 114–129.

33. The memorandum in part reads:

"In the process of judicial selection, the Department of Justice will work closely and cooperatively with the Senate leadership, the Judiciary Committee Chairman and individual members. Both the Attorney General, on behalf of the President, and the Senate leadership are firmly committed to the principle that federal judges should be chosen on the basis of merit and quality.

"By virtue of the Senators' familiarity with the members of the Bar in their respective States, the Attorney General, in making recommendations to the President for judicial appointments, will invite Republican members to identify prospective candidates for federal district judgeships. Senators are strongly encouraged to submit the names of several candidates, preferably from three to five names, to the Attorney General for a particular vacancy. This information should be shared at the earliest practicable time with the Attorney General's designated representative so that any questions or reservations as to merit or appropriateness of the proposed candidates can be identified sufficiently early to allow meaningful consultation."

34. *Washington Post* editorial, "Picking the Reagan Judges," quoted in Mayo H. Stiegler, "Selecting Federal Judges during the Reagan Administration," *Judicature* 64 (1981): 427.

35. W. Gary Fowler, "Judicial Selection under Reagan and Carter: A Comparison of Their Initial Selection Procedures," *Judicature* 67 (1984): 269.

36. Ibid., p. 272.

37. Fowler, "A Comparison of Initial Recommendation Procedures," pp. 323–324.

38. This discussion is drawn from "Senatorial Courtesy History," *Congressional Quarterly Weekly Report*, 3 February 1979, p. 192.

39. Chase, *Federal Judges*, p. 7, and Harris, *Advice and Consent*, p. 317.

40. Grossman, *Lawyers and Judges*, p. 39.

41. Richardson and Vines, *Politics of Federal Courts*, p. 67.

42. Walter F. Murphy, *Elements of Judicial Strategy* (Chicago: University of Chicago Press, 1964), pp. 73–78, and "Chief Justice Taft and the Lower Court Bureaucracy: A Study in Judicial Administration," *Journal of Politics* 24 (1962): 453; Laurence H. Tribe, *God Save This Honorable Court: How the Choice of Supreme Court Justices Shapes Our History* (New York: Random House, 1985), p. 129. See also Grossman, *Lawyers and Judges*, pp. 39–42, and Chase, *Federal Judges*, p. 34.

43. Grossman, *Lawyers and Judges*, p. 42.

44. For a discussion of the Senate's screening role in Supreme Court nominations, see Tribe, *God Save This Honorable Court*.

45. Chase, *Federal Judges*, p. 7.

46. Neff, *District Judge Nominating Commissions*, p. 17. Neff notes that Judiciary is the only committee to use such a device.

47. "Report Card on Judicial Merit Selection," *Congressional Quarterly Weekly Report*, 3 February 1979, p. 12. See also Slotnick, "Reforms in Judicial Selection," p. 60.

48. Goldman, "Carter's Judicial Appointments," p. 353.

49. "Senatorial Courtesy History," p. 192.

50. Stiegler, "Selecting Federal Judges," p. 60.

51. Philip Kurland, "Our Troubled Courts," *Nation's Business*, May 1971, p. 79.

52. Chase, *Federal Judges*, pp. 20–23.

53. Max Farrand, *Records of the Federal Convention*, vol. 2 (New Haven:

Yale University Press, 1911), p. 292; noted in John R. Schmidhauser, *Judges and Justices: The Federal Appellate Judiciary* (Boston: Little, Brown and Company, 1979), p. 13.

54. Much of this discussion is derived from the careful study of Grossman, *Lawyers and Judges,* especially ch. 3.

55. Ibid., p. 50.

56. Ibid., pp. 53, 55.

57. William Mitchell, "Appointment of Federal Judges," *American Bar Association Journal* 17 (1931): 574, reprinted in Schmidhauser, *Judges and Justices,* p. 21.

58. Grossman, *Lawyers and Judges,* p. 58.

59. Ibid., p. 64.

60. ABA, "Report of the Standing Committee on Federal Judiciary," *ABA Reports* 82 (1957): 433, noted in Grossman, *Lawyers and Judges,* p. 72.

61. Neff, *District Judge Nominating Commissions,* p. 11.

62. Elliot Slotnick, "The ABA Standing Committee on Federal Judiciary: A Contemporary Assessment—Part I," *Judicature* 66 (1983): 353.

63. Goldman, "Reaganizing the Judiciary," p. 316.

64. Ibid.

65. Grossman, *Lawyers and Judges,* pp. 108–113, 138–139.

66. Neff, *District Judge Nominating Commissions,* p. 15. Neff notes that the informal and formal assessments are not always identical if new information is received.

67. An exception to this was Harry Truman, who was hostile to the ABA (Grossman, *Lawyers and Judges,* p. 67).

68. Neff, *District Judge Nominating Commissions,* p. 16.

69. Grossman, *Lawyers and Judges,* p. 212.

70. Philip B. Kurland, "The Appointment and Disappointment of Supreme Court Justices," *Law and Social Order* 183 (1972): 212.

71. Schmidhauser, *Judges and Justices,* p. 26.

72. Neff, *District Judge Nominating Commissions,* p. 16, and Elliot Slotnick, "The ABA Standing Committee on Federal Judiciary: A Contemporary Assessment—Part II," *Judicature* 66 (1983): 385.

73. Schmidhauser, *Judges and Justices,* p. 23.

74. Fowler, "Judicial Selection under Reagan and Carter," p. 268.

75. See Lawrence Baum, *The Supreme Court* (Washington, D.C.: Congressional Quarterly Press, 1981), p. 31.

76. Grossman, *Lawyers and Judges,* pp. 43–45.

77. See, for example, Kurland, "Appointment and Disappointment," p. 213.

78. Chase, *Federal Judges,* p. 25. This section is drawn from the Chase discussion of the FBI reports.

79. Title 28, U.S.C. §134 (b) (1982); cited in Grossman, *Lawyers and Judges,* p. 23.

80. Richardson and Vines, *Politics of Federal Courts,* p. 72.

81. Grossman, *Lawyers and Judges,* p. 24. For a discussion of the Conti-

Table N-1. *Relevance of Party in Lower Court Appointments, 1884–1962*

President	Judicial Appointments from Party of President	
	%	N
Cleveland	100.0	(N = 37)
Harrison	89.7	(N = 29)
McKinley	95.7	(N = 23)
T. Roosevelt	97.2	(N = 72)
Taft	82.2	(N = 35)
Wilson	98.6	(N = 72)
Harding	97.3	(N = 44)
Coolidge	94.1	(N = 68)
Hoover	85.7	(N = 49)
F. Roosevelt	95.9	(N = 194)
Truman	92.8	(N = 125)
Eisenhower	94.8	(N = 174)
Kennedy	92.6	(N = 108)

Sources: For appointments before Truman; Evan A. Evans, "Political Influence in the Selection of Federal Judges," *Wisconsin Law Review* (1958): 350–351; other information and discussion from Richardson and Vines, *Politics of Federal Courts,* p. 68.

nental system see Henry J. Abraham, *The Judicial Process* (New York: Oxford University Press, 1980), ch. 2.

82. See Table N-1.

83. William P. Rogers, "Judicial Appointments in the Eisenhower Administration," *Journal of the American Judicature Society* 41 (1957): 39–40.

84. *New York Times,* 20 May 1961, quoted in Chase, *Federal Judges,* p. 51.

85. Comments taken from Nixon's letter to Senator William Saxbe, reprinted in *New York Times,* 2 July 1970, and a speech reprinted in "A New Chief Justice: A New Court Era," *Congressional Quarterly Weekly Report,* 23 May 1969, p. 798.

86. Goldman, "Carter's Judicial Appointments," p. 353; Fowler, "Judicial Selection under Reagan and Carter," p. 268.

87. For the Meese quote, see "Judging Reagan's Judges," *Time,* 6 October 1980, p. 69. See also Goldman, "Reaganizing the Judiciary," pp. 327–329; Nadine Cohodas, "Reagan's Judicial Selections Draw Differing Assessments," *Congressional Quarterly Weekly Report* 41 (1983): 83–84.

88. J. Woodford Howard, Jr., *Courts of Appeals in the Federal Judicial System* (Princeton: Princeton University Press, 1981), p. 90. The quotes in this paragraph are from that work.

3. The Judicial Selection Process in a Presidential Transition

1. Richard L. Schott and Dagmar S. Hamilton, *People, Positions and Power: The Political Appointments of Lyndon Johnson* (Chicago: University of Chicago Press, 1983). This book, an excellent study of a different appointment process, nevertheless provided important insights and some guides for this investigation. See also interview, Schott with Walter W. Jenkins, Austin, Texas, 14 December 1976, and interview, Schott with Bill D. Moyers, New York, 20 June 1978.

2. Harold W. Chase, *Federal Judges: The Appointing Process* (Minneapolis: University of Minnesota Press, 1972), p. 165. See ch. 2 in this book for an in-depth look at the Kennedy process and ch. 5 for a discussion of Kennedy's "legacies" to the Johnson administration. My section dealing with the early Johnson appointments is derived partially from Chase's discussion. See also Victor Navasky, *Kennedy Justice* (New York: Atheneum, 1977).

3. Chase, *Federal Judges*, p. 167.

4. Telegram cited in letter, David Rabinovitz to Pierre Salinger, 3 December 1963, Ex FG 530/ST 49/A, WHCF, LBJ Library, hereafter cited as Rabinovitz letter to Salinger.

5. *New York Times*, 20 November 1963, p. 32:7.

6. Cited in Rabinovitz letter to Salinger.

7. *New York Times*, 3 December 1963, p. 42:1.

8. Rabinovitz letter to Salinger.

9. Letter, Salinger to Rabinovitz, 23 December 1963, Ex FG 530/ST 49/A, WHCF, LBJ Library. See also memorandums exchanged between Salinger and Kenneth O'Donnell, 11 December 1963 and 12 December 1963, Ex FG 530/ST 49/A, WHCF, LBJ Library, which indicate O'Donnell's reply was "We are still all for him."

10. Memo, Robert F. Kennedy to president, undated, Ex FG 530/ST 49/A, WHCF, LBJ Library.

11. *New York Times*, 8 January 1964, p. 22.

12. The lack of recess appointments contrasts with the extensive use by Presidents Eisenhower and Kennedy. Eisenhower made twenty-five appointments for 14 percent of his total, and Kennedy in his short time made twenty-eight such appointments, or 22 percent of his total. Chase notes that not one of the purely Johnson appointments in the first two years was a recess appointment, and Johnson made no recess appointments during the rest of his term. Johnson's last attorney general, Ramsey Clark, opposed recess appointments on principle and also as a result of his perception of the problems of the Rabinovitz appointment. See Chase, *Federal Judges*, p. 184, and Richard Harris, *Justice* (New York: E.P. Dutton, 1970), p. 156.

13. See letter, Senator William Proxmire to president, 7 January 1964, and letters and telegrams to president, 8–17 January 1964, Ex FG 530/ST 49/A, WHCF, LBJ Library.

14. Letter, David Rabinovitz to Lawrence O'Brien, 14 January 1964, Ex FG 530/ST 49/A, WHCF, LBJ Library.

15. Memo, Robert Kennedy to president, 9 January 1964, Ex FG 530/ST 49/A, WHCF, LBJ Library.

16. Memo, Paul Popple to president, 16 November 1964, Ex FG 530/ST 49/A, WHCF, LBJ Library. See also the rather touching letter from Rabinovitz's wife to the president, May 1965, Ex FG 530/ST 49/A, WHCF, LBJ Library, which pleads for Johnson's support.

17. Letter, Ralph Huitt to George Reedy, 15 October 1964, and memo, Reedy to president, 17 October 1964, Ex FG 530/ST 49/A, WHCF, LBJ Library.

18. Letter, Robert Kennedy to president, 2 September 1964, Ex FG 530/ST 21, WHCF, LBJ Library.

19. Memo, Nicholas deB. Katzenbach to president, 2 September 1964, Ex FG 530/ST 21, WHCF, LBJ Library.

20. *Los Angeles Times*, 30 September 1965, quoted in Chase, *Federal Judges*, p. 220 n. 27.

21. Chase, *Federal Judges*, p. 173. Again, Chase's book provides background for my discussion.

22. *New York Times*, 30 September 1965, p. 2.

23. *New York Times*, 19 October 1965, p. 1.

24. Memo, Ramsey Clark to president, 3 November 1965, Ex FG 530/ST 21/A, WHCF, LBJ Library.

25. Letter, Francis X. Morrissey to president, 3 November 1965, Ex FG 530/ST 21/A, WHCF, LBJ Library. Donald Jackson suggests that the Morrissey battle may have caused a change in Johnson's judicial selection process: "Including the Morrissey nomination, six of Johnson's first fifty-six appointments drew gasps of 'not qualified' from the ABA. A strong advocate of senatorial courtesy, Johnson preferred to go along with senatorial nominations. After the Morrissey debacle and a long meeting with ABA leaders, however, he changed course. From then on, all his nominees had ABA backing . . . . The Johnson judges remained partisan Democrats, but their intellectual and professional quality rose visibly." (Donald D. Jackson, *Judges* [New York: Atheneum Publishers, 1980], p. 264).

26. See memos, letters regarding Garrity from 25 April 1966 to 3 July 1966, at Ex FG 530/ST 21/A, WHCF, LBJ Library.

27. Chase, *Federal Judges*, p. 50.

28. Ibid., p. 181.

29. Ibid., p. 19.

30. Ibid., p. 181.

31. Fortas' role, as well as that of other judges, will be discussed in the next chapter.

32. Memo, Joseph F. Dolan to Kenneth O'Donnell, 5 May 1964, and letter, O'Donnell to William C. Doherty, 13 May 1964, General FG 505/FG 216, WHCF, LBJ Library.

33. Memo, Robert Kennedy to president, quoted in memo, Dolan to Mike Manatos, 4 May 1964, Ex FG 505/2, WHCF, LBJ Library.

34. Memo, Katzenbach to O'Donnell, 27 December 1964, Ex FG 500, WHCF, LBJ Library.

35. Memo, Katzenbach to O'Donnell, 23 January 1964, Ex FG 500, WHCF, LBJ Library.

36. Memo, Dolan to Manatos, p. 2.

37. *New York Times,* 10 May 1964, p. 67.

38. For a good discussion of the politics of these appointments, see Jack Zaiman, "U.S. Court Vacancy: The Background Moves," *Hartford Courant,* 1 March 1964, p. 3B.

39. See letter, Robert Kennedy to president, 3 September 1964, and reply letter, president to Robert Kennedy, 3 September 1964, Ex FG 135/A, WHCF, LBJ Library.

40. As Moyers noted, Jenkins' role in appointments had been very important "across the board, because everything went through Jenkins." (Interview, Schott with Moyers, New York, 20 June 1978).

41. *New York Times,* 16 September 1964, p. 1.

4. The Developed Johnson Process of Judicial Selection

1. See memo, Marvin Watson to president, 12 February 1965, filed Ramsey Clark Name File, WHCF, LBJ Library: "Ramsey says that they have no file in the Justice Department on him, which means that for the past five years he has not been considered for an appointment within the judiciary."

2. On memo, Clark to president, 17 June 1968, Larry Temple Aides File, Box 1 (1852), "Federal Judgeships; concerning circuit vacancies" there is "original to night reading."

3. Letter, Abe Fortas to president, CF FG 535, WHCF, LBJ Library:

"Again, my dear friend, I am obligated and honored by your confidence and generosity—to an extent which is beyond my power adequately to acknowledge.

"But after painful searching, I've decided to decline—with a heart full of gratitude.—Carol thinks I should accept this greatest honor that a lawyer could receive—this highest appointive post in the nation.—But I want a few more years of activity. I want a few more years to try to be of service to you and the Johnson family. And I want—and feel that in justice I should take—a few more years to stabilize this law firm in the interest of the young men who have enlisted here.

"This has been a hard decision—but not nearly as hard as another which had the virtue of continuing association with your trials and tribulations and greatness.

"I shall always be grateful.
　　　　　　　　　Abe"

Porter in his oral history reports that the president read the letter aloud to his family and "there were copious tears wept," p. 292. The reference in the third paragraph is to Fortas' previous rejection of the attorney generalship.

4. See letter, William T. Coleman, Jr., to president, 2 September 1966, filed Box 3 (1408), Office Files of Harry C. McPherson, Jr., LBJ Library.

5. Transcript, Abe Fortas Oral History Interview, 14 August 1969, p. 25, LBJ Library.

6. Transcript, Homer Thornberry Oral History Interview, 21 December 1970, p. 33, LBJ Library.

7. Telegram, president to Ray McNichols, 15 April 1964, Ex FG 530/12/A, WHCF, LBJ Library. See similar telegram, 3 March 1964, Ex FG 530/31/A, WHCF, LBJ Library.

8. For more on the Macy operation, see John W. Macy, Jr., *Public Service: The Human Side of Government* (New York: Harper & Row, 1971); Richard L. Schott and Dagmar S. Hamilton, *People, Positions, and Power: The Political Appointments of Lyndon Johnson* (Chicago: University of Chicago Press, 1983); and transcript, John W. Macy, Jr. Oral History Interviews, LBJ Library, hereafter cited as Macy Oral History.

9. Schott and Hamilton, *People, Positions, and Power*, pp. 14–15 (footnote omitted), citing interview with Macy.

10. Transcript, Larry E. Temple Oral History Interview, 12 June 1970, tape 2, p. 2, LBJ Library, hereafter cited as Temple Oral History.

11. Macy Oral History, 26 April 1969, tape 3, p. 8.

12. Memo, Macy to Watson, 1 March 1967, Ex FG 500, WHCF, LBJ Library.

13. Memo, Clark to Macy, 29 January 1965, Ex FG 500, WHCF, LBJ Library.

14. Memo, McPherson to Macy, 15 March 1965, Box 3 (1408), Office Files of Harry C. McPherson, Jr., LBJ Library.

15. See, for example, memo, Macy to president, 12 August 1968, Ex PE 2, WHCF, LBJ Library.

16. Memo with attachments, Macy to president, 14 May 1965, Ex FG 530/ST 41/A, WHCF, LBJ Library.

17. Memo with attachments, Macy to president, 1 May 1967, Ex FG 530/ST 38/A, WHCF, LBJ Library.

18. Memo, Barefoot Sanders, Jr., to Watson, 1 September 1967, Ex FG 500, WHCF, LBJ Library.

19. Memo, William J. Hopkins to Macy, 12 October 1967, Ex FG 505/5A, WHCF, LBJ Library.

20. Johnson recognized the importance of the Justice Department in this and other matters and was very concerned with and involved in the selection of the attorney general and the deputy attorney general. See transcript, Ramsey Clark Oral History Interview, 30 October 1968, tape 1, p. 19 and following, LBJ Library, hereafter cited as Clark Oral History, and transcript, Nicholas de B. Katzenbach Oral History Interview, 12 November 1968, tape 1, p. 7 and following, LBJ Library.

21. Memo, Kenneth P. O'Donnell to Katzenbach, 27 December 1963, filed Ex FG 505/FG 216, WHCF, LBJ Library.

22. Memo, Jack J. Valenti to Katzenbach, 30 March 1966, CF FG 535, WHCF, LBJ Library.

23. There are those who suggest that the long delay in appointment was due to Johnson's suspicion of Katzenbach as a "Robert Kennedy man." See Harold W. Chase, *Federal Judges: The Appointing Process* (Minneapolis: University of Minnesota Press, 1972), p. 182. I tend to discount this, since Ramsey Clark, a Johnson man, remained in that status as acting attorney general for six months before he was appointed. See also transcript, Clark

M. Clifford Oral History Interview, 15 December 1969, tape 6, p. 7, LBJ Library.

24. Transcript, Interview with Ramsey Clark, 5 March 1977, p. 17, LBJ School of Public Affairs project.

25. Clark Oral History, p. 17, and memo, Bill D. Moyers to Perry Barber, 10 December 1964, filed Ramsey Clark Name File, WHCF, LBJ Library, which reads "Ramsey Clark is analyzing contents for President."

26. Memo, Katzenbach to president, 3 February 1965, Ex FG 500, WHCF, LBJ Library.

27. This is from a letter Ernest L. Friesen wrote to Chase in *Federal Judges*, p. 144.

28. Memo with attachments, Clark to president, undated (approximately June 1966), Ex FG 505/5/A, WHCF, LBJ Library.

29. Directive on memo, Macy to president, 13 August 1966, Ex FG 505/5/A, WHCF, LBJ Library.

30. Memo, Clark to president, 3 February 1966, Ex FG 530/ST18/A, WHCF, LBJ Library.

31. See the discussion of the Clark appointment in Schott and Hamilton, *People, Positions, and Power*, pp. 87–93. They write that Johnson originally told Clark he would not consider Clark for the position because his father, Tom C. Clark, was a justice of the Supreme Court. See also transcript, Edwin Weisl, Jr. Oral History Interview, LBJ Library. Weisl, while still in the position of assistant attorney general under Ramsey Clark in 1969, criticized Clark and suggested that Clark had planted seeds in Johnson's mind that Attorney General Katzenbach was disloyal in order to get rid of Katzenbach and assume his position.

32. Memo, Cliff Carter to Marvin Watson, 9 January 1967, Ex FG 530/ST 16/A, WHCF, LBJ Library. For Clark's role after a deputy was appointed, see memo, Sanders to president, 7 October 1967, Ex FG 505/5/A, WHCF, LBJ Library, in which Sanders notes that "Ramsey has checked carefully," and memo, Clark to president, 28 February 1968, Ex FG 505/7/A, WHCF, LBJ Library, discussing an intentional leak to the press about the consideration for nomination being given to Otto Kerner.

33. Memo, Warren M. Christopher to Temple, 26 November 1968, Ex FG 11-8, WHCF, LBJ Library.

34. Transcript, Warren M. Christopher Oral History Interview, 31 October 1968, tape 1, p. 9, LBJ Library.

35. See the exchange of correspondence, 9 April–8 May 1968, concerning a vacancy on the Eighth Circuit. Christopher suggested a candidate from South Dakota, but that state's senator was George McGovern, Democrat, who was supporting Robert F. Kennedy's bid for the White House. This suggestion was vetoed by the White House, and a candidate of Senator Quentin N. Burdick (D-N.D.) was nominated, even though North Dakota had already "had its turn." Ex 505/8/A, WHCF, LBJ Library.

36. See memo, Christopher to Sanders, undated (approximately March 1968), Ex FG 505/7/A, WHCF, LBJ Library.

37. Chase, *Federal Judges*, p. 138. I use much of Chase's description of the assistant deputy's duties contained in pp. 55ff and pp. 138ff.

38. Ibid., p. 144.

39. Memo, Watson to president, 8 September 1966, filed Ramsey Clark Name File, WHCF, LBJ Library.

40. Memo, Sanders to Watson, and memo, Watson to president, 12 January 1967, Ex FG 530/ST/16/A, WHCF, LBJ Library.

41. See memo, Clark to president with Sanders' initials, 9 January 1967, Ex FG 530/ST 38/A, WHCF, LBJ Library.

42. Memo, Macy to president, 1 May 1967, Ex FG 530/ST 13/A, WHCF, LBJ Library.

43. See memos, similar to that expected from the deputy attorney general, from Sanders to president, 5 May 1967 and 13 May 1967, Ex FG 530/ST 9/A, WHCF, LBJ Library.

44. This is described in a memo, Christopher to Temple, 26 November 1968, Ex FG 11-8, WHCF, LBJ Library.

45. Temple Oral History, 11 August 1970, tape 5, p. 24.

46. Memo, Katzenbach to O'Donnell, 23 January 1964, Ex FG 505/FG 216, WHCF, LBJ Library.

47. See memos, Watson to president, 12 February 1965, Valenti to president, 14 July 1965, filed in Ramsey Clark Name File, WHCH, LBJ Library; memo, Macy to Lawrence F. O'Brien, Box 27 (1537), "Dirksen, Senator Everett M.," LBJ Library.

48. Temple comments that "Marvin was viewed by the President as being his key primary personal staff man and I underscore personal. . . . The President had known Marvin for many years [and] had just infinite confidence in him and Marvin kind of was part brother, part son, sort of in the eyes of the President" (Transcript of interview, Richard T. McCulley with Larry E. Temple, 25 July 1980, LBJ School of Public Affairs project, p. 17, hereafter cited as Temple Interview).

49. Quoted in Schott and Hamilton, *People, Positions and Power*, p. 20. For a good discussion of Watson's role, see chapter 2, from which much of my discussion was drawn.

50. Ibid., p. 26, quoting Moyers Interview, 20 June 1978. Moyers writes: "Some of us believed *that* was a serious failure of the Johnson White House, that Marvin was altogether too narrow a man, who interpreted Lyndon Johnson too literally and was too quick to carry out the darker and more primitive passions of the president into policy and personnel." See also transcript, Harry C. McPherson, Jr. Oral History Interview, especially tape 3, p. 30, and tape 5, p. 37, LBJ Library.

51. Memo, Clark to Watson, 22 June 1966, Ex FG 530/ST 9/A, WHCF, LBJ Library, and see communications to Watson in June 1967, Ex FG 500, LBJ Library.

52. Memo, Sanders to Watson, 1 September 1967, Ex FG 500, WHCF, LBJ Library.

53. Memo, Clark to Watson, 3 February 1967, Ex FG 530/ST 15/A, WHCF, LBJ Library.

54. Memo, Watson to president, 22 November 1967, Ex FG 530/ST 32/A, WHCF, LBJ Library.

55. See letter, District Judge _____ to Watson, 4 August 1967, LE/JL, WHCF, LBJ Library, which reads, "Dear Marvin, Many thanks for your note re the upcoming vacancy on the 9th Circuit Court of Appeals."

56. Memo, Irvine Sprague to Watson, 25 January 1968, Ex FG 530/ST 5/A, WHCF, LBJ Library.

57. Memo, Sanders to president, 18 November 1967, Ex FG 530/ST 32/A, and memo, Christopher to Sanders, February 1968, Ex FG 505/7/A, WHCF, LBJ Library.

58. See letter, Joseph A. Califano, Jr. to Representative Frank Annunzio (D-Ill.), 12 March 1968, Ex FG 500, WHCF, LBJ Library; memo, Mike N. Manatos to Watson, 6 February 1968, Ex FG 500, WHCF, LBJ Library; and memo, McPherson to Clark, 24 October 1967, Box 3(1408), Office Files of Harry C. McPherson, Jr., LBJ Library.

59. Memo, Sanders to president, 5 March 1968, filed Warren Christopher Name File, WHCF, LBJ Library.

60. Temple Oral History, 12 June 1968, tape 2, p. 2.

61. Transcript, Temple Interview, p. 14.

62. Memo, Temple to Ramsey Clark, 7 February 1968, Ex FG 500, WHCF, LBJ Library.

63. Temple Oral History, 1970, tape 5, p. 15.

64. Memos, Temple to president, 13 July 1968, Ex FG 505/5; 16 July 1968, Ex FG 500; and 1 August 1968, Ex FG 505/3A, WHCF, LBJ Library.

65. Memo, Sanders to Christopher, 7 June 1968, Temple Aides File, Box 1 (1852), "Federal Judgeships," WHCF, LBJ Library.

66. President Taft continued his interest when he became chief justice. See Walter Murphy, "Chief Justice Taft and the Lower Court Bureaucracy," *Journal of Politics,* 24 (1962): 453.

67. Schott and Hamilton, *People, Positions and Power,* quoting Macy interview, 26 April 1969, ch. 1, p. 10.

68. *ABA Reports* 91 (1966): 487. See also Chase, *Federal Judges,* p. 183.

69. Memo, Valenti to president, 14 July 1965, Ex FG 505, WHCF, LBJ Library.

70. Memo, Watson to president, 5 April 1966, Ex FG 500, WHCF, LBJ Library.

71. Memo, Watson to president, 23 June 1966, Ex FG 500, WHCF, LBJ Library.

72. Memo, Manatos to president with Wayne L. Morse letter attached, 26 November 1968, Ex FG 500, WHCF, LBJ Library.

73. Memo, Clark to president, 3 August 1966, Ex FG 505/FG 216, WHCF, LBJ Library.

74. Memo, Watson to president, 31 March 1966, Ex FG 505/4, WHCF, LBJ Library.

75. Memo, Sanders to president, 5 March 1968, Ex FG 505, WHCF, LBJ Library.

76. Memo, president to Sanders, 29 June 1967, Personal Papers of H. Barefoot Sanders, "Judicial Vacancies, 1967," LBJ Library.

77. Memo, Watson to president, 31 March 1966, Ex FG 505/5, WHCF, LBJ Library; and see transcript, James P. Coleman Oral History Interview, 29 April 1972, p. 42, LBJ Library.

78. Memo, Valenti to president, 18 June 1965, Ex FG 505, WHCF, LBJ Library.

79. Memo, James Jones to president and Manatos, 18 September 1968, Ex FG 505, WHCF, LBJ Library.

80. Letter, David L. Lawrence to president, 19 August 1966, Ex FG 505/3, WHCF, LBJ Library.

81. Memo, Watson to president, 23 June 1966, Ex FG 500, WHCF, LBJ Library.

82. Memo, Sanders to president, 3 June 1967, Ex FG 505 4, WHCF, LBJ Library; memo, Sanders, for the record, 7 June 1967, Personal Papers of Sanders, "Memos," LBJ Library.

83. Memo, Sanders to president, 3 June 1967, Ex FG 505 4, WHCF, LBJ Library. Sanders recollected that session where Johnson met with several candidates and combined small talk and policy views:
"The meeting lasted about 30 minutes. The President met and had his picture taken with each one, and then made an informal talk. He stressed the importance of equal justice for all regardless of race, economic condition or social status. He mentioned that Federal judges tend to get arrogant and that he hoped they would act as though they had to stand for election every once in a while. He urged them not to remain on the bench past retirement age but to take advantage of retirement eligibility and stand aside for younger people.
"He pointed out that each had come through a careful selection process, that he was proud to have them as Johnson nominees, and that he did not expect to hear anything about their judicial service that would be a disappointment to him. When the meeting broke up he suggested that they each seek out the Senators and Congressmen who have recommended them and thank them once again. The meeting was off the record" (Memo, Sanders to Marie Fehmer, 19 May 1967, Personal Papers of Sanders, "Memos," LBJ Library).

84. Memo, Watson to president, 4 March 1965, Ex FG 505/FG 216/A, WHCF, LBJ Library.

85. See, for example, memo, Watson to president, 1 March 1965, Ex FG 505/FG 216/A, WHCF, LBJ Library, in which Johnson had checked "Yes" to "Judge [Edward A.] Tamm wants to come in and personally thank you for his promotion," and memo, S. Douglass Cater, Jr. to Juanita Roberts, 17 July 1967, Ex FG 530/ST 38/A, WHCF, LBJ Library.

86. Letter, Thomas Masterson to president, 31 July 1967, Ex FG 530/38, LBJ Library.

87. Ibid.

88. This role meant a great deal to senators, sometimes in ways not usu-
ally thought of. This can be seen in a memo to Larry O'Brien concerning
Senator William Proxmire (D-Wis.), who was concerned about the loss of
$20,000 in campaign contributions if certain judicial nominations were not
delayed (Memo, Claude Desautels to O'Brien, 1 October 1964, in Office
Files of Lawrence F. O'Brien, Box 28 [1537, 1545], "Proxmire, William [D]
Wisconsin," WHCF, LBJ Library).

89. Memo, Sanders to Clark, 23 March 1967, Personal Papers of Sanders,
"Judicial Vancancies, 1967," WHCF, LBJ Library.

90. See letter, president to Senators John Pastore (D-R.I.), and Claiborne
Pell (D-R.I.), 9 March 1965; accompanying memo, Valenti to attorney general, Ex FG 505/1, WHCF, LBJ Library; letter, president to Claiborne Pell,
forwarded to Macy, 24 March 1966, Ex FG 500, LBJ Library.

91. See, for instance, memos, Clark to president, 9 June 1966 and 16 July
1968, Ex FG 500, WHCF, LBJ Library. The first memo contained senatorial
recommendations for both circuit and district judgeships and the second has
columns for "Name," "Court," and "Recommended and Supported by,"
under which are usually senators' names.

92. See almost all nomination files, including memo, Clark to president, 9
January 1967, Ex FG 530/ST 38/A, WHCF, LBJ Library.

93. See, for example, memo, Katzenbach to president, in which Katzenbach recommends that the president go along with the preference of Senator
Joseph S. Clark (D-Pa.) for a Pennsylvania candidate for a Third Circuit vacancy. Memo, Katzenbach to O'Donnell, 23 January 1964, Ex FG 505/FG
216, WHCF, LBJ Library.

94. For example, see memo, Clark to Watson, 30 August 1966, Ex FG 505/
FG 216, WHCF, LBJ Library, which presents the Justice Department's recommendations (without any input from senators) for what Clark referred to as
"probably the most important judicial vacancy existing"—on the Court of
Appeals for the District of Columbia. But note that senators often tried
nevertheless to suggest nominees. See Ex FG 505/FG 216 and Ex FG 530/FG
216, WHCF, LBJ Library, for these endorsements from Senators Sam Ervin
(D-N.C.), Mike Mansfield (D-Mont.), Robert Byrd (D-W.V.), Walter Mondale
(D-Minn.), and others.

95. Memo, Katzenbach to O'Donnell, 23 January 1964, Ex FG 505/FG 216,
WHCF, LBJ Library.

96. Memo, Moyers to president, 9 August 1965, Ex FG 530/ST 35, WHCF,
LBJ Library.

97. Memo, Christopher to Temple, 26 November 1968, Ex FG 11-8,
WHCF, LBJ Library, p. 6.

98. Memo, Clark to Watson, 28 September 1966, filed Name File of
Ramsey Clark, WHCF, LBJ Library.

99. Memo, Watson to president, with attached letter from Orville L.
Freeman, 27 May 1966, CF FG 505, WHCF, LBJ Library.

100. But sometimes one senator would be or appear more powerful and the
White House would have to be very diplomatic. See memo, Claude De-

sautels to Manatos, 13 October 1964, Office Files of Lawrence F. O'Brien, Box 28, (1537, 1538), "Proxmire, Senator William (D) Wisconsin," WHCF, LBJ Library.

101. See memo, Sprague to Watson, 25 January 1968, Ex FG 530/ST 5/A, WHCF, LBJ Library, and many other files in this folder.

102. Memo, Sanders to president, 17 April 1967, Ex FG 530/ST 38/A.

103. Memo, Manatos to Watson, 17 April 1967, Ex FG 500, WHCF, LBJ Library.

104. Memo, Valenti to president, 23 April 1966, Ex FG 505/7, LBJ Library. (See also accompanying memos.)

105. Memo, Jones to president, 5 May 1967, Ex FG 530/ST 13/A, WHCF, LBJ Library.

106. Memo, Carter to president, 16 December 1963, Ex FG 530/ST 40, WHCF, LBJ Library.

107. Memo, Sanders to president, 18 April 1967, in Personal Papers of Sanders, "Judicial Vacancies, 1967," WHCF, LBJ Library. This entire situation is discussed in Chapter 6.

108. Memo, Watson to president, 24 March 1966, filed Abe Fortas Name File, "Fortas, Abe–1966," WHCF, LBJ Library; letter, William O. Douglas to president, 29 March 1966, Ex FG 530/ST 37, WHCF, LBJ Library.

109. These included Sanders and Matthew Byrne. For more on these and on the Fortas nomination, see ch. 6.

110. Memo, Christopher to Temple, 8 August 1968, Temple Aides File, Box 1 (1952), "Federal Judgeships," WHCF, LBJ Library.

111. See the discussion of the Cecil Poole nomination in ch. 6. Poole was later appointed to the district court by Gerald Ford and then to the Court of Appeals for the Ninth Circuit by Jimmy Carter.

112. Sheldon Goldman makes this claim and points to the nominations of Thurgood Marshall to the court of appeals in 1962 and of Constance Baker Motley as district judge (Goldman, "Judicial Appointments to the United States Courts of Appeals," *Wisconsin Law Review,* Winter 1967, pp. 186, 191, citing several newspaper reports). And Senator James Eastland (D-Miss.) also delayed Marshall's hearings on confirmation to the Supreme Court.

113. Memo, Christopher to Temple, 10 April 1968, Ex FG 530/ST 32/A, WHCF, LBJ Library. Senator Jacob Javits (R-N.Y.) explained to the press his hold was because of a need to look at the "whole set of judges" in the area (*New York Times,* 14 December 1967, p. 68:5).

114. Memo, Sanders to president, 17 April 1967, Ex FG 530/ST 38/A, WHCF, LBJ Library.

115. Temple Interview, p. 16.

116. Ramsey Clark always opposed recess appointments and Johnson never overruled Clark's wishes in this regard. See memo, Deputy Attorney General Clark to president, 3 November 1965, Ex FG 530/ST 21/A, WHCF, LBJ Library, which states Clark's reasons for opposing recess appointments.

117. *New York Times,* 14 December 1967, p. 68:5.

118. But sometimes delay was perceived to work the other way and pressure the White House. In the Pennsylvania situation involving Senator Hugh

Scott's hold, Sanders suggested to the president that the "present deadlock may soon result in criticism from the press and bar in Philadelphia, directed primarily at the Administration even though the deadlock is due to Senator Scott's insistence" (Memo, Sanders to president, 13 April 1967, Personal Papers of Sanders, "Judicial Vacancies, 1967," WHCF, LBJ Library).

119. Transcript, Interview, Dagmar Hamilton with Nicholas Katzenbach, 26 February 1977, p. 26, LBJ School of Public Affairs project.

120. Memo, Macy to president, 11 October 1965, Ex FG 530/49/A, WHCF, LBJ Library. The agreement apparently arose after the David Rabinovitz nomination when the senators both agreed to endorse James Doyle for that vacancy if former Governor John Reynolds would receive the next nomination to a Wisconsin district court.

121. Leon Jaworski supports this point and notes that it held valid for Presidents Eisenhower and Kennedy as well: "I think that sometimes [the committee] irked them a little bit, but at the same time they also found it to be tremendously valuable, because it kept out those who certain senators wanted to push into judgeships who really were not competent. And it was a great buffer really, and a great protection to them; because they could say, 'Well, the American Bar Association has turned them down'" (transcript, Leon Jaworski Oral History Interview, 23 December 1968, p. 15, LBJ Library). This rating also served when a less competent candidate was urged by others. For example, the California congressional delegation was pushing one candidate; Irvine Sprague, congressional liaison for Johnson was able to tell them that the "problem is with the American Bar Association which informally says ____ is not qualified" (Memo, Sprague to Henry Wilson, 10 May 1967, Office Files of Irvine Sprague, Box 5 [1567], "Patronage, California," WHCF, LBJ Library).

122. See Joel B. Grossman, *Lawyers and Judges* (New York: John Wiley & Sons, 1965); Harold W. Chase, *Federal Judges* (Minneapolis: University of Minnesota Press, 1972); and Henry J. Abraham, *Justices and Presidents: A Political History of Appointments to the Supreme Court* (New York: Penguin books, 1975), especially pp. 22–31.

123. See Clark Oral History, 5 March 1977, tape 1, p. 9, and the comments of Jaworski in his Oral History, p. 17. Jaworski recalled that Vice President Johnson did not always agree with the committee or its member Jaworski in all ratings.

124. *ABA Reports,* 89 (1964): 483.

125. *New York Times,* 19 February 1964, p. 24:4.

126. This correspondence is found in Ex FG 500, September 15–October 7, 1964, WHCF, LBJ Library. An interesting sidelight is the 22 September letter from Jaworski to Jenskins urging, for political reasons largely, that the president reaffirm the ABA's role:

"This was done by both Pres. Eisenhower and President Kennedy and I am hopeful that the President concludes he can continue the practice. I am certain that the Republican nominee will voice his reaffirmation of this practice.

"If the President agrees to go along with the course heretofore followed, please see to it that a reply goes forward to Lewis Powell by not later than Oct. 2 or 3—There is a deadline of Oct. 5 for the publication of the next ABA news issue, *which is read by some 115,000 lawyers all over the country*—This will be the last issue before the November one which comes about the middle of that month."

127. Chase, *Federal Judges*, pp. 138–144.

128. Abraham, *Justices and Presidents*, p. 24.

129. Chase, *Federal Judges*, p. 174.

130. *ABA Reports* 91 (1966): 159.

131. Chase, *Federal Judges*, p. 144.

132. *ABA Reports* 91 (1966): 159.

133. Ibid., p. 177.

134. Letter, Samuel Rosenstein to Temple, 5 May 1968, filed Warren M. Christopher Name File, WHCF, LBJ Library.

135. Abraham, *Justices and Presidents*, p. 25.

136. Letter, Jenner to president, 14 February 1967, Ex FG 500, LBJ Library.

137. Letter, Clark to Jenner, 27 February 1967, Ex FG 500, WHCF, LBJ Library.

138. Memo, Clark to president, 5 March 1968, "Department of Justice–General," Box 1 (1982) Office Files of Larry Temple, WHCF, LBJ Library, which quotes Jenner's report to ABA House of Delegates.

139. See Temple Oral History, tape 5, and memo, Temple to president, 22 May 1968, Ex FG 530/ST 5/A, WHCF, LBJ Library: "I have Jenner's 87-page report on Poole in my office. In that report, Jenner told his committee that he personally found all of the objections to Poole unfounded."

140. Memo, Sanders to president, 17 April 1967, Personal Papers of H. Barefoot Sanders, "Judicial Vacancies, 1967," WHCF, LBJ Library. Sanders writes: "California Central—ECF [Ernest C. Friesen] to discuss with Jenner," and "Florida Northern—ECF to discuss with Jenner."

141. See, for example, memo, Watson to Alex Dickie, 24 June 1967; memo, John Gonella to Jones, 3 May 1968, Ex FG 500, WHCF, LBJ Library; and memo, Sanders to Temple, 11 July 1968, Ex FG 500/3, WHCF, LBJ Library.

142. See memo, Sprague to Watson, 27 November 1967, Ex FG 530/ST 5/A, WHCF, LBJ Library, regarding California delegation approval of district court nominees; see also memo, Sprague, undated (approximately January 1968), entitled "Appointments requested by California Congressional Delegation," Office Files of Irvine Sprague, Box 5 (1567), "Patronage, California," WHCF, LBJ Library.

143. Memo, Henry Wilson to president, 29 September 1966, filed Ramsey Clark Name File, WHCF, LBJ Library.

144. Memo, Watson to president, 20 July 1965, Ex FG 535, WHCF, LBJ Library.

145. Letter, Representatives Rivers, Dorn, et al., to president, 19 March 1966, Ex FG 505, WHCF, LBJ Library.

146. Several judges wrote endorsements of Fortas and Thornberry, in File Pertaining to Abe Fortas and Homer Thornberry, Box 2, "Chronological File: 1 July 1968–6 July 1968," LBJ Library; see also memo, Clark to Watson, 23 June 1966, Ex FG 505/5/A, WHCF, LBJ Library; and letter, Judge Walter Ely to president, 17 June 1968, Ex FG 505/9, WHCF, LBJ Library; and letter, Sarah T. Hughes to president, 11 August 1964, Gen FG 530/5543, WHCF, LBJ Library.

147. Johnson wrote, "Send to Bill Douglas and Abe Fortas for further guidance" on memo, Watson to president, 24 March 1966, filed Abe Fortas Name File, WHCF, LBJ Library.

148. Transcript, Earl Warren Oral History Interview, 21 September 1971, p. 31, LBJ Library. But note that Johnson continued, "What do you think about Abe Fortas?" And Warren replied, "I think Abe would be a good Chief Justice."

149. Memo, Fortas to president, 20 July 1967, Ex FG 505/9, WHCF, LBJ Library; letter, Tom C. Clark to Jenkins, 11 March 1964, Ex FG 505/9, LBJ Library; letters, Douglas to president, 15 September 1967, Ex FG 505/9, 2 February 1968, Ex FG 500, 26 March 1964, Ex FG 505/2, WHCF, LBJ Library; and letter, Hugo Black to president, 10 June 1968, Ex FG 505/9, WHCF, LBJ Library.

150. Letter, Fortas to president, 29 July 1965, "Fortas, Abe (1964–1967)," in Files Pertaining to Abe Fortas and Homer Thornberry, Box 1, LBJ Library.

151. Memo, "VM" to president, 7 October 1965, "Abe Fortas" in Files Pertaining to Abe Fortas and Homer Thornberry, Box 1, LBJ Library. The following references are also from that box, unless noted.

152. See letter, Fortas to president, 12 March 1968, which advocated escalation of the war into North Vietnam, and memo, Robert Kennedy to president, 30 November 1965, which concerned Kennedy's complaints.

153. Memo, Fortas to president, October 15, 1965, WHCF, LBJ Library.

154. Letter, Fortas to Valenti, 23 February 1966 (Valenti forwarded the recommendation to Ramsey Clark); and letter, Fortas to president, 30 March 1966, which forwarded Justice Douglas' recommendation and discussed the Maurine B. Neuberger and Wayne L. Morse feud. Johnson asked Fortas to recheck the situation and give further guidance on the Allan Hart candidacy in correspondence 2–30 March 1966, filed Abe Fortas Name File, WHCF, LBJ Library.

155. Memo, Fortas to Watson, 23 January 1967, which notes a 9–5 record and a 29–3 record as civil rights attorney. In a note two years before, Fortas informed Johnson that Solicitor General Marshall had done "a splendid job" in arguing a labor case, which Johnson passed along to Marshall (Letter, Fortas to president, 20 October 1965, filed in "Fortas, Abe [1964–1967]," WHCF, LBJ Library).

156. Memo, Temple to president, 8 April 1968, Ex FG 530/FG 216/A, WHCF, LBJ Library.

157. Letter, Douglas to president, 18 June 1968, filed Warren M. Christopher Name File, WHCF, LBJ Library.

158. Memo, Christopher to Temple, 26 November 1968, Ex FG 11/8, WHCF, LBJ Library.

159. Letter, David L. Lawrence, DNC from Pennsylvania, to president, 19 August 1966, Ex FG 505/3, LBJ Library; memo, Watson to president, 10 September 1966, Ex FG 530/ST 16, WHCF, LBJ Library, noting resolution of State of Kansas Democratic Executive Committee. See memo, "Carol" to Jim Jones, 2 August 1968, in Larry Temple Aides File Box 1 (1852), "Judgeships," WHCF, LBJ Library: "J. R. Miller, Chairman of the Kentucky Democratic State Central Executive Committee, called you concerning a Federal judgeship. He understands that ___ is being considered for Judgeship of the Sixth Circuit Court of Appeals, Chairman Miller feels if Mr. ___ got this post, it would be 'disasterous.'" See also letter, Louis Martin, deputy chairman of the DNC, to Watson, 18 August 1966, Ex FG 530/ST 35, WHCF, LBJ Library, concerning a judicial candidate; it is also interesting to note that at least two members of the DNC, Bert Combs and Frank Theis, were appointed to federal judgeships. See memo, John Criswell to Watson, 21 January 1967, Ex FG 505, WHCF, LBJ Library.

160. Letter, Adlai Stevenson to Moyers, 21 October 1964, Ex FG 530/ST 49, WHCF, LBJ Library; Letter, Ambassador William C. Doherty to president, 23 April 1964, Gen FG 505/FG 216, WHCF, LBJ Library; Letter, Governor Buford Ellington to president, 18 July 1968, Gen FG 505/6, WHCF, LBJ Library; memo, Watson to president, 17 January 1967, Ex FG 500, WHCF, LBJ Library (this memo concerns Governor John Connally of Texas and his willingness "to try to furnish names that would be acceptable for the judgeship"); memo, Jim Jones to president, 15 July 1968, Ex FG 500, WHCF, LBJ Library, which discusses meeting with Governor Harold Hughes of New Jersey. See also memo, Temple to president, 16 July 1968, Ex FG 500, LBJ Library, which notes Hughes supported certain candidates.

161. Letter, Watson to Mayor Richard L. Daley, 27 March 1968, Ex FG 500, WHCF, LBJ Library; memo, Temple to president, 16 July 1968, Ex FG 500, WHCF, LBJ Library, which notes candidates "supported by" Mayor Joseph Barr; memo, Temple to president, 1 August 1968, Ex FG 505/3/A, WHCF, LBJ Library. And see recommendation from Mayor Henry Maier of Milwaukee, in telegram, 12 July 1968, Gen FG 530/ST 49, WHCF, LBJ Library.

162. Letter, Orville L. Freeman, secretary of agriculture, to president, 27 May 1966, C.F. FG 505/8, WHCF, LBJ Library; letter, Postmaster General John Gronouski to president, 18 November 1964, Ex FG 530/ST 49, WHCF, LBJ Library, which supports David Rabinovitz and John Reynolds for Wisconsin District Court.

162. Letter, Dwight D. Eisenhower to president, 15 March 1966, and memo, Watson to president, 10 September 1966, both Ex FG 530/ST 16, WHCF, LBJ Library; letter, Harry S. Truman to president, 1 April 1965, Ex FG 535, WHCF, LBJ Library, in which Truman made a recommendation for the Supreme Court.

164. Memo, Vice President Hubert H. Humphrey to president, Ex FG 535, WHCF, LBJ Library, which passed on interest of California Supreme Court

Justice Stanley Mosk in a Supreme Court vacancy (Humphrey stated: "I am not presuming to urge Mosk's appointment)"; and memo, William Connell, Humphrey aide, to Watson, 14 June 1967, Ex FG 500, WHCF, LBJ Library, which states, "As you know, the Vice President tries hard to stay out of Judicial appointment matters other than those that relate directly to Minnesota. However . . . " And Humphrey suggested in 1966 that Johnson appoint what would be "the first Negro to a southern Federal Judicial post. . . . This appointment would be in the Johnson tradition of important breakthroughs where opposition can be minimized" (letter, Humphrey to president, 9 May 1966, Ex FG 505/4, WHCF, LBJ Library). Although Johnson did not follow Humphrey's suggestion exactly, he did appoint Humphrey's nominee, Spottswood Robinson, to the District of Columbia Circuit judgeship. As senator, Humphrey's suggestions were not especially welcomed by the Justice Department; see memo, Katzenbach to O'Donnell, 23 January 1964, Ex FG 505/FG 216, WHCF, LBJ Library.

165. Letter, Peyton Anderson, publisher, to Tom Johnson, 13 March 1967, Ex FG 500, WHCF, LBJ Library; memo, Tom Johnson to president, 27 June 1968, Ex FG 500, WHCF, LBJ Library, which discussed conversation with editor of *Atlanta Constitution*; and letters, Charles A. Wright, University of Texas Law School professor, to Clark and Temple, 7 November 1967 and 20 June 1968, Gen FG 500, WHCF, LBJ Library.

166. Letter, president to Weisl, 15 March 1965, Ex FG 505/2, WHCF, LBJ Library, responding to a recommendation; memo, Watson to president, 12 May 1966, CF FG 500, WHCF, LBJ Library, which passes on Weisl's suggestion that the president meet with the ABA Committee on Federal Judiciary (which Johnson did); letter, James Rowe to president, 1 April 1966, Ex FG 500, WHCF, LBJ Library; letter, president to Rowe, 7 April 1966, Ex FG 500, "The Judicial Branch 11/23/63–3/10/67," WHCF, LBJ Library; letter, Rowe to president, 16 February 1968, CF FG 530/FG 216, WHCF, LBJ Library; and see restricted letter, Jaworski to Valenti, "re prospective judge nominees in Texas," 27 April 1966, CF FG 500, WHCF, LBJ Library; and memo, Jim Jones to president, 24 June 1968, Ex PE 2, WHCF, LBJ Library, regarding Thomas Kuchel.

167. See the Abe Fortas Name File, WHCF, LBJ Library.

168. See memo, Macy to president, 10 August 1965, Ex FG 530/32/A, on which the president wrote, "What about Ed Weisl, Sr.??" Macy responded in another memo to president, 30 August 1965, that "He has been consulted and he approves." Only then did Johnson check "Approve" on the judicial nomination. See also memo, Clark to Watson, 10 October 1966; memo, Jenkins to president, 28 March 1964, Ex FG 530/32/A, WHCF, LBJ Library; and memo, Sanders to president, 13 April 1967, Personal Papers of H. Barefoot Sanders, Jr., "Judicial Vacancies, 1967," WHCF, LBJ Library, which reads "Pollack is recommended by Edwin L. Weisl, Sr., and is acceptable to Senator Robert F. Kennedy."

169. See Jaworski Oral History, 23 December 1968, p. 15.

170. Memo, "Sue" to Sanders, 27 January 1967, Personal Papers of H. Bare-

foot Sanders, Jr., "Judicial Vacancies, 1967," WHCF, LBJ Library, which reads "FBI is being ordered today for Milton Pollack."

171. Politicking by the candidates is usually a final element in the broth. Because rival candidacies with supporting coalitions usually spring up at each vacancy, a prospect can seldom wait passively for the call. Though a few eminent attorneys had only "to let it be known that I was available," most nominees participated actively, though usually discreetly, in campaigns to mobilize sponsors and support. These may include incumbents on the federal bench. One Southern judge put the matter bluntly: "I don't mean that I waited for people to pound on my door. People don't get judgeships without seeking them. Anybody who thinks judicial office seeks the man is mistaken. There's not a man on the court who didn't do what he thought needed to be done" (J. Woodford Howard, Jr., *Courts of Appeals in the Federal Judicial System: A Study of the Second, Fifth and District of Columbia Circuits* [Princeton, N.J.: Princeton University Press, 1981], pp. 100–101).

172. See memo, Watson to president, 28 March 1966, Ex FG 530/ST 43, WHCF, LBJ Library. See letter, James Moriarty to Manatos, 14 June 1967, Ex FG 530/ST 5, WHCF, LBJ Library; letter, Watson to Judge Andrew Hauk, 28 July 1967, Ex FG 505/9, WHCF, LBJ Library, and letter, Hauk to Watson, 3 July 1967, Ex FG 505/9, WHCF, LBJ Library (Judge Hauk seemed especially active in pushing his nomination and promotion). See also letter, John V. Singleton to Valenti, 8 June 1965, Gen FG 530/ST 43, WHCF, LBJ Library; letter and memo, Humphrey to president, 18 April 1967, Ex FG 535, WHCF, LBJ Library. One of the more interesting self-promotions was a letter sent by a candidate to many friends asking them to urge their senators to endorse him, attached to letter, Darrell Coover to Jake Jacobsen, April 1967, Gen FG 505/5, WHCF, LBJ Library.

173. See memo, Liz Carpenter to president, 23 March 1967, Ex FG 505/3, WHCF, LBJ Library; letter, Mrs. Walter Prescott Webb to president, 20 June 1965, Ex FG 530/ST 43, WHCF, LBJ Library; memo, Valenti to president, 14 July 1965, Ex FG 505, WHCF, LBJ Library; letter, William Holloway to Watson, 9 July 1968, Gen FG 505/10, WHCF, LBJ Library.

174. Letter, Dean Acheson to president, 28 June 1968, Ex FG 505/9, WHCF, LBJ Library, upon which Johnson wrote "Larry, prepare reply; warm one & prompt—L."

175. See the discussion of the Rabinovitz nomination; telegram, A. Phillip Randolph to president, 26 January 1966, Ex FG 530, ST 32/A, WHCF, LBJ Library; and memo, Ramsey Clark to Walter Reuther (approximately August 1968), Gen FG 505, WHCF, LBJ Library.

176. Letter, Drew Pearson to president, 18 November 1968, CF FG 535, WHCF, LBJ Library, in which he asked the president to request Arthur Goldberg's nomination as chief justice; memo, McPherson to president, 20 July 1965; and letter, Anthony Lewis to McPherson, 1 December 1965, both Box 3 (1408), Office Files of Harry C. McPherson, Jr., LBJ Library. In the memo, McPherson passed on Lewis' suggestion of Paul Freund or Burke Marshall to replace Goldberg on the court. (Johnson replied, "I don't think correspon-

dents ought to be advocates lest it interfere with their 1st amendment objectivity—L.") In the second, Lewis recommended Archibald Cox for an appointment.

177. Letters, Danny Thomas to president, 14 February 1967, and Jack Benny to president, 27 June 1967, both Ex FG 530/ST 5, WHCF, LBJ Library, recommending Judge Benjamin Landis.

178. Letter, Billy Graham to president, 21 June 1968, Ex FG 535/A, WHCF, LBJ Library. Graham wrote: "I just heard on the news that Chief Justice Warren has resigned. If this news report proves to be correct, it is my prayer that you will give serious consideration to balancing the Court with a strong conservative as Chief Justice. I am convinced that many of the problems that have plagued America in the last few years are a direct result of some of the extreme rulings of the Court, especially in the field of criminology. I believe that our mutual friend, Governor John Connally, would make an ideal and popular choice. He might not be popular with the extreme liberals and radicals who are already fighting you anyway but he would make a great Chief Justice." See also Letter, Stanley Marcus to president, 23 November 1966, Ex FG 500, WHCF, LBJ Library.

5. The Criteria of Choice

1. See Joel B. Grossman, *Lawyers and Judges* (New York: John Wiley and Sons, Inc. 1965), and Joseph C. Goulden, *The Benchwarmers*, (New York: Ballantine Books, 1974), especially pp. 40ff., for a critical analysis of the ABA Committee's standards and composition.

2. Transcript, John W. Macy, Jr., Oral History Interview, 26 April 1969, tape 3, pp. 14–17, LBJ Library, hereafter cited as Macy Oral History; John W. Macy, Jr., *Public Service: The Human Side of Government* (New York: Harper & Row, 1971), p. 227; Richard L. Schott and Dagmar S. Hamilton, *People, Positions, and Power: The Political Appointments of Lyndon Johnson* (Chicago: University of Chicago Press, 1983), pp. 4–8. The following discussion is taken from these sources.

3. These criteria are illustrated by a report Macy made to the cabinet discussing appointees. See Macy Oral History, pp. 11–13.

4. See memo, Warren M. Christopher to Larry E. Temple re David Stahl, 1 August 1965, Ex FG 505/3/A, WHCF, LBJ Library; letter, Myer Feldman to Bill D. Moyers, 13 October 1965, Ex FG 505/2/A, WHCF, LBJ Library.

5. Memo, Macy to president, 28 April 1965, Ex FG 530/49/A, WHCF, LBJ Library.

6. Harold W. Chase, *Federal Judges: The Appointing Process* (Minneapolis: University of Minnesota Press, 1972), p. 144.

7. Transcript, Larry E. Temple Oral History Interview, 12 June 1970, tape 2, p. 3, LBJ Library.

8. Unless otherwise noted, all of the tables in this chapter are derived from Sheldon Goldman's data in "Characteristics of Eisenhower and Kennedy Appointees to the Lower Federal Courts," *Western Political Quarterly*

18 (1965): 755–762; "Johnson and Nixon Appointees to the Lower Federal Courts," *Journal of Politics* 34 (1972): 935–951; "Judicial Backgrounds, Recruitment and the Party Variable: The Case of the Johnson and Nixon Appointees to the United States District and Appeals Courts," *Arizona State Law Journal* 1974: 211–222; "Carter's Judicial Appointments: A Lasting Legacy," *Judicature* 64 (1981): 344–355; and "Reaganizing the Judiciary: The First Term Appointments," *Judicature* 68 (1985): 313–329.

9. See memo, H. Barefoot Sanders, Jr., to president, 25 January 1968, Ex FG 530/ST 5/A, LBJ Library, concerning experience on San Diego Municipal Court and California Superior Court; and memo, Ramsey Clark to president, 11 April 1968, Ex FG 530/ST 32/A, WHCF, LBJ Library, stressing legislative experience and state legal experience.

10. See memo, Clark to president, 7 October 1965, Ex FG 505/2/A, LBJ Library, concerning experience on Pennsylvania's Court of Common Pleas; and memo, Nicholas Katzenbach to president, 9 June 1966, Ex FG 505/6/A, WHCF, LBJ Library, again concerning district judge promotion.

11. See, for instance, memo, Temple to president, 27 September 1968, Ex FG 530/ST 5/A, WHCF, LBJ Library, concerning U.S. attorneys and district judgeships.

12. Transcript, Ralph A. Dungan Oral History Interview, 18 April 1969, p. 19, LBJ Library.

13. Macy, *Public Service*, p. 87; and Macy Oral History, tape 3, pp. 15 and 12.

14. Memo, Temple to president, 3 April 1968, Ex FG 530/FG 216/A, WHCF, LBJ Library. Temple mentions that the president had raised a question previously about Patricia Roberts Harris for a judgeship but because of her lack of trial experience, the ABA would rate her low.

15. Memo, Christopher to Temple, 30 March 1968, Ex FG 530/FG 216/A, WHCF, LBJ Library. Christopher, who seemed to be the leading proponent of women for judgeships, noted the difficulties, real or perceived, of finding acceptable female nominees:

"Although there are thousands of women lawyers in the United States, it seems difficult to find outstanding women candidates for Federal judgeships. In four years the president has named only one woman to a life-time Federal judicial post—Constance Motley in New York—and an additional female appointment would be highly desirable at this time.

"While it is fairly clear that Mrs. [June L.] Green is the most highly regarded woman lawyer practicing in the District of Columbia with substantial trial experience, her qualifications do not compare with those of the very best men such as [Gerhard A.] Gesell. Her practice has been primarily in the Torts and Domestic Relations field and some have commented that she does not have "big time" legal experience. Few women have such experience, and if a female appointment is thought desirable, I think Mrs. Green's appointment would do credit to the President. Her character and temperament (the latter often a problem in female candidates) are unanimously praised."

16. Memo, Christopher to Temple, 9 July 1968, Ex FG 505/9/A, WHCF, LBJ Library.

17. Memo, Temple to president, 13 July 1968, Ex FG 505/9/A, WHCF, LBJ Library.

18. See the interesting letter to the president from India Edwards, 13 March 1967, Ex FG 500, WHCF, LBJ Library, which urges appointment of women judges.

19. Macy Oral History, tape 3, p. 14.

20. Memo, Clark to president, 5 March 1968, "Department of Justice–General," Temple Aides File, Box 1 (1852), LBJ Library.

21. Memo, Temple to president, 13 July 1968, Ex FG 505/9/A, WHCF, LBJ Library.

22. Macy Oral History, tape 3, pp. 14 and 12; and see draft press release, 11 June 1966, Ex FG 530/ST 5/A, WHCF, LBJ Library, which reads: "The group is relatively young. Four are in their forties and six are in their early fifties. None are over sixty."

23. Transcript, Adrian A. Spears Oral History Interview, 11 June 1971, p. 21, LBJ Library.

24. Memo, Douglass Cater to Juanita Roberts, 17 July 1967, Ex FG 530/ST 38/A, WHCF, LBJ Library. See also memos, Sanders to Marie Fehmer, 19 May 1967 and 7 June 1967, Sanders Personal Papers, "Memos," LBJ Library. Sanders reports on several informal sessions Johnson had with prospective nominees in which Johnson "urged them not to remain on the bench past retirement age but to take advantage of retirement eligibility and stand aside for younger people."

25. Letter, John D. Butzner to president, 5 July 1967, Ex FG 505/4/A, WHCF, LBJ Library.

26. Transcript, Ramsey Clark Oral History, 5 March 1977, tape 1, pp. 7–9, LBJ Library, hereafter cited as Clark Oral History.

27. Memo, Robert F. Kennedy to president, 10 March 1964, Ex FG 530/ST 49/A, WHCF, LBJ Library.

28. Memo, president to George E. Reedy, 21 September 1967, Ex FG 530/ST 22/A, WHCF, LBJ Library.

29. Memo, W. Marvin Watson to president, 25 July 1967, Ex FG 535/A, WHCF, LBJ Library.

30. *Chicago Daily Defender*, 1 July–7 July 1967, in Ex FG 535/A, WHCF, LBJ Library.

31. Transcript, Thurgood Marshall Oral History Interview, 10 July 1969, p. 10, LBJ Library.

32. Schott and Hamilton, *People, Positions, and Power*, p. 6, quoting Bill D. Moyers Interview. "I don't doubt for a moment that the New Deal, Franklin Roosevelt, populist side of Lyndon Johnson, which was set aside for those years he was in the Senate representing a broader constituency of a very conservative state, kept reasserting itself powerfully, sincerely, and effectively while he was in the White House."

33. Memo, Lee C. White to president, 24 August 1965, Ex FG 500, WHCF, LBJ Library, concerning appointment of Jim Watson to a "black" seat on the

Customs Court: "The Customs Court vacancy was created by the retirement of a Negro appointed by President Truman."

34. Clark Oral History, tape 3, p. 17.

35. An eighth black, Cecil Poole of California, was nominated to the district court in 1969 but was one of the nominees whose names were withdrawn by the Nixon administration. (See Chapter 7 for further discussion.)

36. Memo, date unknown (approximately February 1966) "Motley, Constance B., D-N.Y.," Macy Office Files, LBJ Library.

37. Memo, Watson to president, 27 April 1966, Ex FG 500, WHCF, LBJ Library. The president did not want to see them, writing "See at [Attorney] Gen—I'll see if necessary—L."

38. Letter, Joseph A. Califano, Jr., to Frank Annunzio, 12 March 1968, Ex FG 500, WHCF, LBJ Library. Letter, Annunzio to Califano, 3–5 March 1966, Ex PE 2, WHCF, LBJ Library, notes that only four Italians had been appointed to federal courts by Johnson as of 1967, and argues that "this is indeed a sad record." Jack J. Valenti, too, while in the administration and while out of government, was anxious for Italian-American nominees. See letter, Valenti to president, 26 June 1968, Temple Aides File, Box 1 (1852), "Federal Judgeships," WHCF, LBJ Library.

39. Memo, Peter W. Rodino, (D-N.J.) to Califano, 24 May 1967, Gen FG 535, WHCF, LBJ Library; memo, Clark to Sanders, 19 April 1967, Sanders Personal Papers, "Judicial Vacancies, 1967," LBJ Library.

40. Memo, Joseph F. Dolan to Mike N. Manatos, 4 May 1969, Ex FG 505/2, WHCF, LBJ Library.

41. Letter, Congressman John H. Dent (D-Pa.) to president, 16 January 1968, Ex FG 503/3, WHCF, LBJ Library.

42. Memo, Annunzio to Califano, 16 September 1966, Ex FG 530/13/A, WHCF, LBJ Library.

43. Memo, James Falcon to Manatos, 22 June 1967, Ex FG 530, ST 35/A, WHCF, LBJ Library.

44. Manuel L. Real was appointed to a district court in California; memo, Katzenbach to president, 3 September 1966, Ex FG 530/ST 5/A, WHCF, LBJ Library. Two other Hispanics were appointed to the district court in Puerto Rico.

45. J. Woodford Howard, *Courts of Appeals in the Federal Judicial System* (Princeton: Princeton University Press, 1981), p. 90.

46. Grossman, *Lawyers and Judges*, p. 33.

47. Schott and Hamilton, *People, Positions, and Power*, pp. 7–8.

48. Goldman, "Judicial Backgrounds," p. 218.

49. Macy Oral History, tape 3, p. 13.

50. Memo, Macy to president, 11 February 1966, Ex FG 505/3/A, WHCF, LBJ Library. Unfortunately for the GOP, no qualified Republicans were found in that instance (memos, Sanders to Watson, 11 and 12 July, 1967, Sanders Personal Papers, "Memos," LBJ Library).

51. Memo, Clark to Watson, 3 August 1965, Ex FG 505/3, WHCF, LBJ Library; letter, Democratic National Committee member David Lawrence to president, 19 August 1966, Ex FG 505/3, WHCF, LBJ Library.

52. Memo, Watson to president, 4 May 1967, and memo, president to Macy, 5 May 1967, Ex FG 530, ST 13/A, WHCF, LBJ Library.

53. Schott and Hamilton, *People, Positions, and Power*, pp. 6–7.

54. See, for instance, letter, Joe Hickey to president, undated, (approximately January 1966), Ex FG, 505/10, which reminds Johnson of Hickey's "solicitation of friends, etc.," and letter, Tom C. Clark to Walter W. Jenkins, 11 March 1964, Ex FG 505/9, enclosing 1960 "Johnson for President" advertisement signed by prospective nominee.

55. Memo, Watson to president, 12 September, Ex FG 530/ST 42, WHCF, LBJ Library.

56. Memo, Clark to president, 10 October 1966, Ex FG 530/ST 9/A, WHCF, LBJ Library.

57. Memo, Clark to Watson, 3 February 1967, Ex FG/135-10/ST 15/A, WHCF, LBJ Library.

58. Memo, Watson to president, 22 November 1967, Ex FG 530/ST 32/A, WHCF, LBJ Library. This memo also mentions that the candidate's supporters are also "supporting the President 100%."

59. Memo, Temple to president, 3 and 8 April 1968, Ex FG 530/FG 216/A, WHCF, LBJ Library.

60. See memo, Watson to president, 13 October 1966, Ex FG 530/ST 32, WHCF, LBJ Library, discussing Robert Kennedy candidate whom Johnson vetoed, and letter, Eugene Gillmore to president, with attachments of newspaper story on feud, 19 March 1968, Ex FG 530/ST 32, WHCF, LBJ Library. And see memo, Temple to president, 19 April 1968, Ex FG 505/8/A, WHCF, LBJ Library, which notes that Johnson wanted to call personally a nominee from New York to inform him that his name had been submitted to the Senate rather than allowing Senator Kennedy to inform the nominee and get the political appreciation. Regarding the loyalty of a candidate's endorsers, note, for instance, that Senator Hugh Scott (R-Pa.) got his nomination approved, possibly because of his support of the president "on Viet Nam (as opposed to Clark's harassment)" (memo, Manatos to Watson, 17 April 1967, Ex FG 500, WHCF, LBJ Library). Note also that George M. McGovern's (D-S.D.) candidate did not receive a nomination, possibly because McGovern supported Kennedy (memo, Christopher to Temple, 13 March 1968, Ex FG 505/8, WHCF, LBJ Library; and see memo, Temple to president, 25 April 1968, Temple Aides File, Box 1 [1852], "Judgeships," WHCF, LBJ Library).

61. As Macy commented, in the early years the standard of "loyalty" was "relatively easy to meet, but as the dissensions brought on by the Vietnam war increased, the standard reduced the available field" (Macy, *Public Service*, p. 227). See also Schott and Hamilton, *People, Positions, and Power*, p. 7: "By late 1966 or early 1967 the question of loyalty to the president on the Vietnam War loomed large in Johnson's consideration of prospective appointees."

62. Transcript, Harry C. McPherson Oral History Interview, undated, tape 9, p. 4, LBJ Library, hereafter cited as McPherson Oral History.

63. Robert A. Carp and Claude K. Rowland, "The Effects of Appointing President on Judicial Policy Decisions: A Comparison of Nixon, Johnson,

Kennedy, and Eisenhower Federal District Judge Appointees" (unpublished manuscript, 1982).

64. See memo, Temple to president, 23 March 1968, Ex FG 530/24/A, WHCF, LBJ Library, which notes that "[William C.] Keady has a long record as a Lyndon Johnson man and that he is still a strong supporter of the President." And after Johnson pulled out of the campaign for nomination, he still directed that Watson make sure that the endorsers of a candidate "will follow us at convention"; memo, Temple to president, 10 May 1968, Ex FG 530/ST 8, WHCF, LBJ Library; see also memo, Temple to president, 27 September 1968, Ex FG 530/ST 5/A, WHCF, LBJ Library, which notes loyalty criterion even this late.

65. See memo, Tom Johnson to Marvin Watson, 24 March 1967, Ex FG 500, WHCF, LBJ Library.

66. Clark Interview, LBJ School of Public Affairs project, p. 34.

67. Letter, White to Aaron Henry, 18 May 1965, Gen FG 505, WHCF, LBJ Library.

68. Memo, Watson to president, 23 June 1966, Ex FG 500, WHCF, LBJ Library.

69. See the series of reports on the civil rights position of various candidates from the South in Ex FG 530/ST 9/A, Ex FG 530/ST 10/A, and Ex FG 530/ST 18/A, WHCF, LBJ Library.

70. Memo from president, 14 August 1966, Ex FG 505/5/A, WHCF, LBJ Library.

71. Memo, Sanders to Ernest C. Friesen, 7 March 1967, Sanders Personal Papers, "Judicial Vacancies, 1967," LBJ Library.

72. Memo, Clark to president, 3 February 1966, and memo, Macy to the president, 8 February 1966, Ex FG 530/ST 18/A, WHCF, LBJ Library.

73. Memo, Clark to president, 30 January 1967, Ex FG 530/ST 18/A, WHCF, LBJ Library; memo, Christopher to Temple, 22 March 1968, Ex FG 530/ST 24/A, WHCF, LBJ Library.

74. Memo, Sanders to president, 7 October 1967, Ex FG 505/5/A, WHCF, LBJ Library.

75. Memo, ? to Watson, 23 June 1966, Ex FG 505/5/A, WHCF, LBJ Library, which reports Judge John M. Wisdom's view that Judge Robert A. Ainsworth is "completely trustworthy on civil rights. He says he has never seen any weakness in Ainsworth on civil rights."

76. Memo, Sanders to president, 3 June 1967, Ex FG 505/4, WHCF, LBJ Library; memo, Sanders to Marie Fehmer, 19 May 1967, in Sanders Personal Papers, "Memos," LBJ Library.

77. S. Sidney Ulmer, "Social Background as an Indicator to the Votes of Supreme Court Justices in Criminal Cases: 1947–1956 Terms," *American Journal of Political Science* 17 (1973): 622–630; Richard E. Johnston, "Supreme Court Voting Behavior: A Comparison of the Warren and Burger Courts," in *Cases in American Politics*, ed. Robert L. Peabody (New York: Praeger, 1976); Sheldon Goldman, "Voting Behavior on the United States Courts of Appeals Revisited," *American Political Science Review* 69 (1975):

491–506; Robert A. Carp and Claude K. Rowland, "A Longitudinal Study of Party Effects on Federal District Court Policy Propensities," *American Journal of Political Science* 24 (1980): 291–305; C. Neal Tate, "Personal Attribute Models of the Voting Behavior of U.S. Supreme Court Justices: Liberalism in Civil Liberties and Economic Decisions, 1946–1978," *American Political Science Review* 75 (June 1981): 355. This article contains a good review of previous research on background characteristics and voting behavior and points out that personal attributes may be closely linked to both attitudes and votes.

78. Rowland and Carp, "The Effects of Appointing President on Judicial Policy Decisions," p. 22. They conclude that "the linkage between presidential appointment and judicial policy making is an important extension of presidential policy propensities and an important determinant of judicial outcomes." See also their "Presidential Effects on Federal District Court Policy Decisions: Economic Liberalism, 1960–1977" (unpublished manuscript, 1981), and *Policymaking and Politics in the Federal District Courts* (Knoxville: University of Tennessee Press, 1983).

79. Tate, "Personal Attribute Models," pp. 362, 363.

80. Ibid., p. 362.

81. Ibid., p. 357. The calculations in the following section were performed using the Tate data.

82. Laurence H. Tribe, *God Save This Honorable Court: How the Choice of Supreme Court Justices Shapes Our History* (New York: Random House, 1985), pp. 50–76. See also Robert C. Scigliano, *The Supreme Court and the Presidency* (New York: Free Press, 1971).

83. Fred P. Graham, "The Fortas Liberalism," *New York Times*, 22 June 1966.

84. Claude K. Rowland and Robert A. Carp, "The Influence of Background Characteristics on the Voting Behavior of Federal District Judges" (paper presented at the annual meeting of the American Political Science Association, New York, 1978), p. 27.

85. Rowland and Carp, "Effects of Appointing President," p. 13. The table is from that work. But note that although the Johnson cohort is more liberal, it is not "pro-defendant" entirely. This perhaps reflects the Johnson selection process emphasis on nominees with moderate or conservative views on criminal justice.

86. Rowland and Carp, "Presidential Effects," p. 5. The following table is from this study.

87. Schott and Hamilton, *People, Positions, and Power*, p. 8.

88. McPherson Oral History, tape 1, p. 18.

89. Lyndon B. Johnson, *The Vantage Point* (New York: Holt, Rinehart & Winston, 1971), p. 545.

6. Case Studies in Judicial Apointment

1. Much of the discussion on Judge McNichols' appointment is drawn from a personal conversation with him, 24 November 1981, Moscow, Idaho, hereafter cited as McNichols Interview.

2. Memo, Nicholas Katzenbach to Kenneth O'Donnell, 27 December 1963, filed Ex FG 505/FG 216, WHCF, LBJ Library.

3. "McNichols, Ray (D-Idaho)," Office Files of John Macy, LBJ Library.

4. Telegram, president to McNichols, 15 April 1964, Ex FG 530/12/A, WHCF, LBJ Library.

5. McNichols Interview.

6. All of the references to memos (unless noted) and most of the background information in this section come from "Motley, Constance B., D-N.Y.," Box 411, Office Files of John Macy, LBJ Library.

7. Memo, John B. Clinton to Macy, 12 October 1965, in Macy Files.

8. Memo, Macy to president, 17 January 1966, Ex FG 530/ST 32/A, WHCF, LBJ Library.

9. Black leaders, including A. Phillip Randolph, warmly approved. See telegram, Randolph to president, 26 January 1966, Ex FG 530/ST 32/A. Johnson directed his aide Jack Valenti to "write him a real nice letter." The appointment also received some letters of criticism based on racial and ideological criticisms, which Macy's office answered. See Macy Files, September 1966.

10. Memo, Ramsey Clark and H. Barefoot Sanders, Jr., to president, 15 May 1967, Ex FG 505/4/A, WHCF, LBJ Library.

11. *New York Times*, 5 April 1966, p. 18:2; 25 August 1966, p. 28:2; and 31 August 1966, p. 33:1.

12. Memo, Sanders to W. Marvin Watson, Jr., 26 June 1967, Ex FG 500, WHCF, LBJ Library.

13. Letter, John Butzner to president, 5 July 1967, Ex FG 505/4/A, WHCF, LBJ Library.

14. Donald D. Jackson, *Judges* (New York: Atheneum Publishers, 1974), p. 265.

15. Letter, James Rowe to president, 1 April 1966, Ex FG 500, "Judicial Branch, 11/23/63–3/16/67," WHCF, LBJ Library.

16. Memo, Mike N. Manatos to Clark, 28 July 1966; memo, Henry Wilson to Watson, 21 January 1967 (copy sent to Clark); and letter, William Spong to Wilson, 2 September 1966, all in Ex FG 500, "Judicial Branch, 11/23/63–3/16/67," WHCF, LBJ Library.

17. Memo, Sanders to Clark, 21 March 1967, filed in Personal Papers of H. Barefoot Sanders, "Judicial Vacancies–1967," WHCF, LBJ Library. Unless noted, all of the documents cited in the remainder of this section are from that file.

18. Memo, Sanders to Clark, 23 March 1967.

19. Memo, Sanders to Ernest Friesen, 23 March 1967.

20. Memo, Sanders to Clark, 3 April 1967.

21. Memo, Sanders to president, undated (approximately 8 April 1967); memo, Sanders to president, 8 April 1967.

22. Memo, Clark to president, 16 May 1967.

23. Memo, Sanders to Clark, 9 May 1967.

24. Concerning Jones and civil rights, see memo, Sanders to president, 3 June 1967, Ex FG 505/4, WHCF, LBJ Library. For other quotes see memo, Sanders for the record, 7 June 1967, filed Personal Papers of Sanders, "Memos," WHCF, LBJ Library.

25. Memo, Sanders to Watson, 26 June 1967.

26. Memo, Sanders to George E. Christian, 26 June 1967.

27. Memos, Sanders to Watson, 11 July 1967 and 12 July 1967.

28. Memo, Sanders to Clark, 29 June 1967, and memos, Sanders to president, 21 August 1967 and 27 August 1967. Sanders' headaches were not quite over even yet. Congressman Porter Hardy (D-Va.) was concerned about the question of which district judge would have seniority and thus the choice of assignment in Norfolk and kept contacting Sanders to request that John MacKenzie's commission be signed first to give him seniority over Richard Kellam. MacKenzie's was not.

29. Transcript, Earl Warren Oral History Interview, p. 31, LBJ Library, hereafter cited as Warren Oral History.

30. Transcript, Warren M. Christopher Oral History Interview, 31 October 1965, p. 8, LBJ Library, hereafter cited as Christopher Oral History.

31. See the general discussion in Henry J. Abraham, *Justices and Presidents* (New York: Penguin Books, Inc., 1975), pp. 259ff., and the description of the first Fortas nomination and of the Fortas-Thornberry battle in Robert Shogan, *A Question of Judgment* (Indianapolis: Bobbs-Merrill Company, 1972). On general patterns, see Lawrence Baum, *The Supreme Court* (Washington, D.C.: Congressional Quarterly Press, 1984), ch. 2, and for anecdotal information on the Johnson nominations, see William O. Douglas, *The Court Years, 1939–1975* (New York: Random House, 1980); Merle Miller, *Lyndon: An Oral Biography* (New York: G. P. Putnam's Sons, 1980); and Jack Pollack, *Earl Warren* (Englewood Cliffs, N.J.: Prentice-Hall, Inc., 1979).

32. There are actually conflicting stories on the attitude of Arthur Goldberg. Justice William O. Douglas states that Goldberg "allegedly asked to be moved from the Court to the United Nations, though in later years he vehemently denied this and called LBJ and denounced him for spreading the contrary story" (Douglas, *The Court Years*, p. 251.) And Johnson in *The Vantage Point* (New York: Holt, Rinehart and Winston, 1971), p. 543, says that he had heard from Ambassador John Kenneth Galbraith and others that Goldberg "would step down from his position to take a job that would be more challenging to him," and when he asked Goldberg about these reports while flying to Adlai Stevenson's funeral, Goldberg told him "these reports had substance." Johnson further states that the next day Goldberg "called Jack Valenti and told him that the job he would accept was the U.N. ambassadorship . . ." Abraham reports from a private conversation with Goldberg that he stepped down only because he hoped he could negotiate a peace and that

he was also "influenced by a clearly implied understanding of an ultimate return to the Court" (Abraham, *Justices and Presidents*, p. 259).

33. Warren Oral History, p. 29.

34. Quoted in Shogan, *A Question of Judgment*, p. 108.

35. Letter, Goldberg to president, 26 July 1965, Ex FG 535/A, WHCF, LBJ Library. In a return letter accepting the resignation on 28 July 1965, Johnson replied; "As I have told you personally—and as I have said publicly to the Nation—I am grateful to you for your willingness to relinquish the position on the Court so that your country may have the benefit of your services in the continuing efforts for peace which we shall make at and through the United Nations."

36. Transcript, Paul A. Porter Oral History Interview, 2 October 1970, p. 29, LBJ Library, hereafter cited as Porter Oral History.

37. Johnson, *Vantage Point*, p. 544. The president implies that he did not start the consideration until after Goldberg discussed the U.N. ambassadorship with him and also says that he "conferred with many friends and advisers, including [Abe] Fortas, about a possible successor to Arthur Goldberg" and only after studying these lists did he conclude Fortas was the right choice. Yet he also reports that Fortas tried to decline soon after the day of the flight to Illinois.

38. Shogan, *A Question of Judgment*, p. 110.

39. Transcript, Abe Fortas Oral History Interview, 14 August 1969, p. 24, LBJ Library, hereafter cited as Fortas Oral History. The text of the letter (which Fortas did not keep) appears in ch. 4, n. 3.

40. Johnson, *The Vantage Point*, p. 545.

41. Shogan, *A Question of Judgment*, p. 111.

42. Ibid., p. 110.

43. Letter, Douglas to president, 21 July 1965, Ex FG 535/A, WHCF, LBJ Library. Apparently it had some effect; Johnson wrote to thank Douglas and said "Your note helped so much. I showed it to Abe yesterday, and I believe that it helped him to make the decision we wanted him to make" (letter, president to Douglas, 28 July 1965, Ex FG 535/A, WHCF, LBJ Library).

44. Douglas, *The Court Years*, p. 318.

45. Memo, Watson to president, 20 July 1965, Ex FG 535, WHCF, LBJ Library, and *New York Times*, 16 July 1965, p. 1:6.

46. Porter Oral History, p. 30.

47. Fortas Oral History, p. 25. Justice Douglas reports the story this way: "Sometime later I heard over the radio a flash announcement that Abe was appointed. I got in my jeep and raced from Goose Prairie, Washington, our residence, to Yakima to reach a phone. En route I was flagged down by the Forest Service, through whom Lyndon had sent a message. When I got Lyndon on the phone he told me what had happened. At 11:55 they finished and at 11:59 they walked to the door that opened on a press conference. Lyndon asked Abe to be present while he read the Vietnam statement, and Abe agreed.

"With his hand on the doorknob, Lyndon turned to Abe and said, 'Before announcing this statement, I am going to announce your appointment to the Court.'

"Abe was taken aback, saying they had been over that many times and his answer was still in the negative.

"Turning full face to Abe, Lyndon said, 'This Vietnam statement that you approved says fifty thousand more boys are going to Vietnam—perhaps to die. No one is ever going to shoot at you on the Court. Tell me, how can I send them to battle and not send you to the Court?'

"Abe was silent a second and finally said, 'Okay, you win.'

"When Lyndon told me the story over the phone, I said, 'You bagged a good Justice, Mr. President.'" (Douglas, *The Court Years*, p. 318).

48. Johnson, *The Vantage Point*, p. 545.

49. Those opposed to Fortas' appointment were Carl Curtis of Nebraska, Strom Thurmond of South Carolina, and John Williams of Delaware. See Abraham, *Justices and Presidents*, p. 263; *New York Times*, 12 August 1965, p. 13:4 and 5 October 1965, p. 6:3.

50. Transcript, Thurgood Marshall Oral History Interview, p. 10, LBJ Library, hereafter cited as Marshall Oral History.

51. Memo, Hubert H. Humphrey to president, 18 April 1967, Ex FG LBJ Library.

52. Letter, Cliff Carter to president, 19 April 1967, 535, WHCF, LBJ Library.

53. Letter, Manatos to Harry Byrd, 27 April 1967; letter, Rowe to president, 18 May 1967, Ex FG 535, WHCF, LBJ Library. (Rowe recommended Paul Freund.)

54. Letter, Senator Everett M. Dirksen (R-Ill.) to Watson, 24 May 1967, Ex FG 535, WHCF, LBJ Library.

55. See the *New York Times* reports of 16 July 1965, p. 1:6, which reported that Johnson had considered Marshall for the Goldberg vacancy, and of 30 July 1965, p. 29:7, which reports Johnson's comments at the Fortas announcement that he had considered naming a woman to the Court and will do so when one is the best person available.

56. Abraham, *Justices and Presidents*, p. 267.

57. Marshall Oral History, p. 14.

58. Ibid.

59. The discussion of the Marshall announcement and confirmation is taken from Abraham, *Justices and Presidents*, p. 267, and *New York Times*, 14 June 1967, p. 1:7, 14 July 1967, p. 12:2, 4 August 1967, p. 60:1, and 31 August, p. 1:2.

60. Letters and telegrams to president, 13–19 June 1967, Ex FG 535/A, WHCF, LBJ Library. Chief Justice Warren wrote expressing his confidence in Marshall.

61. Abraham, *Justices and Presidents*, p. 268.

62. See letters, Mrs. Thurgood Marshall to president, 4 October 1967, Ex FG 535/A, WHCF, LBJ Library; and Clarence Mitchell to president, 5 October 1967, Gen FG 535/A, WHCF, LBJ Library, in which he thanked the

president for coming in "unobtrusively to witness the oath taking by a new Associate Justice of African descent."

63. Memo, James Jones to president, 11 June 1968, Ex FG 535, WHCF, LBJ Library.

64. Memo for the record by Jones, 13 June 1968, Ex FG 535/A, WHCF, LBJ Library.

65. Letter, Warren to president, 13 June 1968, Ex FG 535/A, WHCF, LBJ Library. He was seventy-seven.

66. See Christopher Oral History, pp. 9–11, LBJ Library.

67. Quoted in Shogan, *A Question of Judgment*, p. 148.

68. Memo for the record by Macy, 6 September 1968, Ex FG 535/A, WHCF, LBJ Library.

69. Christopher Oral History, p. 9.

70. See transcript, Clark Clifford Oral History Interview, 7 August 1969, tape 4, p. 6, LBJ Library, hereafter cited as Clifford Oral History; as well as transcript, Larry Temple Oral History Interview, hereafter cited as Temple Oral History; transcript, H. Barefoot Sanders, Jr., Oral History Interview, LBJ Library, hereafter cited as Sanders Oral History; and Johnson, *The Vantage Point*, p. 545. Johnson reports that Clifford suggested appointing as associate justice a Republican from the Middle West to avoid charges of favoritism and that Ed Weisl informed him that Senator Richard Russell of Georgia was lukewarm about Fortas but would "enthusiastically support" Homer Thornberry. Johnson notes, "I thought that Russell's stand would provide strong insurance against a Southern filibuster opposing Justice Fortas."

71. Letter, Albert E. Jenner, Jr. to Clark, 26 June 1968, Ex FG 500, WHCF, LBJ Library.

72. Temple Oral History, tape 6, p. 4.

73. The New York *Daily News* headlined on June 22, p. 1: "Earl Warren to Quit Court. LBJ Faces Row on Successor" (quoted in Pollack, *Earl Warren*, p. 276).

74. Press conference No. 128, 26 June 1968, Files Pertaining to Abe Fortas and Homer Thornberry, "Chronological File 6/13/68–," WHCF, LBJ Library.

75. Fortas Oral History, p. 33.

76. Thornberry Oral History, pp. 38–39.

77. See Shogan, *A Question of Judgment*, p. 150, and memo, Manatos to president, 25 June 1968, Ex FG 535/A, WHCF, LBJ Library.

78. Memo, William J. Hopkins to Jim Gaither, 24 June 1968, and memo, Clark to Jim Gaither, 24 June 1968, Ex FG 535, LBJ Library. A few weeks later, after charges of cronyism had been raised, Warren Christopher sent a memo dealing with the many other close relationships between appointing presidents and Supreme Court justices in the past. He included excerpts from Walter F. Murphy's *Elements of Judicial Strategy* (Chicago: University of Chicago Press, 1964), and repeated a conversation with Professor Charles Fairman, who had asked "Who better for a nominee to have as his friend than the President? Would Senator Griffin prefer that the nominee be a friend of a friend of the President? Or perhaps a friend of a tycoon? Or of a

big contributor? Or of a shady lobbyist?" (memo from Christopher [to president], 12 July 1968, Ex FG 535, WHCF, LBJ Library). And see memo, Gaither to Joseph A. Califano, Jr., 24 June 1968, filed Files Pertaining to Abe Fortas and Homer Thornberry, "Chronological File 6/13/68–6/25/68," WHCF, LBJ Library.

79. Memo, Sanders to president, 28 June 1968, Files Pertaining to Fortas and Thornberry, "Chronological File 6/26/68–6/30/68," WHCF, LBJ Library.

80. Telegram, Manatos to president, 29 June 1968, Ex FG 535/A, WHCF, LBJ Library. Nevertheless, the president was astute enough to worry about the firmness of the notes and the tactic of delay. See Temple Oral History, tape 5, p. 41.

81. Memo, Harry C. McPherson, Jr., to president, 28 June 1969, Files Pertaining to Fortas and Thornberry, "Chronological File 6/26/68–6/30/68," WHCF, LBJ Library.

82. Memo, Temple to president, 13 July 1968, Files Pertaining to Fortas and Thornberry, "Chronological File 7/7/68–7/13/68," WHCF, LBJ Library.

83. Memo, Manatos to president, 25 June 1968, Files Pertaining to Fortas and Thornberry, "Chronological File, 6/13/68–6/26/68," WHCF, LBJ Library.

84. Memo, Manatos to president, 26 June 1968, Files Pertaining to Fortas and Thornberry, "Chronological File 6/13/68–6/26/68," WHCF, LBJ Library.

85. Memo, Manatos to president, 2 July 1968, Files Pertaining to Fortas and Thornberry, "Chronological File 7/1/68–7/6/68," WHCF, LBJ Library.

86. Transcript, Mike N. Manatos Oral History Interview, p. 23, hereafter cited as Manatos Oral History. He notes that the package of both Fortas and Thornberry may have hurt the Fortas confirmation: "I recall talking to one senator who said that 'Mike, I can go along on Abe Fortas. . . . But I served with Thornberry over in the House, and he just isn't qualified to be a member of the Supreme Court'" (p. 39). Clifford suggested this problem might arise also, but Johnson "was very fond of Homer Thornberry" (Clifford Oral History, p. 29).

87. For more on this, see Shogan, *A Question of Judgment.*

88. Fortas appeared before the Senate Judiciary Committee (the first chief justice nominee to do so) and "became the target of fifteen years of conservative fury against Warren Court decisions" (Pollack, *Earl Warren*, p. 280). Thurmond's contribution to the debate included "Mallory! Mallory! I want that name to ring in your ears." (The *Mallory* case was decided in 1957; Fortas went on the bench in 1965.) Pollack also reports that anti-Semitism was a factor in Fortas' defeat: One senator "was overheard to exalt after a hearing: 'I think we've got that Jew-boy son of a bitch in a box now'" (ibid., p. 281). McPherson also makes that claim: "There was no question there was a lot of anti-Semitism in the whole struggle. One Southern Senator . . . said to another Southern Senator, 'You're not going to vote for that Jew to be Chief Justice, are you?'" He sums up the most significant causes for the Fortas defeat: "There was a lot of anti-Semitism as well as a lot of anti-Court. And primarily it was political on the part of the Republicans to save the nomination for Nixon" (McPherson Oral History, tape 4, p. 38).

89. This outcome was forecast by James Eastland before Fortas was even nominated. Manatos, on 25 June, reported to Johnson that Eastland "informed me that Abe Fortas cannot be confirmed as Chief Justice. . . . Eastland indicates also there will be a filibuster against Abe Fortas should his name be submitted to the Senate" (memo, Manatos to president, 25 June 1968, in Files Pertaining to Fortas and Thornberry, "Chronological File 6/13/68–6/25/68," WHCF, LBJ Library).

Some seven months after Fortas withdrew his name and some four months after Johnson left the White House, another and more serious storm arose concerning Justice Fortas' financial dealings. In May 1969, *Life* magazine (aided, some claim, by leaks from the White House) reported that while on the High Court, Fortas had accepted a large fee from the Louis Wolfson Foundation. Wolfson, a wealthy industrialist and philanthropist, was later imprisoned for selling unregistered stocks. Fortas had returned the $20,000 fee, but there were reports that the IRS was investigating whether taxes had been paid on the income and other reports that the Fortas–Wolfson Foundation contract called for the foundation to provide Fortas with $40,000 a year for as long as he or his wife should live. In the midst of these charges and the resulting public criticism and talk of impeachment, Attorney General John Mitchell visited Chief Justice Warren to divulge more damaging information on Fortas. When this visit leaked out, pressure mounted further. On 15 May 1969, Fortas announced his resignation from the Supreme Court. He insisted that he was guilty of no wrongdoing but was leaving because of his concern for the welfare of the Court. By resigning, he became the first justice to leave the Court under pressure of public criticism. Much of this section was taken from Shogan, *A Question of Judgment.*

90. Warren Oral History, p. 33. For a discussion of the confirmation battle, see Shogan, *A Question of Judgment,* and references therein. It should be pointed out that Warren served for another year until President Nixon appointed Warren Burger.

91. Manatos Oral History, p. 40.

92. Memo, Mary Rather to president, 2 October 1968, Ex FG 535, WHCF, LBJ Library, appending Tommy Corcoran's letter about Rowe.

93. Letter, Willard Deason to president, 3 October 1968, Ex FG 535, WHCF, LBJ Library.

94. Memo, Charles Murphy to president, 3 October 1968, and letter, Ernest Gruening to president, 2 October 1968, Ex FG 535, WHCF, LBJ Library. The son of former Chief Justice Harlan F. Stone suggested the president elevate Justice Hugo Black (letter, Marshall H. Stone to president, 3 October 1968, Ex FG 535, WHCF, LBJ Library).

95. Memo, Murphy to president, 3 October 1968, Ex FG 535, WHCF, LBJ Library.

96. Memo, DeVier Pierson to president, 3 October 1968, Ex FG 535, WHCF, LBJ Library.

97. Memo, Pierson to president, 5 October 1968, Ex FG 535, WHCF, LBJ Library.

98. Letter, Drew Pearson to president, 18 November 1968, CF FG 535, WHCF, LBJ Library.

99. Memo, Sanders to president, 9 December 1968, Ex FG 535, WHCF, LBJ Library.

100. Warren Oral History, p. 33.

101. Ibid.

7. The Last Year and the Transition

1. Richard Harris, *Justice: The Crisis of Law, Order, and Freedom in America* (New York: E. P. Dutton & Company, Inc., 1970), p. 86.

2. Memo, Ramsey Clark to president, 21 May 1968, Ex FG 500, WHCF, LBJ Library.

3. Memo, Clark to president, 13 May 1968, Ex FG 530/ST 10, WHCF, LBJ Library.

4. Letter, Richard B. Russell to president, 1 July 1968, "Russell Letter," filed Larry Temple Aides File, LBJ Library, and memo, Temple to president, 3 May 1968, Ex FG 530/ST 10, WHCF, LBJ Library. Temple states, "Senator Russell has previously indicated great interest in this appointment to the Department of Justice." The transcript of the Larry Temple Oral History Interview, 11 August 1970, tape 5, p. 14 and following, LBJ Library, hereafter cited as Temple Oral History, contains a great deal about the Alexander Lawrence episode.

5. That speech had been inserted into the *Congressional Record*, 2 February, 1959, p. S1539, by none other than Senator Russell.

6. Memo, Tom Johnson to James Jones, 7 May 1968, Ex FG 530/ST 10, WHCF, LBJ Library.

7. Memo, Jones to Juanita Roberts, 2 July 1968, Ex FG 530, WHCF, LBJ Library.

8. Memo, Clark to president, 13 May 1968, Ex FG 530/ST 10, WHCF, LBJ Library.

9. Memo, Temple to president, 20 May 1968, filed Abe Fortas Name File, "Fortas, Abe, May 1968," WHCF, LBJ Library.

10. Memo, Jones to president, 24 June 1968, filed Abe Fortas Name File, "Fortas, Abe, May, 1968," WHCF, LBJ Library.

11. See Temple Oral History. Johnson pushed forward even against the advice of Leon Jaworski. Memo, Temple to president, 15 May 1968, "Department of Justice–General," filed Temple Aides File, LBJ Library.

12. Ibid., and memos, Tom Johnson to president, 7 and 22 June 1968, Ex FG 530/ST 10, WHCF, LBJ Library.

13. Memo, president to Temple and H. Barefoot Sanders, Jr., 28 June 1968, "Russell Letter" filed Temple Aides File, LBJ Library.

14. Temple Oral History, tape 5, p. 29.

15. Letter, Russell to president, 1 July 1968, "Russell Letter," filed Temple Aides File, LBJ Library.

16. Reported in Robert Shogan, *A Question of Judgment* (Indianapolis: Bobbs-Merrill Co., 1972), p. 159.

17. Temple Oral History, tape 5, p. 33.

18. Johnson tried to contact Abe Fortas for his views on the draft, but the Justice was out of town. Memo, Harry C. McPherson to president, 2 July 1968 (7:40 p.m.), "Russell Letter," Temple Aides File (1852), LBJ Library. Perhaps Fortas was contacted later.

19. Letter, president to Russell, 3 July 1968, "Federal Judgeships," filed Temple Aides File, Box 1 (1852), LBJ Library. There are drafts of this letter located in a file devoted to the letter, entitled "Russell Letter" in Temple Aides File, Box 1 (1852), LBJ Library.

20. Memo, Tom Johnson to president, 12 July 1968, Ex FG 530/ST 10, WHCF, LBJ Library.

21. Temple Oral History, tape 5, p. 37.

22. Letter, Albert Jenner to Clark, 10 July 1968, Ex FG 530/ST 10/A, WHCF, LBJ Library.

23. Memo, Clark to president, 12 July 1968, Ex FG 530/ST 10/A, WHCF, LBJ Library, and Temple Oral History, tape 6, p. 35.

24. Johnson's good will only went so far. When President-elect Richard Nixon's request to see the Heineman Task Force Report on Government Reorganization was relayed to the president, he responded "Hell no—and tell him I'm not going to publish my wife's love letters either!" Memo, Charles Murphy to president, 22 November 1968, Ex FG 11-8, WHCF, LBJ Library.

25. See Harris, *Justice,* ch. 2, for an excellent discussion of the transition, focusing on the Justice Department.

26. Ibid., p. 161.

27. Temple Oral History, tape 7, p. 45.

28. Letter, Temple to John Ehrlichman, 16 December 1968, Ex FG 11-8, WHCF, LBJ Library. The Warren Christopher memo is located in memo, Christopher to Temple, 26 November 1968, Ex FG 11-8, WHCF, LBJ Library.

29. Letter, Ehrlichman to Temple, 18 December 1968, Ex FG 11-8, WHCF, LBJ Library.

30. Temple Oral History, tape 7, p. 46.

31. Memo, Clark to president, 10 July 1968, Ex FG 500, WHCF, LBJ Library.

32. See memo, Temple to ?, 8 October 1968, Ex FG 500, WHCF, LBJ Library. Nan Robertson of the *New York Times* on 4 August 1968 charged that "Johnson has also paid off debts of varying kinds by nominating 35 Federal judges for lifetime jobs. Fifteen vacancies are still to be filled, and it is considered certain the President will leave none of them empty" (quoted in Harold W. Chase, *Federal Judges: The Appointing Process* (Minneapolis: The University of Minnesota Press, 1972), p. 180.

33. Memo, Mike N. Manatos to president, 10 October 1968, Ex FG 500, WHCF, LBJ Library.

34. Martin and Susan J. Tolchin, *To the Victor . . . Political Patronage from the Clubhouse to the White House* (New York: Random House, 1971), p. 171. Sanders had originally been scheduled for appointment to the Fifth Circuit but instead his nomination was submitted to the Senate on 25 September for the District of Columbia Circuit (memo, Christopher to Temple, 25

September 1968, Ex FG 505/FG 216/A, WHCF, LBJ Library). He first cleared the nomination with Senators Ralph Yarborough, (D-Tex.), and John Tower (R-Tex.), since he still maintained Texas residency (memo, Sanders to ·Temple, 25 September 1968, filed Ralph Yarborough Name File, LBJ Library). David Bress was originally recommended for nomination in August 1967, but his name was submitted as a nominee for the district judgeship from the District of Columbia only in August 1968 (memo, Temple to president, 12 July 1968, Ex FG 530/FG 216/A, WHCF, LBJ Library).

35. Harris, *Justice*, p. 157.

36. Ibid, p. 156.

37. Letter, Sanders to president, 16 October 1968, Ex FG 506/FG 216/A, WHCF, LBJ Library. Sanders' letter also states: "And I appreciate, and will always remember with great pride, all that you did to try to secure Senate confirmation of the nomination. There are not many, if any, people who have had the President of the United States go to bat for them the way you did for me. I have no regrets whatsoever about the matter and I hope that the President will have none."

38. Memo, Charles Maguire to president, 16 October 1968, and letter, Sanders to president, 17 October 1968, Ex FG 505/FG 216/A, WHCF, LBJ Library.

39. Memo, Christopher to Temple, 12 December 1968, Ex FG 500, WHCF, LBJ Library.

40. Memo, Temple to president, 4 January 1969, "Mostly Temple Memos Nov 68–Jan 69," Box 3 (1852), Office Files of Larry Temple, LBJ Library.

41. Memo, Clark to president, 6 January 1969, "Mostly Temple Memos Nov 68–Jan 69," Box 3 (1852), Office Files of Larry Temple, LBJ Library.

42. Memo, Manatos to president, 8 January 1969, Ex FG 500, WHCF, LBJ Library. Obviously Johnson had a right to be concerned about senatorial reaction after the Fortas defeat and the lapsing of the previous nominations. This is indicated by the Temple and Clark memos, and by his reply to a request from Senator Harry Byrd (D-Va.) in December 1968 to nominate a Byrd candidate: "Tell him President does not want to make any nominations unless he has lead pipe assurance of confirmation" (memo, Temple to president, 16 December 1968, Ex FG 530/ST 46, WHCF, LBJ Library).

43. Apparently Clark had called Mitchell when he sent in his memo recommending resubmissions on 6 January 1969. Clark described the five cases and noted that Johnson did not plan to fill the other twenty existing vacancies, that Nixon could expect about twenty new vacancies each year and that a judgeship act for sixty-seven new positions was pending (quoted in Harris, *Justice*, p. 158). My discussion of this episode relies on the Harris discussion, various oral histories, and the 27 January controversy as reported in the *New York Times*, 28 January 1969.

44. Harris, *Justice*, p. 158, and Temple Oral History, tape 6, p. 11.

45. Memo, Temple to president, 9 January (5:10 p.m.), Ex FG 11-8, WHCF, LBJ Library.

46. These efforts are documented in Ex FG 11-8, 11/1/68–1/20/69, Box 69, LBJ Library (especially in Johnson's opening statement to the cabinet meet-

ing of 4 December 1968, which noted that this was not the time to adopt
new policies) and in Temple Oral History, tape 7. But in the last three days of
his tenure, Clark filed three major antitrust cases, arguing that they needed
to be filed then or they would have been lost (Harris, *Justice*, p. 128; Clark
Oral History, tape 5, p. 26; Larry Temple Interview, LBJ School of Public Affairs project, p. 36). This caused a great deal of public outcry and apparently
added to the deterioration of the Johnson-Clark relationship in the last few
days of the administration. This is illustrated by an occurrence two days before the end of the Johnson presidency. John Macy turned in Clark's letter of
resignation, effective 20 January, and a suggested letter of acceptance. The
suggested letter was full of praise for Clark as a "beacon for us all," with
courage and vision as his hallmarks, and ended with "we will see each other
often in the years to come." Johnson responded with a directive to Temple:
"Just rewrite this—and say nothing—just something like—it's the end of a
time together for us" (memo, Macy to president with attachments, 18 January 1969, Ex FG 135/A, WHCF, LBJ Library). And Clark was one of the few
cabinet members not invited to Johnson's Inaugural Day luncheon (transcript, Clark Oral History Interview, 5 March 1977, tape 5, p. 27, LBJ
Library).

47. *New York Times*, 24 January 1969, p. 18:2 and 28 January 1969, p. 1:6.

48. Harris, *Justice*, p. 159. For the Clark, Mitchell, and Nixon statements,
see *New York Times*, 28 January 1969, pp. 1:6 and 12:5.

49. Quoted in Harris, *Justice*, p. 159. Temple reports that during this episode, Clark called requesting a copy of the 9 January memo reporting the
Mitchell conversation. But Temple told Clark that the ex-president would
have to approve release of it because it involved him. Clark did not want to
get Johnson involved in the furor and so the memo was never released
(Temple Oral History, tape 6, p. 13).

50. Quoted in *New York Times*, 28 January 1969, p. 1:6.

51. Ibid., p. 12:5.

52. Harris, *Justice*, p. 169.

53. *New York Times*, 28 January 1969, p. 1:6.

8. Conclusion

1. Harold W. Chase, *Federal Judges: The Appointing Process* (Minneapolis: University of Minnesota Press, 1972), p. 185.

2. Ibid., p. 184, and Alan Neff, *The United States District Judge Nominating Commissions: Their Members, Procedures and Candidates* (Chicago: American Judicature Society, 1981), p. 19.

3. See, for example, Donald D. Jackson, *Judges* (New York: Atheneum,
1972), and Victor S. Navasky, *Kennedy Justice* (New York: Antheneum,
1977), ch. 5. Navasky reports on the nomination of Harold Cox, Mississippi
Senator James Eastland's college roommate (pp. 251–252):

"Robert Sherrill has charged in *The Nation* that the appointment came
about in a Senate corridor where Eastland spotted the Attorney General and
accosted him with this quasi-threat: "Tell your brother that if he will give

me Harold Cox I will give him the nigger" [meaning Thurgood Marshall]. A less conspiratorial explanation: In addition to gratitude for favors done, the Kennedys were reluctant to antagonize needlessly the powerful chairman of the Senate Judiciary committee so early in the game.

"Whichever version one believes, the critical fact is that the Cox appointment did not stand alone. It was part of a pattern."

4. Joel Grossman, *Lawyers and Judges: The ABA and the Politics of Judicial Selection* (New York: John Wiley & Sons, 1965), p. 219. See also J. Woodford Howard, Jr., *Courts of Appeals in the Federal Judicial System* (Princeton: Princeton University Press, 1981), p. 18: "For all the rhetoric decrying the penetration of politics into the judicial process, it is far from certain that political considerations should be eliminated from the selection of judges, even if they could be. So long as . . . judges participate in governing the country much is to be said for courts being responsive, as distinct from responsible, to the governed. Political appointment serves to harmonize federal judicial power with popular tolerances and concomitant lawmaking coalitions in other branches of government."

5. See, for example, Robert A. Carp and C. K. Rowland, *Policymaking and Politics in the Federal District Courts* (Knoxville: University of Tennessee Press, 1983), and C. Neal Tate, "Personal Attribute Models of the Voting Behavior of U.S. Supreme Court Justices: Liberalism in Civil Liberties and Economics Decisions, 1946–1978," *American Political Science Review* 75 (1981): 355–367.

Index